```
B HUG
Grey Champi
More than a

17.95
```

More Than an Actor

THE STORY OF PETER H.

W. GREY CHAMPION

Copyright © 2018 W. Grey Champion
All rights reserved
First Edition

PAGE PUBLISHING, INC.
New York, NY

First originally published by Page Publishing, Inc. 2018

ISBN 978-1-64138-344-8 (Paperback)
ISBN 978-1-64138-345-5 (Digital)

Printed in the United States of America

Preface

THE LATE PETER H. WAS a celebrity, a gifted British actor who had fans around the world when he died at the age of sixty-one. As with any celebrity, especially in the entertainment business, the facts of his life are an open book, instantly available through an internet search: where he was born and when, his family, schooling, career, marriages, a chronology of his many roles on stage and screen, some of which one may still enjoy. Even television interviews are still available in this new age. But surely, all this information is superficial. As public as he was, constantly exposed, it was always the actor's mask he carefully presented. Who was the private man, and why should we care to know him?

Many fans of the late Peter H., who, like myself, never knew him personally, remain devoted to his memory. They will identify him immediately, though I have chosen to write this as fiction, and my reason is not simply the lack of more personal information. To say, as many have in tribute, that Peter was gifted, remarkable, special is supreme understatement. He was physically magnificent yet, in spite of that distraction, intelligent, charismatic, kind, and decent, possessing all the most human and humane qualities one may mention. At the same time, he fought demons: he was bisexual before the term "gay" gained currency, and he was bipolar, what is also called manic-depressive. To do justice to such an amazing and unique human being, at the same time exploring in some depth that darker side, I can see no alternative to fiction.

The book is based on what I have learned of Peter from a variety of sources as well as my observations, but I have my own viewpoint, naturally, which fiction also allows me to express. I will not pretend to know what really went on in his mind. But that is the larger point: we cannot know the mind of another. We shy away, especially from mental illness, close our eyes, deny its reality. Having an older brother who is bipolar, I have personal experience of its true horrors, which are routinely minimized by those ignorant of it, and which even modern medicine still has not conquered. To what degree the manic moods contributed to Peter's personality is a moot question. He himself believed they gave him the spark, the edge, as an actor, and he was brilliant.

But his charm from all reports came through from childhood in all areas of life. More than an actor, he was an exemplary and successful person. What really makes his story compelling, however, is that interwoven with that success, in an arguably causal relationship, was tragedy, dogging him without mercy. That so fine and talented a man should have a successful life is expected; that he should manage to do so in the face of the several misfortunes that I shall recount is a tale of courage, of superior humanity, which should be remembered and celebrated. I came upon him through his work after he had died, and upon learning more about his background and life story, I was surprised that no one had written a biography. It is a story that begs to be told.

My avoidance of last names and place-names in the first chapter is meant simply to underscore a creative portrayal of people and places, not to fool anyone to whom these will be obvious. For the early years of his life until that time when he adopted his stage name, I will call him Peter H. I will further attempt to alert the reader when I have made an informed guess concerning him, using the editorial "we" in hope that others will share my portrait of Peter. The endnotes, however, are written in first person singular, being a way to show how I have arrived at both fact and fiction based on it. Readers may prefer to skip these and follow the story as that of a fictional person, reading the notes last.

So based on the facts, I offer you my fictional account of an extraordinary person, a man who was more than an actor and who left a deep impression on so many, deeper and more lasting than the celluloid upon which it was so often conveyed.

W. Grey Champion
May 2014

Introduction

The drawing room was growing dark in the early twilight of autumn, but a fire blazed and crackled. In front of it on the settee, mother and child sat wrapped in a blanket, while the old Airedale terrier sprawled on the hearth rug at their feet. The antique mantle clock struck half past five, showing its disrepair by missing the second note in each quarter. Opposite on the mantle stood a vase of red roses, beginning to hang their heads but still perfuming the room, while at the window sat a large pot of brilliant yellow mums. Outside, the verdant English countryside was burnished both by the season and the glow of sunset.

Peter sat on his mother's lap cradled in her left arm. "Mummy, are you sad that summer is over?"

"No, no, darling, not at all. I love the summer, but winter gives everything the chance to rest." Her hands, holding the child, mingled the smells of lavender soap and mint. She had been in the potting shed, transplanting some mint for the greenhouse, loving as she did to have it in her tea all winter. "Shall I read to you, Peter?" she asked. A copy of *Wind in the Willows* lay on the table beside them.

"No, Mummy, I want to hear the fire and listen to your heartbeat." He lay his head on her shoulder, and she pressed it against her, kissing his soft hair, its baby blonde slowly giving way to brown. "I love you more than anything," he said, wrapping his little arm around her neck.

"I love you too, dear, very, very much," she replied, hugging him gently.

"Do you love me more than John?"

"You boys are each one different, Peter, so I love you differently. How do *you* love your brother?" John was the oldest of four, and Peter the youngest.

"I love him because he is smart and helpful."

"And what about Michael?" Mother continued.

"I love Michael because he draws good pictures of animals and people," Peter said, "and Patwick because he is fun to play with." The baby lisp in his speech was still endearing.

"So you see? I love each of you more than anything, and each just for being who you are. Is that all right, child?" With the keen instincts of a mother, she refrained from telling him that he really was her very special angel, the dearest and most beautiful, and that her love for him ran very deep indeed.

"Mummy, are the trees sad when summer is over?"

"Least of all, dear. They need to rest all winter long. But, Peter, are you sad?"

"No, I'm not sad either, because my birthday is coming! How much longer, Mummy?"

"You were born on the third of November, less than two weeks away now. You will be six years old!"

Peter heaved a big sigh of satisfaction, closed his eyes, and fell instantly to sleep in that spontaneous way that childhood allows. His mother continued holding him, while the room became quite dark but for the firelight. She took such comfort merely from the feel of his legs curled in her lap under the blanket. Through the window, she could just see the workmen leaving in their truck and hear the crunch of its wheels on the gravel. They were building a bomb shelter onto the house. England had been at war with Germany for over a month.

Chapter 1

As soon as Mrs. H.[1] lay eyes on her newborn son, she gasped with joy, exclaiming, "He has the face of an angel!" The nurse handing the baby over to his mother agreed, as did Nanny C.[2], who sat by the bedside as she had for three earlier births. Infant Peter was the youngest of four boys, and not only the most beautiful baby anyone had ever seen but the sweetest as well, never crying, never cranky or petulant.

He entered a happy family of affluent circumstances in a small community of Warwickshire[3] in England. His father was a retired army colonel, decorated for his service in World War I, then employed in his family manufacturing business. He was a horseman and an archer, and the family property was enough for him to pursue those skills, both of which were fading as the twentieth century proceeded. It was 1933 when his youngest son was born.

Colonel H.[4] had a military bearing and discipline, but by no means the stiff austerity one might ascribe to the career soldier. He was well loved by his troops, and in civilian life, he was active and highly regarded in the community. As a father, he took great joy watching his four sons grow, helping them find their way in life and, of course, teaching them to ride and to shoot longbow.

The heart of Peter's family, however, was his mother, about whom all that need be said is that she was half Irish and descended of a Quaker clan. The Society of Friends has had meetings in Ireland for some centuries, though the incongruity of their respective stereotypes makes the fact hard to believe: the pugnacious Irish versus the pacifist Quaker; the abstemious Quakers in contrast to the intemperate Irish. Put these together, and you had in Mrs. H. the best traits of both. She was jolly and fun-loving, kind, tolerant, and charitable—in short, just the woman to be the beloved mother of four energetic boys. She came from a family of successful tea merchants[5] and was ten years younger than her husband.

Surely it was thanks to the loving ways of their mother that Peter's older brothers were as delighted at his arrival as his parents were. Aside from the occasional good-natured rivalry, there was no serious discord between them, and they loved the idea of a younger brother to play with, to teach. And so Peter came home to the lovely nursery, which had been added to the home just after the family moved in five years before.

The room, which was large and on the ground floor, had a southern exposure, welcoming the baby with light and warmth that autumn. Peter[6] was born on 3 November. The furnishings were old but comfortable, having served the other children over the years. There was a bassinet, a crib, a rocking chair, a dresser, a pram—all in an old Edwardian style. White sheer curtains hung at the windows and blew softly whenever one was cranked open to air the room. The weather was still fair and mild that November. From the rocker, Mrs. H. could look out upon the pasture and the family's several horses as she nursed her newborn. The house where Peter grew up was, indeed, attractive, one of the stately manor houses that graced their small village, not far from Coventry. It dated from the seventeenth century. Peter's maternal grandmother, who lived less than an hour away by car, was a frequent visitor. It was she who came from a long line of prominent Quakers, right there in the English Midlands where Quakerism began, also in the seventeenth century; and many generations of her family had made their way in the tea business. Her husband, Arnold B., brought the Irish connection.

Granny B.[7] was not overly concerned about her daughter, who was thirty-three when this fourth son was born. Mrs. H. had done well with her first three, and she had an experienced and devoted helper in Nanny C. Of course, Granny had heard that this newborn was extra special, but she was skeptical. She called at teatime. The oldest two boys were away at school, but she greeted Patrick, age 5, the next oldest, as she arrived.

"Patrick, dear, you are not the youngest anymore! What do you think of your new brother?"

"He is very pretty, Grandma!" said the boy, hugging his grandmother around the hips. "Come and see him." And he led the way to the nursery.

The family had moved to this house just after Patrick was born, from a smaller place in the same village[8], which had been a wedding gift from the Colonel's people ten years earlier. The three older boys were born at that previous house, but of course with the third child larger quarters were necessary. In fact they no sooner had moved in than an addition was begun, that being this lovely nursery, where Granny B. was now meeting her newest grandson.

"Betty, my dear," she said softly in case the baby was asleep, "it's your mother."

Mrs. H.—her given name was Elizabeth—rose from the rocking chair, holding Peter, and the two women embraced, hugging the baby between them.

"Oh, Mum, I have been so anxious to see you!"

"But how are you, darling? I hope you are not overdoing things too soon."

"No, no, I have Ellen," Nanny C.'s given name, "and Bill is keeping the boys busy at the Archery Club." Colonel H. was Henry William.

"Now," said Granny, "let me have a look at this child."

She took him from her daughter's arms and cradled him, pulling back the soft, blue receiving blanket slightly. "Well, Betty, it's fortunate he is your fourth, or you would have been in for a very long labor. Look at the size of his head, will you!"

Betty laughed. "Ellen said something of the kind as well. But that angelic face, Mother, and the quick smile!"

"Oh yes, I quite agree, he is special indeed. And I see by the color of the blanket that you knew to expect a boy! Was Bill disappointed?"

"Just a little, I think. Isn't it odd? I was fine either way."

"It's God's endorsement of the splendid way you handle boys! Do we have a name then?"

"The first name for Saint Peter—all the boys have saint names."

"Saints John, Michael, and Patrick—a nod to your Irish blood." Granny winked at little Patrick, who had taken over the rocking chair, and beamed upon hearing his name.

"Then Jeremy," Betty continued, "because the other boys like the name, and William after his father."

"Wonderful! And the christening?"

"In two weeks, at the village church, following Sunday service." Then came a loud rumpus from the back of the house, as though one of the horses had gotten in through the kitchen door. "That will be John and Michael coming home from school. They will have tea in the kitchen with Ellen and Cook"—the cook was Lily K.[9]—"and Jennie will bring us our tea here in the nursery."

Jennie V.[10] was one of the housemaids. The family employed seven staff members, three of whom lived with them: the nanny, the cook, and the housekeeper, one Joyce J.[11] They had as well a gardener, a driver, and two housemaids, who lived in the village.

By now baby Peter was nodding off, so his grandmother put him gently into the crib. Patrick climbed out of the rocking chair. "May I go to the kitchen, Mummy?"

"Yes dear, you run along."

This nursery was large enough for chairs and a table, upon which presently Jennie the maid placed the silver tea tray. The teapot was not silver but china, an heirloom, and the cups and saucers unmatched. In true English fashion, there were scones and cakes and curds and jams, and still in a corner of the tray, there was room for a bud vase with a single rose.

"How in the world, Betty, do you still have a rose out of your garden in November?"

"It is from the bush by the back door, sheltered by the house. I think it opened up its last bloom just for the baby!"

"You can be so fanciful, dear."

Mrs. H. began pouring the tea. "Please help yourself, Mother. Lily baked your favorite cinnamon scones when she heard you were coming, and she's made jam from the wild blackberries."

"Oh, wonderful! I must thank her before I leave." They were quiet for a while, fixing their tea in the English style, with cream and sugar. "It's been five years since you had a newborn, Betty. How are you feeling about it?"

"Oh, you know me, Mother, strong as an ox! But don't worry, I'm glad for the chance to slow down a bit. We won't be hosting the Hunt Breakfast, for example."

"No breakfast at the Grange?" said Granny in mock horror. The house and fifteen acres upon which it sits had been known as the Grange since 1920 when it was given that name by the former owner. Formerly it had been Elm Cottage. Granny B. continued, "Where will it be then?"

"At Nailcote."

"Miss Katherine?[12] She is ninety-two!"

"But you know how she and her brother John loved the Hunt. He is fairly spry at eighty-even, and the staff will do everything."

"Will Bill be riding to hounds then?"

"Oh yes."

"And you?"

"No, no, no, baby Peter and I will be rocking peacefully, enjoying the early sunsets."

While Granny B. was quite naturally the first visitor, others soon began calling to greet the baby, never failing to remark about his beauty. His smile was especially unusual, not really cherubic, though in later years it could be called impish, nor such that might be attributable to gas. His Aunt Margaret[13] upon seeing him declared this special smile to be "ethereal." She was the younger sister of Colonel H. and paid a visit with her daughter Daphne[14], age 5. They came on a windy autumn afternoon, when Peter, not yet a month old, was napping in the bassinet. Young Daphne crept up to him, awestruck at her first experience of a newborn. As the wind rattled the shutters at the nursery windows, the baby stirred and smiled up at his visitors. Daphne was in love.

There was nothing for it at that point but that Aunt Margaret had to hold the baby, wrapped in his warm blanket, as the chilly wind was seeping in. Tea was brought then, and as they sat and sipped and chatted, Peter was handed round between mother and aunt, and even cousin Daphne, feeling very grown-up at being allowed to hold him.

"Will you be hosting the Hunt Breakfast this year, Betty?" Margaret asked.

"Oh no, dear, it will be at Nailcote. Mother asked the same thing!"

"Well, we don't want you *overdoing*," and they laughed.

Before long the early dusk of late November came on, and the sun, even in its southern trajectory, disappeared from the nursery windows. The visitors, wanting to leave before dark, bade their adieu. "Now, Betty, don't hesitate to call me if I can help you in any way. Promise me!"

"Yes, Margaret, thank you, but you know how devoted Ellen is to me and the children." Margaret and Daphne drove off in the old motor car, the model that still resembled, to some extent, an actual carriage, Daphne looking back at the house, one she loved for its gables and its vine-covered brick, thinking with excitement, "A beautiful home for a beautiful new cousin!"

*　*　*

While Peter's mother was a very fit and active woman, we may surmise with some confidence that she might, with equanimity, forgo riding with the Hunt so soon after giving birth and might even cut back on archery practice, which interest she shared with her husband. On the other hand, she would surely have kept up with her charitable activities, which included the Red Cross, the Women's Institute, and the village church of St. John the Baptist.

There can be no doubt that the Colonel and his family were Church of England, but the family of Elizabeth H. was Quaker, going back in that same region surrounding Birmingham where the sect arose, and nearly as far back as its origin. It was there around 1650 where a young George Fox, founder of the Society of Friends, wandered on a spiritual journey, unsatisfied by the orthodoxy of an atrophied Church hierarchy. He was an earnest and very religious person, who felt this spiritual yearning intensely and who, in his wandering, sensed a personal closeness with God. He reported in his journal that "when my troubles and torments were great, then was

His love exceeding great," and it was in this circumstance that he had a vision.

Modern people tend to be inured by the skepticism of science with respect to the so-called visions reported from centuries past, which might have resulted after all from certain toxins of improper fermentation, or from ergotism, which was not uncommon when grains became moldy. Both phenomena might be expected to cause hallucination. Nevertheless, George Fox believed without doubt that Christ had come to him personally to renew among his followers his message of faith and compassion, simple and peaceful living. This direct and personal aspect of the encounter led to the novel idea in Quakerism that the lay person can receive the divine word without a priestly intermediary. Moreover, in contrast to Calvinism, the Quaker view holds that man is a child of God, not a depraved sinner.

Quakerism spread slowly from the heart of England around the globe, most notably taking root in the New World, where Pennsylvania served as a refuge from the inevitable persecution. William Penn, the colony's first governor, brought it with him in 1682. The movement was unusually enlightened for its time, or even our own for that matter. Renouncing all violence, it is pacifist with regard to war, upholds the highest virtues of honesty, integrity, and sincerity, and requires of the individual believer that he return God's love through service to his fellow man. The family of Elizabeth H. from the eighteenth century onward were exemplary Quakers. Their prosperous business, even today, allows the family foundation to support great works of charity. But she herself was much more than the wealthy, aloof mistress of the manor. Stories abound of her personal generosity and involvement, and in those times, there was no lack of opportunity to serve one's fellows.

The years between the two world wars in Britain saw the upper classes doing quite well. Even the middle class enjoyed a decent lifestyle. But among the working class and in rural areas, there was persistent poverty, unemployment, and homelessness. So if a band of gypsies wandered into the fields surrounding the Grange, Elizabeth would see to it that they were fed, bathed, and given clean clothing; or if a homeless man, a hobo as they were called, showed up at the door, he would likewise receive her assistance. Then there came the evacuees from Coventry during the air raids. But we are getting ahead of our story!

In the person of Elizabeth H. the influence of Quakerism, great though it was, mixed in equal measure with her father's Irish gene. She was, as a result, not only charitable and generous to a fault, but also gregarious, lighthearted, vivacious, willing, and able as only the Irish are to enjoy life and to bring others along on the ride. The Grange often came alive with gaiety and celebration, not alone the Hunt Breakfast, but every August there was Archery Week. Eventually the whole family became expert at the sport, including Peter. Dances were held to the accompaniment of the Colonel's brother, Leslie, on the grand piano. Large groups of Boy Scouts might be entertained at the house, like the forty or more who came one Parish Sunday and posed for a snapshot, with the Colonel and Mrs. H. at the center.

And that is where this active, energetic, civic minded couple always stood in their community—at the center. Having enjoyed prosperity, both had a keen sense of *noblesse oblige*, and of service in the cause of any social good. The Colonel had served his country in World War I, the Great War, as a Second Lieutenant in the Royal Horse Artillery, which involved horse drawn cannon. As a good horseman, he was well suited to the duty; and by the end of the war he had received both the Distinguished Service Order and the Military Cross. Returning home, he rejoined the family business in Birmingham and married; but work and family did not hinder him from serving as Deputy Lieutenant of Warwickshire, nor from numerous other positions of leadership in local affairs. His wife, whose work with charities we have enumerated, also took an interest in local politics. These parents were indeed a fine example for their four boys, John, Michael, Patrick and Peter.

* * *

It was a typical school night after dinner with the family gathered in the drawing room. Mrs. H. sat with Patrick on the sofa by the fire, reading to him from *The Jungle Book*, while John helped Michael with his spelling. Baby Peter slept in the nursery, well within earshot. The Colonel was seated at the secretary writing a letter to his mother. His father had died just a year earlier at age 73, at home in Bexhill-on-Sea. For the time being his widowed mother, though nearly 320 kilometers away, was managing, with visits from his sister Margaret.

He got up to stir the fire, which was crackling warmly, and threw on another birch log. Then interrupting his wife, he asked, "When is the christening?"

"It will be the third Sunday in advent at one o'clock, with a lunch after at the Parish Hall. Perhaps Margaret can bring your mother up on the train."

"I will suggest it."

John and Michael worked quietly in the corner, John quizzing his brother on the spelling list. "Bird," he said.

"B-e-r-d," replied Michael.

"No Michael, b-i-r-d," whereupon Michael would write the correct spelling on his homework paper, and draw a small picture beside it. He loved to draw and was good at it.

John was the oldest, then age 9, and typical of first place in birth order, felt a sense of responsibility that showed itself in a seriousness and maturity beyond his years. It came as no surprise when later in life he entered the clergy. He loved his younger brothers and was especially thrilled with this new baby. When he and Michael had finished with the spelling list, he asked his mother, "May we look in on Peter before we go to bed, Mum?"

"You may, my dears, but tiptoes and whispers." She kissed them both, and off they went to the nursery, where Peter slept in his crib. Michael started to speak, and John shushed him, so Michael whispered, "Isn't he wonderful?! Can I kiss him?"

"No, no," said John very softly, "you will wake him." They tiptoed up the stairs together and to bed.

The Grange was not large by modern standards, but was considered grand in those days; each owner over the years had made additions. Still, more recent listings of it indicate that it is a two story house of six bedrooms, three baths, and two staircases. The front shows two large and two smaller gables above the lower stories, so there may have been usable attic rooms. But with three live-in staff members, we may surmise that the parents had one bedroom, and the boys bunked two to a room. In fact, later in life when Peter was asked about his Eton years, he said he had felt lonely having a room to himself, implying that at home he shared his room, probably with Patrick, as soon as he left the nursery.

One thing we cannot assume, however, is that four boys can grow up together in perfect harmony. Boys can be highly competitive, so while love and loyalty was in all probability deep between them, there surely must have been occasional friction. One may have been better at archery, for example, causing jealousy; or another may have become possessive of one of the animals, of which there were always several, theirs being a semi-rural community. There were horses, a pony, donkeys, and always a family dog. In any event, their parents would have used any and all childish squabbles, with the assistance of Nanny, to mold good character, nurture maturity, and restore peace in the household.

The sons of Colonel H., for that matter, no doubt felt pressure to excel. He was quite a father to live up to: a military officer, a decorated veteran, a successful man of business, a community leader. He was ten years older than his wife, and could be short-tempered at times; but they had met at Woodbrooke, an estate near Birmingham that had been in Elizabeth's family for generations, and which had been turned into a Centre for Quaker Studies. What was he doing there, a soldier, an army man? We may only conjecture, but it is surely a gross misunderstanding to believe that a soldier must love war, especially a man who had just lived through and fought in the bloodiest conflict in the history of his country. That he should come home and marry a woman with Elizabeth's background is not really unusual at all.

In those days, no one could have had an appetite for conflict after the enormous toll of the Great War. Some few, notably Winston Churchill and John Maynard Keynes, felt that the Treaty of Versailles was so economically punitive against Germany that the battle was not over. But the British on the whole did their best to ignore Chancellor Hitler and his aggressions. Neville Chamberlain, himself from a prominent Birmingham family, was much in favor for his policy of appeasement, or at least a "working accommodation" with the Fascists, that would shield the country from European unrest, alas, only for a time.

* * *

It was a crisp and clear late autumn morning in December, Sunday the seventeenth, and the family was up early as usual to get themselves ready for church. But today there was an air of keen excitement, being the day baby Peter would be baptized. The Colonel's sister, niece Daphne, and his mother had arrived the day before and were staying at the Grange, while Elizabeth's parents would be coming to the christening at one o'clock. Granny B. had three sisters, Peter's great aunts, who were also coming, as well as Elizabeth's own sister, Christine, and two brothers, Richard and Arnold Junior. The church would be packed, and the Parish Hall buzzing like an overturned beehive hosting the luncheon.

The house was of course decorated for Christmas, holly wreaths at the doors and on the gable windows, mistletoe hung in the archways, a pine tree covered in ornaments in the drawing room, this latter causing a small dispute. "It's my tree!" cried Patrick with a great pout. "I found it. I saw it first."

"But Patrick," said Nanny, trying to calm him, "John cut it down."

The Colonel intervened. "I'm your father, Patrick; the tree is mine."

But Mother had the last word. "Patrick dear, it is your tree, but you are such a good and kind little boy that you are sharing it with all of us. Isn't that right?"

"Yes Mummy," he conceded reluctantly, upon which his father picked him up.

"We were saving the angel for Christmas Eve, Patrick; but since today is also a special day, I will let you do the honors and place it on top of the tree." He reached the ornament from the mantel and walked to the tree, where Patrick, still in his father's arms, proudly affixed it to the top. It was a lovely thing with a white silk robe and white china face, hand painted.

Gazing at it in wonderment, Patrick said quietly, "It looks just like baby Peter, doesn't it, Daddy?" The Colonel set him down gently.

"Indeed so, child. Now run and get your coat."

Outside the village church of St. John the Baptist, cars and bicycles were pulling up along the lane for the morning service. There was a hoar frost on the lawn and the head stones in the churchyard and even on the stone cross, which stood high upon its base of five octagonal steps. Worshippers arriving early gathered there and chatted, their breath forming clouds in the chill. Presently, the church bells began pealing from the tower, so resonant in the stillness as to suggest that all six were sounding. The church has stood there for many centuries.[15]

This morning the sanctuary was generously adorned for the Christmas season. The scents of pine and boxwood were fresh from the wreaths decking the nave; the chancel had bouquets of white chrysanthemum, and a cross of holly was secured to the front of the pulpit. The family pew was directly beneath the pulpit, and when they all had filed in, it was crowded. The baby had been left at home with Nanny C., who would bring him along later for the christening.

Oh, it was a fine service that morning! The choir sang beautifully, a medley of favorite carols, and the rector, Reverend W.[16], spoke eloquently on the joy and the promise of birth. The valetudinarian whose coughing so often drowned out the sermon had been encouraged to come to early service, so the congregants were happily attentive, even the children. Before closing the rector invited anyone who wished to do so to remain for the Service of Baptism and to luncheon in the Parish Hall.

It would be a long day for Mrs. H. but a joyous one, and she was as she said, strong as an ox. Despite the cold, she went outside to greet the other family members arriving. First came her parents, and her mother said that brothers Richard and Arnold and their wives would be coming together, but younger sister Christine had caught the flu and by no means wanted anyone else to succumb. Granny B.'s three sisters then pulled up, all packed into the Daimler. The eldest, Jessie, was then 67, while Granny herself was 60, and Helen and Margaret[17] were younger. Later in his life, Peter referred to his great aunts as "very elegant old darlings," so they must have been on the day of his christening. Though it was not yet winter, Aunt Jessie was already in her sable coat and hat, the subtle dark brown of the fur shimmering in the clear, cold air beneath jet black tips. All three wore pearls, long ropes of pearls, in keeping with a very special occasion. Jessie embraced her niece, who felt the cool softness of fur against her cheek.

"Dearest Betty, how do you manage to be so beautiful with all you do, and now a new baby? I hope this is your last."

"Oh yes, Auntie, thank you. Four is our tradition, is it not? I now have four, Mother had four of us, and Grandmother had you four girls!"

"Then your four boys will even things out," Jessie concluded, and they all laughed.

"I don't know, Jessie," Aunt Margaret added, "you know the old saw, when so many boys are born, it forebodes a war." She turned to Mrs. H., put an arm around her, and kissed her cheek gently. "You are radiant today, my dear, as usual."

"No politics today, sister!" was Jessie's retort. "Now where is this child? I am dying to see him!"

No sooner had she said it than Lou W., the family's driver[18], arrived bearing Nanny C. and the baby. Peter was well swaddled in a very soft white knitted woolen gown, and a cap to match tied under his chin. Ellen handed him to his mother, and his great aunts were as sincere in their admiration as they were profuse in there praise.

Baby Peter was wide awake and beaming. "The face of an angel!" said Aunt Helen.

"Everyone who sees him has said that, Auntie, and he has a soul to match," Mrs. H. responded.

"Then you are truly blessed of heaven, my dear. Now let's get him in where it is warm," and with that Aunt Jessie led the way into the sanctuary.

The Service of Baptism is not a long one. Mrs. H. stood at the baptismal font opposite the pulpit holding the baby, beside the

Colonel. Her older brother Richard and his wife Anne stood with them as the godparents. Baby Peter smiled throughout, even as he was blessed with the water, the rector pronouncing, "I name thee Peter Jeremy William H. in the name of the Father . . ."

The family alone filled many pews that day, and many though not all congregants from the morning service had stayed on. They egressed to the hymn, *O holy Jesus, Lord divine, we pray thee guard this child of thine* . . . played by the organist, Arthur G.[19] Family and friends lingered in the vestibule to glimpse the star of the day, his parents and brothers gathered round as proud as they could be; and then on to lunch, a sumptuous one in the traditional country fashion.

* * *

Peter's mother, Elizabeth, was a beautiful woman; her aunts were not exaggerating. She was equally as elegant a darling as they. Her dark hair contrasted with clear, fair skin, in that Celtic image referred to in some quarters as "black Irish," having been brought to that island, it is thought, from southern Europe long ago. Her smiling eyes might have been called hazel, but really were more of a luminous mix of green, blue, and grey. The fine sculpted features of her face and her fine-boned frame belied her strength, as she was in fact an excellent horsewoman and could pull the bow with the best of the Woodmen of Arden[20], the centuries old archery club in Meriden.

When Peter had grown out of infancy, it was clear even as a toddler that he closely resembled his mother. His was the masculine version of a very classic beauty, and nonetheless manly for it. But he also shared her personality, her vigor and fortitude, her jolliness and generosity, her modesty and honest concern for the less fortunate. Both were gregarious, but she perhaps less extroverted. She could enter a room unnoticed, until she had quietly inserted her presence into a conversation. She could make her opinions known, yet unassumingly, her manner always one of grace and dignity. Was it the Quaker influence, a quiet listening for God?

There can be no doubt of her spiritual nature; her oldest son, after all, became a clergyman. But it would not have been one of rigid ideology, or strict orthodoxy. Peter said of his mother later in life that "she had open doors and windows in her soul." From all reports, she had a great and compassionate heart that embraced all creatures, and this love and openness she surely passed on to her sons.

People from all walks of life and strata of society would come to her assured of whatever help she could give. Such egalitarian principles are typically Quaker, while not the British tradition even at that time. In those days, as one old gentleman[21] still living in the village so quaintly put it, "Things were much more *them and us*." Yet when that same gentleman lost his mother in a bicycle accident in 1958, Elizabeth H. was on his doorstep the next day with her condolences and an armful of roses. She had the common touch, and at one time was president of the Women's Institute in the village. This grass roots movement, begun in Canada in 1915, had the purpose of revitalizing rural communities by educating country women in agriculture and home arts. The Institute, or WI, would have its own humble building where monthly meetings were held. Also bespeaking the Quaker spirit was a story Mrs. H. once told on herself concerning certain acts of civil disobedience, a tale she repeated at a village meeting to none other than the constable. This involved a local crossroads where speeding cars were creating a danger. After requests of the council to take action were ignored, she had her own speed limit signs made and erected. When she was prosecuted for the infringement, she was only too happy to have her say in court.

Clearly there was no controlling her, being part Irish after all. But what must her husband have thought of such behavior? The Colonel was a man of uniforms. In his Army regalia, he was imposing, gallant, indeed magnificent, but equally so decked out for the local Hunt, in the regulation red jacket, white breeches, black boots and hat. Then there was a very handsome outfit for the archery club: green jacket, white waistcoat and trousers with the Arden button, and a feathered cap.

At his post as a director in the family business in Birmingham, a brass and tube manufacturing company, he would have worn a finely tailored suit. It was during the Industrial Revolution that Birmingham became known as "the city of a thousand trades." Anything one might name was manufactured there. When the Second World War broke out, these factories were enlisted to arm the nation, which was why the region became a target of air raids by the Luftwaffe. The British were clever enough however to elude attacks on the manufacturing of planes and other armaments.

The Colonel was perhaps a person more inclined toward convention and decorum than his wife. He was a good man of business and, as we have observed, a decorated veteran of the First World War. He was courageous, disciplined, and dedicated to the well-being of his troops. It was at the outbreak of the second war that he was promoted to Lieutenant Colonel, and then age 49, put in command of a training regiment in North Wales. As one often repeated story shows, he would never ask his recruits to do something he himself could not. This he demonstrated one day by riding a motorcycle up a steep hill and back, announcing, "If I can do it so can you!" He was a good soldier, a compassionate officer, a man of the highest character. He wanted at least one of his four sons to follow him into the military, but it was not to be.

* * *

"Patrick, would you please pour the lemonade for you and Peter while I slice the tea bread; that's a good boy." It was elevenses in the nursery on a warm late summer morning, and Nanny sat with her two youngest charges at the old wooden table, sturdy and worn, much like herself.

Nanny C. was a stout woman, well-padded, her graying hair pulled back and thick glasses always perched on her nose. She was rarely seen without her apron on, and in the most practical shoes. She loved her job, and it was apparent through all her years of service that she was devoted to the family, most especially the children.

On this particular morning, Mrs. H. had taken the older boys to Leamington Spa, which at the time was something of a shopping mecca for people in the village. In the prior century, Royal Leamington Spa was noted for the medicinal quality of its mineral springs. With four growing boys, however, Mrs. H. would surely have been a patron of Brett's of Leamington clothing store. The Colonel himself would have had resort to haberdasheries in Birmingham or Coventry, but for the children, Brett's was handy, and John, the eldest, was getting ready to enter his first term at Eton.

Nanny and the boys were joined by Jenny V., the housemaid, a sweet young woman with short hair, in her white dress with its puffed sleeves, an apron over it. Her sister-in-law, Edna, the under nurse, came also, carrying tea for the adults. Cook had made fresh lemonade that day, along with a lemon tea cake, and of course there was lemon curd to put on it.

"Should I help Peter with his lemonade, Nanny?" asked Patrick. Peter was then almost four.

"No, dear, he can feed himself. You could fix him a slice of cake though."

"That's wight, Patwick," said Peter defensively. "I can feed myself!"

"Peter, what's wrong with you? Say 'Patrrrick'!"

"Patwick."

"All 'wight' then, eat your cake."

"Don't tease your brother, Patrick. He's only three."

Patrick was annoyed, but fresh lemonade made everything better.

Peter's mispronunciation of the "r" sound was assumed by everyone to be simply appropriate to his age. Surely he would grow out of it in time, and as long as it was just Patrick teasing him there seemed to be no problem. When he began school, however, and still could not say an "r" properly, a specialist was consulted, who easily determined that the child had ankyloglossia, a congenital oral anomaly involving the lingual frenulum which attaches the tongue to the floor of the mouth. In this condition, it is too short so that the individual is in effect "tongue tied." A wait-and-see approach is often adopted with children, who may be able to compensate. If not, it is correctible with surgery, as it was in Peter's case, though not until he was seventeen.

This day however, Peter had no thought of anything but the delicious taste of cold lemonade and the lovely summer freedom known only to a child. The windows and doors were all open to let in the coolness of morning, and on the breeze blowing the white curtains came the mingled smells of hay and grass, flowers and turned earth—and of animals! Horses, donkeys, and chickens, some of which latter wandered into the kitchen and had to be shooed, to the consternation of the cook, and the glee of the children. But Peter was put in mind of another animal.

"Nanny! Nanny!" he cried eagerly. "May I wide on the donkey this afternoon?" He already showed his love of animals, and Mahal was his favorite of the family's two Irish donkeys.

"Ask your mother, darling, as soon as she gets home," Nanny replied.

When they had finished tea, Nanny and the maid cleared the table, while Peter and Patrick went outside to see the donkeys. "Mind what I said," warned Nanny, handing them carrots to feed the animals. "Your mother will be home soon." She could see the paddock from the window and so could watch them as she helped clean up.

As promised, Mrs. H. soon returned, preceded by John and Michael loaded with parcels. Of course, John would be wearing the Eton uniform, but there were many other needs, undergarments, sweaters, and Michael had gotten a very handsome new Sunday suit and tie. Even Mother had indulged herself in a beautiful, light silk scarf.

Peter ran up to her and tugged on her skirt. She picked him up and kissed his soft cheek. He looked at her coyly from under his brow, his head tilted, in a characteristic manner that only gained in power as he matured. "Mummy, may I wide on the donkey, please?" How could she resist?

"Of course, darling. Let me change clothes and have a bit of lunch. Then I will come outside to help you. Did you have tea?"

"Yes, Mummy, it was lemonade and lemon cake." Then he scampered back to Patrick, who was still leaning against the fence feeding Mahal and Betsy, the second, smaller donkey.

When Mother arrived in more suitable garb, she opened the gate, put the bridle, which had been hanging on a fence post, on Mahal, then led him out of the paddock. Immediately, Peter threw his arms around the creature, who was very tolerant, fortunately. Mother cupped her hands for Peter's left foot, and he hoisted his right leg over Mahal's back, thereby practicing the way he would later mount a saddled horse. Then round the next field they walked. Michael had come out and joined Patrick, but the two soon grew bored of this activity and grabbed their bicycles, heading down the lane toward the village. "Be back by suppertime!" Mother shouted after them, and they waved acknowledgement through the summer dust they were stirring up.

"Mummy," Peter began, "can Mahal come to my bedroom with me?" By this time he was sharing a room on the first floor with Patrick.

"I don't think he could climb the stairs, darling."

"I could teach him!"

"I know you love him, Peter, but you have your toy donkey." She looked him in the eye, and he gave that quick smile that also became characteristic, the corners of his mouth turning up suddenly but briefly.

"It's not the same. Mahal is alive and he loves me back." She kissed his head.

"I love you even more, dear," and on they walked, all three loving every minute.

* * *

"Good heavens, Betty, who are all those people camping in our garden?" The Colonel burst into the house, returning from work on a rainy day sometime around Michaelmas. The scene he encountered in the walled courtyard of the garden—a charming addition that attested to the creativity of Mrs. H.—was colorful to say the least. A band of gypsies had gathered there, a small fire going in the center with a pot hung over it. Their horse and wagon were parked by the fence, and the saddle room in the stable was hung with their wet clothes.

"Darling, I passed them on my way home from the WI meeting. It was pouring rain. What was I to do?" Mrs. H. was notorious for this kind of spontaneous generosity, so the Colonel should not have been surprised. Still, his tolerance must have been tried at times.

"But really, Betty, they will burn the place down!"

"Tut, tut, no such thing! They can help Tom[22] in the garden while they are here."

"While they are here? How long will that be?"

"Oh, who can say? You know gypsies."

The Colonel clearly was not appreciating her insouciance. Not seeing his youngest son, he asked, "And where pray tell is Peter?"

"He is playing with the children. Don't worry, dear, Ellen has an eye on him."

Peter was indeed enchanted by these exotic people, and was thoroughly enjoying the excitement, along with Jasper, the family dog[23]. He had brought out a tin box of small toys and was showing them to a little orphaned girl about his age. He had toy horses and wagons and little metal cars and trucks. With these, he was making quite an impression on her.

"Are your mother and father here?" he asked her.

She was quiet for a bit, then replied softly, "They are both dead, but Grandmama looks after me. She sits over there by the fire."

Peter, unable to imagine being without parents, was dumbstruck by this announcement. His brow suddenly wrinkled, and the most earnest expression clouded his face. "You wait here, please," he told her. He ran into the house and up to his room. When he returned he was carrying his stuffed donkey, which showed the wear of much loving. "I want you to have him to keep you company," he said to the girl.

"Oh no, he belongs to you!" she protested.

"I don't need him anymore. I have a live donkey." Like mother, like son. From the start, Peter had a penchant for the waif.

That evening after supper, he sat by his mother on the settee in the drawing room. Patrick was sprawled on the floor reading Conan Doyle's *The White Company*, his head resting against a sleeping Jasper. Michael perched on a wide window sill, with sketch pad and pencil in hand, capturing the unusual scene outside, while his father and John, who was home for the Michaelmas holiday, were in deep discussion about what sports the young man should go out for. Archery, of course, perhaps tennis or swim team. Rugby was popular at Eton, but rough. The sky had cleared and as twilight came on, strains of gypsy music, with its plaintive sighs on the violin and soulful voices, drifted in through the open windows. Even the Colonel took notice, lowering his voice. Peter's face again took on that serious expression, his brow furrowed quite uncharacteristically for so young a child, as he related to his mother the tale of the orphan girl. When he had finished, Mrs. H. was clearly impressed with his sacrifice of such a cherished toy.

"I am extremely proud of you, Peter!" she told him.

"Mummy, where do people go when they die?" he asked.

"They go back to heaven, dear, to be with God and Jesus."

"But why would they leave a little girl behind, alone?"

"Only God knows that, child, but this little girl is not alone. Her grandmother cares for her, and you brought her much comfort, I am sure, with your gift today." Her arm was around the boy, who then threw his legs over her lap and hugged her tightly.

"Don't ever leave me, Mummy!" he mumbled, his face buried in her bosom.

"Of course not, baby," she whispered and kissed him. Then changing the subject, "Peter, would you like to be in the nativity play at church this Christmas? They still need a shepherd." Just the thought of Christmas brought a wide smile back to his face.

"Oh yes, Mummy, yes! That will be so much fun!"

The morning of Saturday next had Mrs. H. up early and out with her trug and a rose shears to cut roses for the house. Just a quick glance at her garden was enough to reveal her love of this flower. A hedge of red floribundas ran along the back fence, and tea roses were artistically distributed near the house and around the outer perimeter of the courtyard wall. These were the old fashioned roses, bred for their glorious scent, but with colors nonetheless beguiling in their beauty and variety, red and white, cream and pink, and combinations of these. Mrs. H. had greatly improved the layout of the garden at the Grange since taking it on, adding the courtyard, a greenhouse, and potting shed. Along with her many favorite roses, there were areas for annual and perennial cutting flowers, vegetables, and herbs. She and her husband had also put in new stables and a tennis court. Tennis was very popular in those days in Warwickshire, since a native, Maud Watson, became the first woman champion at Wimbledon.[24]

Being late September, there were not many decent roses left; indeed, the hips were already ripening to bright orange. Cook would gather these later for rose hips tea and jam, known to ward off winter colds. But this day the Hunt Breakfast would take place at the Grange, so Mrs. H. hurried to the kitchen to put her cuttings in water. While she was an excellent horsewoman, it was rare at that time for women to ride in the hunt. We might even surmise, being Quaker at heart, that her love of animals might have extended even to the fox.

Colonel H. would of course be in the hunt, and the boys were always enthralled by the spectacle, and a great one it was: the horses; the hunters in their livery, some in top hats, others in caps; and best of all the *hounds*, a pack of them. Frank H., known as "Skinner"[25], for reasons we can only imagine, may have been Master of the Hounds, since he was said to have followed the pack to his dying day. It requires a special gift to control a large pack of hounds with nothing but a flick of the crop above their heads, a sight to behold and to marvel. Skinner also gave riding lessons, and Peter later on became a student. The Master of the Hunt, however, was Tom Bates.

A glorious day it was for a hunt! Autumn was in the air, the hedgerows taking on a russet shade and the native small-leafed lime trees, evidence of an ancient wood, were turning yellow. Motor cars began pulling up early at the Grange, and of course many horses, some arriving in trailers, others tied up to the fence. The hounds were corralled in a nearby field awaiting their Master to finish his breakfast. And it was a generous buffet being served in the large entry room: eggs Benedict, chipped beef, sausage and bacon, fruit salad, melon, freshly squeezed orange juice, and a variety of muffins and breads. Cook had made her famous scones, and Mrs. W., the rector's wife, also known for her baking, contributed a fresh apple cake. In all the commotion, Peter, who was not tall as a child, clung closely to Nanny.

"Let me fill you a plate, darling. What would you like?" she asked him. He took an egg with sausage, melon, orange juice, and a raspberry scone, still warm, with jam; and she sat him in the kitchen where he could eat more quietly. He ate quickly, then went looking for his father, who was also looking for him.

The Colonel cut a striking figure in his hunting jacket, breeches, and boots. As Peter ran up to him, he picked up the boy, and holding him on his hip, asked, "Shall we go see the hounds, son?"

"Oh yes, please, Daddy!" and out they went. The older sons were already hanging by the fence, where the pack created a riotous tumult as only a large congregation of frenetic canines can. There was Michael straddling the top fence rail while balancing his sketch pad. Patrick was reaching over to pet the jumping dogs. John was holding the reins of his father's horse, a bay mare with experience in the hunt, who could manage uncertain terrain without injury.

First setting Peter down, the Colonel then took to his mount. "Hand Peter up to me, would you John?" and up the lad went, to sit in front of his father in the saddle. In the warmth of the early autumn sun, the smell of leather and saddle soap was intoxicating to Peter, and the thrill of being so high off the ground, able to see over heads and across the fields, was better than a donkey ride. The Colonel walked his horse along the fence, toward Spencer's Lane and back again, with Peter in a state of bliss. By that time, Skinner on his horse came trotting toward them, and the men greeted each other.

"A fine mate you have there, Colonel!"

"That he is, Skinner, and loves the horses already. Did you get breakfast?"

"Oh yes, I was here early with the pack. We should be heading out now."

"First the stirrup cup, old chap," and carefully, the Colonel handed Peter back down to John. "There you are, son, now let your brother look after you."

As riders took to their mounts, maids came out from the Grange with silver trays bearing steaming cups of grog, seen to fortify a person in the chill and sure to raise spirits! A quick swig and off they went down the lane toward the village, where they would assemble on the green. The hub of the village was the old stone church; it had a large churchyard and rectory. Then there was a butcher, a baker, a grocer, and the local public house, all surrounding a crossroads[26]. Across from the church was the Reading Room and the Women's Institute, along with the alms houses, available to the poor in the community and supported by the church. There was also a cluster of cottages, built for retired staff of Colonel W. who inherited the Berkswell Estate, which included fourteen tenant farms.[27] The Reading Room was and remains an important local institution, a facility built in 1900 by the father of Colonel W. Father and son were highly esteemed for their philanthropy, as was Peter's father and another wealthy local gentleman, Sir Charles H., a newspaper magnate, who lived at The Moat.[28]

Reaching the green, the hunters gathered by the gate.[29] Horses and riders went quiet, and the ears of every hound stood at attention. When Mr. Bates sounded the hunting horn, Skinner signaled his lead hound, and they were off, the Master keeping them in something of a formation, and the hunters following. They passed through the gate, and just beyond, the dogs picked up a scent. Instantly the pack was off at a run, and the horses too—white and black horses, sorrels, bays and dapple greys—a grand sight for a young boy, and never to be forgotten!

* * *

It should have come as no surprise when as an adult Peter chose a career in acting. Even his father, who frowned upon it as a profession, played a role in "The Normans of Warwickshire" for a pageant put on by the WI in 1930. He was Edric "the Wild," who earned that appellation in 1067 for his rebellion against the usurpation of his land by the conquerors. The Colonel's brother Leslie, who was director of music at Stowe School, must have noticed early on that his young nephew had a good ear and a beautiful voice, useful gifts for a life on stage. Moreover, Peter was a beautiful child and very outgoing, so he took to school and church plays as a duck to water. We would be remiss, furthermore, should we fail to observe that

Stratford-upon-Avon was less than thirty-two kilometers from where he was born.

It may have been the year he turned five that he played a shepherd in the nativity play given by the Sunday school on the last Sunday of Advent. It is hard to tell his age from the picture we have, which shows him swathed in the cloak and headdress of the shepherd's costume, with just his face visible; but we may be sure he was very excited.

"John, John! Will you help me pwactice?" pleaded Peter the day before the event. John would be reading the story of Christmas from the second chapter of Luke as the children enacted it. But at the moment he was engrossed in his book of collected Sherlock Holmes mysteries. Conan Doyle was not that long deceased and was still very popular, his medieval romance novels even more than his mysteries. John was a fan of Holmes, however, and had taken to holding a pipe in his mouth, though he was not yet allowed to light it. Of course he acquiesced to his little brother's plea, feeling very paternal.

"Yes I will, Peter, but first you must recite the chapter and verse." John already tended toward the clerical.

"The Gospel of Saint Luke, chapter two, verse eight," said Peter proudly.

John then began reciting from Luke 2:8, which begins, "And in that region there were shepherds keeping watch over their flock by night." After the heavenly host praises God and proclaims good will toward men, John read on, "'When the angels went away from them into heaven, the shepherds said to one another...'" He glanced at Peter expectantly.

"'Let us go over to Bethlehem and see this thing that has happened, which the Lord has made known to us.'" Peter enunciated this line slowly and loudly, happy there were no "r" sounds to stumble over.

"Very good, Peter. Then what happens?"

"We leave the stage and wait for Mawy and Joseph and the baby to come back. Then we come on with our sheep. Will there be weal sheep, John?"

"Not inside the building, but the crêche is set up, wreaths, a Christmas tree." He lifted his little brother to his knee before asking, "Are you nervous, baby brother?" John was nine years older, already in his teen years.

"Oh no, John, I love pwetending to be a shepherd, and all the other childwen will see my special costume!"

"Well, that's good. You will be fine, and you do make a very convincing shepherd!"

The next morning, Nanny took Peter to the Sunday school. The rest of the family had gone to early service, and the play was to follow. The day was cold, and a light snow had fallen before dawn, dusting the gravestones in the churchyard, the gate to which had blown open and was creaking on its hinge as parishioners arrived. Nanny C., always the one to see to things, latched it as she passed. She carried Peter's outfit in a bag, having dressed him warmly, even to his best new cap, a Harris Tweed he had been given for his birthday, quite special for so young a child. The children in the play donned their costumes in the cloak room, where they also left their coats and hats, scarves and gloves.

The play did indeed go very well, in spite of fidgeting on the part of youngsters in the audience and one squalling infant whose mother took him out of the room. Enthusiastic applause from parents and children followed the performance.

Unaccountably, not Peter's family, nor even Nanny C. had been made aware that each child was to bring a gift for the baby Jesus, these of course to be distributed to poor children in the community. When all the other children began lining up to present their Christmas gifts, which were being laid by the crêche, Peter became upset and ran to where his mother was sitting. "But, Mummy, I didn't bwing anything!"

"I'm sure it will be all right, darling, if we bring something later. There will be time, don't worry," she reassured him.

He stood next to her chair awhile with that serious frown on his face, then bolted toward the cloak room. He was still in his shepherd's costume when he came out, and there was still a line of children filing by the crêche, which was carved of wood with baby Jesus in a rustic looking manger. When it was his turn, Peter laid down his best new tweed cap as his gift. His mother felt her eyes well up with tears and a hard lump form in her throat from the emotion she was trying to conceal. She was enormously proud of her son and so impressed by this young boy, beautiful in every sense. Her love spilled over, as tears came in spite of her.

* * *

By now we may be getting a somewhat idealistic and unbalanced impression of Peter H. as perfect in every way, sweet and generous, good looking, well behaved, without blemish of any sort. But then we would be getting ahead of our story were we to jump to the tale of Mahal, the donkey, and then even Babs the pony, both of whom the child rode into the house and upstairs to his bedroom on separate occasions, to the consternation of Nanny C., who for some time after was unable to see the humor of it. Of course when she did, she made sure that this account of major mischief became legendary. No, Peter was angelic but not an angel; indeed, after he started school his angelic smile was more often characterized as *mischievous*. But we will deal with that in due course.

England between the wars was desperate to recover from the first, to restore stability and prosperity, and above all to remain at peace. But Neville Chamberlain's popularity waned as the distant rumblings of unrest from across the Channel grew louder, with Germany seizing Austria and threatening Czechoslovakia. The many military veterans, such as Colonel H., must have watched these developments with considerable uneasiness. The prowess of the German Luftwaffe meant that England was well within reach of Hitler's destructiveness, and even vulnerable to invasion. After all, the long history of these islands in the North Atlantic is a sad tale of conquering hordes, from the Romans, to the Vikings, and worst of all the Normans. Now they feared, came the Germans. We may safely assume that Peter's father was already envisioning plans for an air raid shelter to protect his family, even as his wife prepared for their biennial hosting of Parish

Sunday, held near 24 June, the feast day of Saint John the Baptist, patron saint of their church.

It was quite an exciting and anticipated event, involving villagers young and old, from all walks of life and strata of society. Festivities began with a parade in which the British Legion[30] would march, as well as the Boy Scouts, Cubs, Girl Guides, and of course a marching band. The parade would wend its way to the church, where a service was held in midafternoon to honor the occasion, following which the parade continued either to the Grange or to Berkswell Hall, the estate of Colonel W., in alternating years. Everyone marching in the parade was treated to tea and an afternoon of fun, particularly enjoyable for the village children.

Mrs. H. was accustomed to entertaining on a grand scale, but this year the Boy Scouts alone would number more than forty. The troop had been started in 1931. So Mrs. H. would be skipping church service to stay home and oversee preparations. Long tables would be set up on the lawn for refreshments: punch bowls with lemonade, pitchers of tea, cookies, cakes, curds and clotted creams, fresh fruit, while inside, the large entry hall would provide much of the same in a quieter atmosphere for the adults; and in the kitchen, away from the heat, several churns would be busy turning out homemade ice cream of different flavors.

Extra staff was needed, of course, to bring this off, and each of the boys was given a task. John was to mind the tree house to ensure no child fell from it; Michael was in charge of donkey rides; and Patrick was to see that little brother Peter stayed out of trouble and had a good time. Patrick also had helped the gardener, Tom H., hide gifts under the shrubs for the treasure hunt. There would be about three dozen prizes: candies, small toys, books wrapped in brown paper, and the grand prize, bringing honor and good fortune for the child who found the most treasures—a very nice small statue of Saint John the Baptist.

We may be sure that Mrs. H. embraced her role as hostess with energy and gusto. She was not a nervous person, but to the contrary, loved people and was exuberantly warm hearted. Her beloved roses were at their peak in this season, and she relished the scent filling the house as she placed bouquets in each room and even on the outdoor tables. Many fragrant blooms also remained on the wisteria vine on the front of the Grange.

At just past four o'clock, the sound of the marching band crescendoed as the parade approached. Peter, who had returned home with the family after service, was upstairs changing his shoes, and ran to his brother John's room to look out the window. He cranked it open, and the warm summer air spilled into the room, with it the pungency of new mulch from under the hedges. The color guard of the Legion led the marchers, all looking smart in their uniforms, even the Cubs, so proud to be parading in step just like their elders. But it was the band that made the day, stepping briskly down the lane.

"What are they playing, John?" asked Peter. "It is so exciting!"

"That's 'the British Grenadiers.'"

"What's a 'gwenadier'?"

"It comes from the word 'grenade,' which is a bomb soldiers throw at the enemy in a war." The Etonian was already taking on a certain erudition, and loved instructing his younger brothers. Patrick came in looking for Peter.

"Come on, the scouts will be here soon and all the other children. Let's go outside!"

"Patwick! They're playing 'The Gwenadiers'! John told me!"

Patrick rolled his eyes at his brother's as yet undiagnosed speech problem. He looked over Peter's head to see the most perfect view of the approaching parade. "Well, let us march downstairs, Peter. What would you like to do first? Get ice cream? There will be races, you know, sack races, relay races."

"I want to wide the donkeys!"

"Very well, but you'll have to wait your turn. What about the treasure hunt?"

"I want the others to get the pwizes. That would be fair."

"Come on, then, ice cream, then donkeys," and off they went tumbling over themselves down the stairs. John followed more sedately, leaving his unlit pipe in his room, to take up his post by the tree house. As he passed through the front hall, though, he grabbed a quick cup of tea with one of Cook's famous scones. Next to them was a very rich and tempting chocolate cake baked by the rector's wife; but John knew that Cook was a bit jealous of Mrs. W.'s baking skill, and the scone was faster.

In the nearby sitting room, his father sat having tea with Colonel W., whose given name was Charles, the two old veterans in a deep discussion concerning the state of the world. With Hitler having invaded Prague in March, could anyone still believe he would stop there? And now Britain had entered a commitment to defend Poland. The handwriting was on the wall for these two military men, and they knew that the Midlands of England would be in the crosshairs because of its factories. There was talk in the village of constructing dugouts, some calling them "bunk holes," as air raid shelters; and the Colonel had been called upon by the War Office to recruit a regiment from the area.

"I understand, Bill, that you already have enlisted six hundred men from Warwickshire. How is it going?"

"Well, Charles, I'm afraid we are still training with broom handles and garden tools, but the men are a jolly good lot, I must say."

Colonel W. laughed. "And the Minister of War is letting it be known that we have 'the finest equipment in the world.'"

"Don't forget we also have Leslie, my musician brother. At least we will be singing on key! Seriously, we need to mobilize quickly, and to conceal our arsenals from enemy aircraft. This whole region will be in danger."

"It will come to war then, you think."

"And soon, old chap. You know Betty and I agreed with Mr. Churchill after Versailles that the reparations were so punishing as to portend further conflict; and any thoughtful person with knowledge of economic conditions in Germany can see why this Hitler fellow has arisen."

"I have never asked you, Bill, but how does Betty feel about war? Her family goes back to the early Quakers."

"What's happening in Europe, Charles, is so outrageous as to lead a pacifist to enlist!" They both laughed, "And Betty is half Irish after all, a bellicose lot!"

"I understand." He lit a cigar, proffered by his host. "You've done a bang up job for Parish Sunday this year. The children love coming to the Grange." In fact, the sound of youngsters laughing and shouting came through the open windows and could be heard throughout the house.

"We try to measure up, Charles," was the bemused response. Peter's parents were relative newcomers to the village, having moved there after their marriage in 1923, while Colonel W. had inherited his estate from his father, who purchased it in 1888.

Before long, finishing their tea, the two made their way outdoors to check on all the activities. Though the summer solstice had just past, shadows already were lengthening, and the younger children were running out of steam. Sir Charles H. was in the thick of things still, however, running the relay races. He was older than both the Colonels, and as a bachelor, loved the village children; he was a big supporter of the scout troop, for example. Was it at his behest, being a newsman, that a photograph was taken that day in front of the Grange of all the four dozen or so Boy Scouts and Cubs, with Colonel and Mrs. H., host and hostess, in the center? Very likely, perhaps.

Finally, when all the prizes had been awarded, nearly all the hidden treasures ferreted out from under the bushes, and the chocolate cake baked by the rector's wife devoured to the last crumb, the remaining guests, who had succumbed neither to fatigue nor stomach ache, gathered in the back field where a bonfire had been laid. Tom the gardener lit it, and the yellow light of the blaze flickered on people's faces in the twilight as they stood or sat in the dewy grass.

Peter ran up to his father, who was standing next to the rector, and raised both arms to be picked up. Of course Daddy obliged, balancing the lad on his shoulder. From this perch, Peter could feel the fire's warmth, welcome after the sun had set, and smell the faint musk of his father's pomade. The scout leaders got the attention of the group and led them in singing such Scout songs as "Campfire's Burning" and "Softly Falls the Light of Day." The sound of voices, muffled in the open air, rose up with the mist over the field. There were enough band members remaining to make up a brass choir; and as it was getting dark, they struck up "God Save the King." Then the rector suggested the vesper hymn, "Now the Day is Over." Peter loved this one and knew all the words. As he sang out, loud and sweet, from his father's shoulder, father and rector looked at each other, smiling their amazement.

* * *

Less than three months had passed when the predictions of Colonel H. came true, and Britain was at war with Germany. The whole country rallied to the cause, and preparations rolled out precipitately. For example, evacuation plans for civilians in cities and towns, including Coventry, went into effect immediately, with rural villages being organized to billet the evacuees. Before any bombs had fallen, volunteers were going house to house matching families with any villagers willing and able to take them in. And by the time Peter's sixth birthday came around in November, the Grange had an underground air raid shelter entered by stairs leading down from the kitchen. Peter thought it was the most exciting place, with cots and tables, vents in the ceiling, a camp stove, and even a camp latrine, behind a curtain for privacy.

But while he was curious about war and bombs, the birthday was all he could think about, because his mother had told him to expect a big surprise. On the day, he awoke early and scampered into his parents' room, where his mother sat at her dressing table. This particular piece of furniture held a strong fascination for Peter. It was of the design with an oval mirror at the center, framing a woman's full torso, and taller sections with drawers on either side. There was Mother's jewelry box, guarding such beautiful heirlooms, small glass perfume bottles with fancy stoppers, and the round box of face powder topped by a sweet smelling puff, soft as fur.

"Mummy, do we hate Germans?" They regarded one another in the mirror, he peering out from under his brow with a precocious solemnity. She reached around for him, and sat him on her knee.

"No, Peter, it is wrong to hate, but the leaders of Germany are doing very bad things to innocent people, and we must do whatever we can to stop them. But what a thing to talk about on your birthday, dear!"

He reached up and put his arms around her neck. "I wish Daddy were here." The Colonel's regiment had gone in August to a training camp near Buddleigh Salterton in Devon nearly three hundred kilometers away.

"I do too, Peter, but he is training young men to be soldiers, and now it is very important for them to be well prepared. He will be home at Christmas, but he has left a *very* special present for you, which you shall see after breakfast. Now, run along and get dressed." She kissed him and off he went. Nanny was in his room and had his clothes ready, knowing how eager he would be. Breakfast, we can be sure, was not so much eaten as gulped. John was back at Eton, and the other boys, even cousin Daphne, were in school, but they would be home in time to share birthday cake, along with Granny and Grandpa B., who were also coming at teatime.

After Peter had eaten, Nanny took a handkerchief to use as a blindfold. Tying it over his eyes, she said, "Take my hand, and I will guide you to your birthday surprise. Cook is coming with us and your Mum is waiting there."

Peter was on tenterhooks of anticipation. What could possibly be awaiting him, guarded with such thrilling secrecy? As he followed, trying unsuccessfully to peak round the handkerchief, Nanny led him carefully out the back door. He felt the cold air on his face, and instantly understood why Nanny had put a sweater on him. They were going down the gravel path to the left toward the stable, and sure enough the smells of hay and manure grew ever stronger as they neared and then entered it. Finally they stopped, and he recognized his mother's shoes as she took his hand and lifted the blindfold. It was a pony!

Grabbing his mother tightly around the waist, he cried, "Oh, thank you, Mummy! Thank you! Thank you! Thank you!" The three women—Lily the cook, nanny Ellen, and Mother—laughed at his exuberance, anticipated naturally. As much as he loved the donkeys, a pony was a step up; and what child who ever lived has not wished for just this very birthday present?

"Happy birthday, darling! This is Babs. Should I help you into the saddle?"

"I can do it, Mummy." The pony already had a very nice leather saddle, and Peter did indeed know to put his left foot in the stirrup and swing his right leg over, holding onto the saddle, with Mother holding the reins.

"I'll be back to the kitchen then, Peter, to start your birthday cake," said Lily. "Your favorite, of course."

"Angel cake?"

"What else!" she laughed, and pulled her coat around her as the wind was nippy.

Mrs. H. led Babs into the paddock with Peter in the saddle, and before long he was gripping the pony with his little legs, and steering her with the reins. How she came to be called "Babs" we may never really know. Could it have been the nickname of a hairdresser in nearby Leamington Spa? The first girlfriend of his oldest brother? Let us assume, given this uncertainty, that Babs came with her name. Of one thing we can be perfectly sure, however, she was the start of Peter's love for the horses.

What an exciting autumn it must have been for young Peter, riding his new pony, and Christmas just around the corner. Colonel H. did come home from army camp as promised and John from Eton, in mid-December. By this time, the Colonel's mother was living at the Grange, having been widowed the year before Peter was born. Redeeming his gift to baby Jesus the previous Christmas, she had replaced Peter's Harris Tweed cap on his birthday, and he looked so smart in it as he trotted over the barren fields on Babs. He would not be in the nativity play this year, but instead had been enlisted to sing a solo with the children's choir, his favorite carol, "Away in a Manger." The sweetness of his soprano voice had greatly impressed the rector, and he had begun learning the rudiments of music notation from Uncle Leslie, who at this time was also serving as an officer in his brother's regiment.

Christmas was a Monday that year, and although people were "jittery," that being the catch word in use, air raids had not yet occurred. The Grange in fact was in a seasonal hubbub, with family even more eager to gather. Elizabeth's parents were staying over until Boxing Day; Granny H., then age 76, was in residence, and the great aunts, those "elegant old darlings," would visit after church Christmas Day.

Before the festivities commenced, however, there was at least one quiet evening when Peter, exhausted from anticipation and not a little queasy from too many Christmas cookies, was able to curl up next to his mother in front of a warm fire, soothed by the sound of her voice.

"'The country lay bare and entirely leafless around him,'" she read from *Wind in the Willows*, "'and he thought that he had never seen so far, and intimately into the insides of things as on that winter day when Nature was deep in her annual slumber and seemed to have kicked the clothes off.'" Peter especially loved this description of "The Wild Wood," the title of chapter three, where Mole, led by Rat, goes searching for Mr. Badger; and the illustrations brought all the little woodland animals to life, dressing and speaking just like proper gentlemen.

When she finished reading chapter three, Mum closed that book and picked up one of nursery rhymes, which the older boys had used in learning to read. Between the efforts of mother and nanny, Peter had learned his letters, though he was the child who wrote "e's" backwards and confused "b" with "d."

"Now you read to me, darling." Mother held the book for Peter.

"'Jack and Jill went up the hill to fetch a pail of water . . .'" He could recite this one by heart, of course.

"How about this one?" Mother said, turning the page.

"'The owl and the pussycat went to sea,'" Peter read haltingly, "'in a . . . bea . . .'" He stopped, trying to sound out the word.

"'Beautiful,'" Mother interjected, "some words have silent letters."

"'In a beautiful pea gween doat.'"

"That's a 'b,' Peter."

"A beautiful pea gween boat,'" Peter finished proudly.

"Very good, Peter! Very good! Now it is your bed time, and *you* are *ready* for it. Nanny will tuck you in." She kissed him and sent him along, showing none of her concern that he might have trouble with reading, and that given the threat of air raids and evacuations it was no time to be sending him off to school. She and Nanny, with some help from his older brothers, would do the best they could.

Nanny had been listening from her chair by the window, where she sat with her knitting—a long forest green woolen scarf, matching Peter's new cap. Unknown to him, it was to be his Christmas present, and was perhaps the start of his lifelong love of such scarves. She set it down and took his hand to lead him up the stairs.

By the time Christmas Eve arrived, the Grange was bustling. The Colonel was home, and John from Eton, and Elizabeth's parents were staying. Peter was to sing at the evening service as well as Christmas morning, and he could hardly eat any dinner he was so excited. Nanny had him bundled up, and his choir robe, carefully pressed, neatly draped over her arm as they set out for church.

There had been no snow, but a dampness to the cold air promised it; the stars, nonetheless, were twinkling. Most of the family were attending in the morning, so not everyone was going on Christmas Eve, except of course Peter's parents and grandparents. Once at the church, he donned his robe eagerly with Nanny's help, and joined the other children in the choir, climbing to the loft. They sat in front of the adult members, causing Peter to feel suddenly very grown-up. He sang his solo beautifully, his boy soprano ringing out to the rafters of the old stone church, sending chills through many a congregant, certainly his mother. He loved to sing and joined in the other carols as well, sometimes switching to the alto parts, which his Uncle Leslie had taught him. By the end of the service, well past his usual bedtime, he was thoroughly exhausted, and wanted only to find his Nanny and go home. Easily foreseeing this, she was waiting at the bottom of the stairs to the choir loft to retrieve the choir robe and bundle him up again. The other children were all raving to him about his solo, and he was gracious if a bit sheepish in his acceptance.

As Nanny buttoned his coat, he yawned and asked, "Why do people think I am special? Anyone can sing."

"Perhaps, darling, but not as beautifully as you do," came the response.

"I can spell 'beautiful,' Nanny! It has silent letters!" he said, with the nimble leap of a child's mind.

As they left the church, a light snow had indeed begun to fall, putting Nanny C. in mind of the Sunday Peter was christened. By morning, the countryside was just barely covered in a thin white blanket, the low winter sun struggling to edge out the clouds.

But regardless of weather, is there any morning more exciting to a child than that of Christmas Day? Peter was up at dawn and flying down the stairs to find his stocking, the one with his name embroidered on it by his Granny B. and hanging by a special hook to the wooden mantle in the drawing room, where the tree also stood. So loaded was the stocking with candy and nuts and fruit that it looked about to fall. Patrick and Michael were close behind Peter, and the three boys sat under the tree to sort the stack of presents. Nanny soon came shuffling down the stairs to supervise the jolly lads, one hand on the railing and the other pulling on her apron. Peter had found the green scarf she had knitted for him, and already had it draped about his neck.

"Thank you, Nanny, thank you! It is so soft and wonderful and matches my cap!" he said, running into her arms. It was in fact his favorite present that Christmas, because it was of a fine lamb's wool, not the Shetland that is so scratchy.

"You are most welcome, dear, I am glad you like it. Now boys, no candy before breakfast!"

John of course had outgrown this childish exuberance, but with all the commotion, he and all in the house were up, and the joyous day rolled out as it commonly does, fulfilling plans and dreams then slowly subsiding into a nostalgic fatigue.

At church, the family pew was as crowded as it had been for Peter's baptism, with the grandparents, aunts and uncles. His mother had to save room for his father, who was detained in the vestibule by the many neighbors questioning him about war preparations: Did the recruits have proper equipment yet? Yes. Were the orders for evacuation of Coventry premature? Yes, in his opinion.

By the time he came down the aisle, a hush had come over the congregation as Arthur G. played the organ prelude. The Colonel was in uniform, and though nearly fifty years old, he was still very fit, in the tall black boots, the medals on his jacket, his cap tucked reverently under his arm. Then over the soft organ music came a rather loud whisper.

"That's my Daddy!" Peter was heard to say to his choir mates from the loft. The Colonel turned on his heel and looking up, with a smile and wink to his son, saluted the choir, as the low murmur of laughter rippled through the nave.

* * *

There was much snow that winter that lingered in long spells of freezing weather. The initial frenzy of war planning cooled down as the expected air raids did not come. Nevertheless, the course of the war on the Continent was followed closely and with considerable anxiety, while careful preparations continued in every community. In Peter's village, for example, sewing tables were set up in the rectory where the women met to make triangular bandages for the Red Cross; and plans for billeting evacuees from the cities went on. Air raid shelters were built, some provided by the government for those without means, and blackout curtains made for every house and building. With Colonel H. still away at training camp, we may assume that Mrs. H. was kept busy, involving herself wherever she could be of help.

In the meantime, Peter was happily distracted with his pony, learning from the stable boy, a local lad hired for several days a week, how to groom her, feed her hay and water, and put on her saddle and bridle, a hackamore, without a bit. As soon as the snow receded enough, he was out every afternoon riding Babs around the paddock, and he was such a natural, he was trusted to do so unattended.

One day in mid-March with the sun warming toward the equinox, but the wind still sharp as ice, Mrs. H. was at a WI meeting, where she was president, and Nanny C. was in the nursery ironing the boys' clothes. The Grange was modern in its day for having its own electric and water sources. Peter was out on Babs as usual.

Nanny began to hear a thudding noise from somewhere in the house, which she thought at first must be a shutter or door banging in the wind. But the sound seemed to be coming from the front hallway; so setting the iron on its heel, she went to investigate. We struggle to visualize the expression of shocked horror at what she found, but her loud, spontaneous shriek conveyed it to all the staff, who came running. There midway up the staircase was Babs, with Peter on her back looking proud as he could be.[31]

"See, Nanny? Babs can climb stairs, I taught her!"

Well, what was Nanny to do? She knew the pony would not back down the steps, so she had to let them continue to the next floor and turn around, but what then? "Jenny," she called to the maid, "go fetch Jack," the stable lad, "and Tom," the gardener, "if you can find them, to come help."

When poor Babs reached the top of the stairs, she was clearly in a fright, so Nanny had to speak softly. "Peter, get down carefully, dear, and go to your room."

"But I want Babs to come with me, Nanny!"

"Please, Peter, your pony needs to go back to her stable."

Crestfallen to put it mildly, Peter stalked off, as Jack and Tom came running in. Tom stood in front of the pony so that she was not able to see downward, while Jack urged her forward one slow step at a time. Once Babs was safely out the front door, Nanny was free to fume, and fume she did.

"Who is going to shovel this manure out of the entryway? Jack, get a shovel, quick before Mrs. H. gets home, and don't scratch the tile!" Joyce, the housekeeper, equally disgruntled, mumbled something about fetching a mop and bucket. Her eyes met Nanny's, and the two just shook their heads, sighing heavily.

"You'll have to tell her" she said.

"I know," replied Nanny.

By the time Mrs. H. came home that day, peace and decorum had been restored; but as she removed her coat, Ellen reported Peter's misdeed. She listened, picturing the outrageous incident in her mind, and her irrepressible Irish side brought a smile to her face, which she tried vainly to conceal from the nanny. At the same time, she could not help recalling the day Peter had asked to bring the donkey to his bedroom, and then the orphaned Gypsy girl, to whom he gave his toy donkey. Had he not told her he no longer needed the toy because he had a live donkey?

"Good Lord!" she remarked to Ellen with as much indignation as she could muster, "I will go up and speak to him, and bring him down shortly for tea, in the nursery."

She found Peter in his room with his head still buried in his pillow.

"Peter, look at me!" She tried to be stern. He rolled over, but averted his glance. "What were you thinking? Horses belong in the barn. Your pony is too large and heavy to come inside. She might have broken something, or hurt herself. Promise me you will never try to bring Babs into the house again."

"I promise, Mummy," he said, his head lowered in shame. But knowing the history of this business, we might be forgiven for suggesting that when his mother wasn't looking, that quick smile came to young Peter's face and a most devilish glint to his eye.

"Come down then for your tea." She got up and took his hand.

Later that day, after dinner, Peter and his mother sat together in the drawing room in front of a crackling fire, blazing all the more for the wind whistling down the chimney. Holy Week was coming up, as Easter came early that year, 24 March in fact; and in keeping with the advancing spring, Peter was learning to read Beatrix Potter's "Peter Rabbit." It is easy to imagine he loved his namesake. Peter swung his legs over his mother's lap, and she picked up the book.

"Shall I begin?" she asked, and not waiting for the reply, since this had become a little ritual, she read, "'Once upon a time there were four little rabbits, and their names were Flopsy, Mopsy, Cottontail, and—'"

"'—and Peter'!" said he on cue, and he continued, "'They lived with their mother in a sandbank, underneath the woot of a vewy big fir tree.'"

Thus the familiar tale unfolded, Mother turning the yellowed pages of the well-worn volume slowly and gently, and Peter never failing to share the terror of the poor rabbit, pursued by Mr. McGregor, when he foolishly disobeys his mother and steals into the farmer's garden. The picture of little Peter Rabbit lying exhausted but safe at home, having escaped with his life, was hard for the child even to look at. Mother closed the book and gave him an extra-long hug.

"You see darling, awful consequences can come when you disobey."

Of course he then realized why she had wanted to read that particular book that evening. But in his own child's mind he really could see no similarity between raiding a garden and bringing a pony into the house.

* * *

The spring of 1940 passed without the sound of the air raid siren, but people were far from complacent, as reports continued of Hitler's relentless advance. British troops were driven back to Dunkirk, whence they were evacuated; and then fascist Italy jumped in on the German side. But the rural villages of England knew they would not be the targets of enemy planes, which would be bombing the cities and especially the centers of manufacturing such as Birmingham and Coventry. The impact on villages like Peter's came in absorbing the large numbers of people fleeing the destruction. Yet blackouts each night were already being enforced, and the countryside seemed eerily still. A Mrs. M.[32], who was secretary of the Women's Institute, and whose only son, Alan, had been wounded and taken prisoner in the early fighting, wrote in her diary, "A sort of deep stillness comes over everything from time to time . . . and the village seems empty in the evenings. One misses young life everywhere."

It was a Tuesday night, 25 June, a quiet, balmy summer night, the darkness punctuated by the sawing of katydids in the hedges and the occasional sweetness of a nightingale. John was home for the summer, but the Colonel was still away at the regimental training camp. Close on to midnight, everyone asleep at the Grange, Mrs. H. awakened to a distant throbbing of engines, the sound growing steadily. Needless to say under the circumstances and with her husband absent she slept with one eye open. Around the side of the blackout curtain she could see the searchlights busy against the night sky. Then the sirens sounded. As she grabbed her robe, the light went on in the hallway. Nanny was already waking the older boys. The two women exchanged apprehensive glances, and Elizabeth said, "I'll bring Peter."

He was still asleep, the deep and innocent sleep of childhood, as she picked him up, blanket and all, and carried him to the stairs. He was an armful by this age. Reaching for her neck, he asked in a drowsy voice, "Where are we going, Mummy?"

"Do you hear the siren, darling? It is a signal to go to the shelter." At the top of the stairs, she put him down. "Now take my hand, and careful on the steps." Nanny was leading the way, turning lights on and off as they went through the house. The other live-in staff, Joyce and Lily, were waiting in the kitchen and would follow the family down to the shelter, which would certainly have been large enough for the household.

Though it was summer, this underground room had the damp chill of a root cellar, and a slight musty smell. There were cots for everyone, each with a thin mattress and bedding. Elizabeth took the one next to her youngest, and after covering him, added her own blanket. John stopped her.

"No, Mum," he said, "Peter can have my blanket. I am not cold." His mother squeezed his shoulder affectionately; at fifteen he was getting a bit too old for Mother's hugs and kisses.

"Thank you, John," she said. "What would we do without you?"

In the morning, reports came of homes and businesses bombed out in Coventry, adding to the tide of evacuees. Throughout that summer, the air raids escalated, coming always at night, in what the Germans called "Operation Moonlight Sonata." The attacks grew longer and more frequent. Residents of Coventry would come in the evenings to their assigned billets in the village, praying that their homes would still be there for them to return to in the morning.

Turning up at the Grange one night came a certain Mr. W.[33], who was of course taken in; and over the next few months, another forty members of his family joined him. Commodious as the place was, this number must have been a terrible strain, on the facilities and the people. The men and boys were put up in the stable, women inside in the staff sitting room.

Except that the adults were being very serious, the young children of the village had no real understanding of what was happening. Peter for example loved having more playmates in the extended family of Mr. W., some his own age. But his mother had cautioned him not to let them ride the pony.

"These are townsfolk, Peter," she told him, "not accustomed to handling animals. You may take them on donkey rides though. Betsy and Mahal can handle it."

We have a picture of these two donkeys, one quite a bit larger than the other, but no indication of which was which; so we are venturing a guess that Betsy was the smaller animal. It was upon Betsy perhaps that Peter's new friends were taking rides one morning in late August. By that time the increasing number of sleepless nights, the roar of engines overhead and the boom of distant explosions until the small hours of morning, were taking a toll on nerves. One boy in particular, somewhat older than Peter, was becoming irascible to the point of belligerence. He sat on the fence as his little sister rode Betsy, Peter leading her around the paddock.

"Why don't you let us ride the pony, Peter? I don't think you know how yourself!" the older boy taunted.

"Of course I know how to wide my own pony!"

"You can't even say 'ride,' Peter!" the exchange continued.

Well, that jab was too much, and Peter blurted out, "I can wide my pony vewy well. I even wode her into the house and taught her to climb the stairs to my bedwoom."

Naturally at that point, proof became the only way poor Peter could save face. To his credit, we should consider that he weighed the matter in his mind. Betsy was smaller and lighter than Babs, and so less able to do damage. Furthermore, he had promised his mother not to ride the *pony* into the house; no proscription stood against a donkey.

The little girl dismounted, and Peter jumped on Betsy's back, riding her out of the paddock and to the front door of the house, several curious children now following.

"Open the door," he commanded the ruffian with authority, and complete confidence in his mount. Into the house and up the stairs they went. At the top, Peter got down, smiling in vindication, but the troublesome boy was not done.

"I bet you can't get her back down the stairs!" he sneered.

Nanny C., who had been in Peter's room folding clothes, came running upon hearing hooves on the staircase once again, and here was Peter yet another time struggling to pull Betsy down the stairs. The other boys were laughing uproariously, while the girls, trying to be helpful, attempted to cajole the poor animal. Betsy of course was braying loudly. It seems that what Peter had failed to realize was that the stubbornness of a mule comes from the donkey's contribution. But Ellen knew this quite well. She said nothing, but flew down the back steps and out the kitchen door. Conveniently, Tom H. was tending to the rose bushes near the house. They looked at each other, and eyebrows were raised.

"Get me a blindfold, Ellen, and tell Jack," he said, coming inside and up the stairs two at a time. Now, it must be observed that the sonority of a man's voice, especially a large man—as Tom was—is far more reliable at seizing a child's attention than a woman's.

"Peter," Tom bellowed, "if I ever have to come into this house again to rescue an animal, your Daddy is going to hear from me!"

The poor lad, now red as a beet with embarrassment, ran into his room, slamming the door. Betsy was small enough that Tom and Jack might have lifted her down the stairs, but that seemed somewhat risky; so with her blindfolded, they raised her front end down a step at a time, while she managed her back legs. No harm was done, except to Peter's pride. When his door was still closed hours later, Nanny started to worry; but too furious to talk to him, she enlisted the oldest brother. "John, will you please go in and ask him what happened?"

John knocked softly, and as he entered the room, Peter sat up on the edge of the bed, drying his swollen eyes. When John had heard the whole story of the bully taunting and mocking Peter, he took his brother's hand and pulled him up. "Come down to the drawing room, and I'll ask Jenny to bring us tea," he said, and this he did, at the same time relating the whole misadventure to Nanny, who then understood immediately, having taken note of the troublemaking boy before. When she later reported the incident to Mrs. H., she emphasized this child's role.

"Thank you, Ellen, I will speak to Mr. W. about him." Mr. W., their temporary boarder, was the boy's grandfather.

That night Peter came late to dinner, his mother and brothers already seated around the table. He could not look at anyone, and he hardly ate a thing, though Cook had obtained a large and delicious capon in spite of shortages at the butcher's. It was a warm night, so after dinner they adjourned to the garden room, throwing open its great windows to the summer breezes. John read his Sherlock Holmes; Michael and Patrick played checkers on the floor; and Mother as always took a book to read to Peter, who seemed to anticipate a rebuke.

"Mummy, are you angry at me?"

"No, darling, I am not. I think Betsy already taught you this lesson." She tousled his hair gently, and they smiled at one another, she thinking to herself that, war or no war, this child needed to be in school!

* * *

As fate would have it, that very day at tea with the rector's wife, Mrs. H. had learned that a certain Miss K.,[34] who had a primary school in Coventry, was billeted in the village, and was actively seeking a place to relocate her school for the duration. This incident with the donkey served to reinforce Mum's intention to offer the Grange for this purpose. What better solution than to have Peter schooled at home? The arrangement was all the more felicitous as Miss K. was a proponent of the Montessori method, an educational philosophy originated by the Italian teacher, Maria Montessori in the 1890s. Its emphasis on channeling a child's natural curiosity and on an active participation in learning would certainly have appealed to Peter's mother. It was in fact Miss K. who before long, having accepted the offer and set up a classroom in the nursery, determined that Peter was dyslexic. With her special attention, and many an evening reading with Mother, he was able to compensate.

The frequent air raids continued over Coventry, Birmingham, and London, sirens usually sounding late at night and the "all clear" some hours after. The countryside was not a target, yet incendiary missiles might be misguided, starting fires in fields or hedges. Air raid wardens were on duty to see to these. The Moat, estate of Sir Charles, incurred damage one summer night to the roof, the greenhouse, and a holly hedge, which went up like a torch.

But on a Thursday evening in November 1940, the fourteenth to be exact, as Mrs. H. sat with the boys after dinner in the drawing room, they were startled by the siren at eight o'clock. John and Michael were both now at Eton, so Mother with Peter, Patrick, and Nanny headed down to the shelter along with Lily and Joyce and anyone else for whom there was space. Many local people, tired of this near nightly ritual, were taking their chances above ground.

The bombing went on for hours. At midnight, Lily made hot cocoa on the camp stove, hoping that at least the children might get some sleep, but Patrick and Peter were wide awake playing cards together. When Peter finally grew sleepy, Patrick switched to solitaire, while Mother and Nanny took turns with Peter in the rocking chair. But the noise was unrelenting. At one point, Joyce went up to the kitchen to have a look out the window, and returned to report that the sky over Coventry was lit a fiery orange.

That was the night in fact that the Germans struck the heart of England: literally, hitting the Midlands; and figuratively, destroying the Coventry Cathedral, one of the country's oldest and most precious. It was not until shortly before dawn that the bombing finally subsided. Patrick and Peter had slept fitfully, but the adults not at all; so, exhausted, they came up to the kitchen at the sound of the "all clear," and then straight to bed. There would have been no classes that day, the local schools already forced to share classrooms with children evacuated from the towns.

No one was allowed into Coventry for some days after, due to the horrendous devastation. When this restriction had been lifted, Mrs. H. went one morning into her greenhouse and gathered a grand bunch of blooms, from chrysanthemums to lilies, asters and Shasta daisies. She had called Lou W. to drive her to Coventry, and he was ready and waiting as she came out with this large bouquet. She laid it gently in the back of the car, and with shears still in her hand, cut a branch of the winter cherry, laden with its autumn blooms, for good measure. Coming into the town, they were stunned by the dreadful destruction: shops and houses burned to the ground, others with windows and doors boarded up, just a shell of the public library remaining. Water mains had been bombed, so that there was no water to put out fires. They got as close as they could to the burned out Cathedral, and there upon the charred altar Elizabeth placed the flowers.[35] Overwhelmed by what they had seen and choking back tears, she and Lou rode home in silence.

That attack on Coventry had been the worst so far, but history records still more intense raids the following year, beginning on Tuesday, 8 April, and then every night until 11 April, 1941, which was Good Friday. Bombers, like a swarm of hornets, came constantly for hours; many were shot down, but the carnage and destruction they wreaked on towns and cities was severe. With the entrance of Russia into the war that June and of the United States in December, however, the tide began turning against Germany. Through it all, the country villages struggled to sustain some normalcy, at least for the children, and to help as best they could their neighbors displaced by the war. Peter had finally begun his formal education in the nursery of his own home with Miss K. and her other students. After a time, though, she found a more permanent site in the next village, by the train station, and only a short walk or bicycle ride from the Grange. Of course, Peter continued in her class, and happy to be really in school, no longer thought about bringing barnyard animals into the house.

* * *

"I think Peter is the cutest boy in the class," Ann G.[36] announced to her girlfriends as they stood together after school. It was a mild

September afternoon, leaves drifting down from the trees in the still warm sun. Peter was nearing his eighth birthday.

"I think he's *dreamy!*" exclaimed another of the girls.

"But he talks funny," the third protested. They were at the age when the potential for puppy love arises.

A group of the boys collecting their bicycles overheard this interchange, and one of them chimed in, uninvited. "Peter talks like a baby. I call him Peter Wabbit!"

"I don't care," Ann continued. "I am inviting him to my birthday party, and you don't need to come!"

Her birthday was about a month before Peter's. At that moment he came out of the school, where Miss K. had been helping him with his reading homework, and the other children, looking at him, were suddenly silent. Their behavior seemed odd, but he got on his bike and heading down the lane called to them, "See you tomorrow!"

The outspoken lad exchanged glances with his chums; and mounting their bicycles, they took off after Peter, who hearing their approach, pedaled as fast as he could. But two of the boys were older. They overtook him, blocking him from the front. All the while the group taunted, "Peter is a baby. Peter is a baby! Peter Wabbit, Peter Wabbit!"

Braking fast, Peter landed in the brambles by the side of the lane. The thorns tore his britches and swiped his face, drawing blood. Their deed done, the hooligans sped away, laughing and hooting, while Peter picked himself up and walked home limping. At the sight of him, Nanny registered horror. "What on earth happened to you, Peter?"

"I fell off my bicycle on the way home," was all he would say, as she cleaned his face. In fact he told no one of the humiliating incident; but the next day when he appeared at school with bruises on his arms and a bandage on his face, Miss K. was suspicious, especially as some of the other boys were sniggering and making faces behind his back. She was well aware that the ringleader of this group had a reputation as a bully.

That evening, Peter told Patrick what had happened, swearing him to secrecy; he needed to confide in his roommate because he was hatching a plot for his revenge. For several months, he had been avidly practicing his archery; with the threat of German invasion, after all, he envisioned defending his family and country in the same manner as the knights of old. He now had a quiver full of various types of arrows and had become quite proficient at hitting his mark.

He stayed awake until all the household was asleep, then crept carefully down the back stairs and out the back door, his bow in hand and the quiver around his shoulder. Quietly walking his bicycle to the lane, so as not to make any sound on the gravel, he set out for the village, and the house of the notorious bully. Fortunately the night was clear and moonlit. When he had gotten close enough, he crouched behind a hedge and took aim. *Swoosh!* One arrow hit the front door. *Swoosh!* Another, dead on, then three more. He had chosen arrows with no distinctive features that might be traced to him or to the archery club, yet they were reliably accurate. The next day, word of this mysterious happening spread through the village. When it reached Mrs. H., she began to put two and two together; and after a phone call to Miss K., she was certain who the archer was.

She confronted him in his bedroom, where he sat at the corner desk, his favorite place for school work because it had windows on two sides. "Peter, tell me the real reason you fell off your bicycle after school." To his mother's surprise, he turned around and stood up, launching into a loud tirade about how the boys had teased him, called him names, how he was outnumbered, and how unfair it was because he could not help how he talked. Needless to say she was taken aback. Where was her sweet, mild-mannered little boy? As the door to the room was open, Nanny C. and the maid Jenny listened outside, having themselves suspected there had been more to the whole affair.

"Peter," his mother continued, when he had finished, "there are better ways of handling bullies than with bow and arrow." This bid for Quaker pacifism, of course, revealed that she knew of his nocturnal escapade. He looked down sheepishly. She took him by the shoulders. "I heard that the arrows landed in a circle around the knocker."

Then he flashed that quick smile of his, and she leaned closer so that she could whisper, "Good shot!" She was half Irish after all.

Peter went to Ann's birthday party along with eight others of their classmates. It was held in the garden at Nailcote Hall, the stately Tudor manse formerly owned by the late Miss Katherine L. In an old photo, the children are pictured seated in a half circle around Ann, who stands in front of her birthday cake, dressed in a pinafore, with a barrette holding her short, straight hair away from her face. Behind her sits Peter, smiling at the camera; and it is at this point that we must describe his smile as *impish*.[37]

* * *

Peter was not a scholar, given his reading and speech problems. School was difficult for him; and after his exposure to the cruelty of other children, his behavior in class deteriorated. He forgot his books or his homework; he would whisper or pass notes, and answer Miss K. with gruff humor. She being an experienced and compassionate teacher understood, but was of course disappointed in the way the boy was dealing with his embarrassment and frustration. She must have been horrified to hear some time later that he would follow his older brothers to Eton.

For the next several years though, Peter found escape at the Cameo Theatre[38] in the next village, not far from school, where he developed his passion for film. His frequent companion, who shared this passion, was his cousin Daphne.[39] She was Patrick's age, yet loved meeting young Peter at the Cameo, the two converging on it by bicycle. There they would have enjoyed Charlie Chan and Shirley Temple movies, Basil Rathbone and Nigel Bruce as Sherlock Holmes and Dr. Watson, *Gone with the Wind*, and Sir Laurence Olivier in *Henry V*. Olivier gradually became Peter's idol, but at that age he had no thought of becoming an actor; he wanted to be a jockey.

"Peter! Peter!" Daphne cried as she sped up to the theatre, quickly back pedaling to brake in front of it. Peter was already waiting for her. "Sorry I'm late," she said breathlessly. "Let's hurry, I don't want to miss any of this one." The Cameo was showing *Rebecca*, with Olivier as Maxim deWinter, and Daphne was also reading the book.

"It's very sad, Daphne." Peter had seen it the day before. He sometimes went to the Cameo two or more times a week, and did not mind seeing a film over.

"I know, I'm reading it for school. But Olivier is the greatest, don't you agree? I'm going to marry him!" Daphne was almost in her teens.

"I would wather see him in Shakespeare myself."

"Oh yes, but *Wuthering Heights* and now *Rebecca*! So romantic . . . You should be an actor, Peter, you would be very good."

"Only if I could wide horses!" He had begun formal riding lessons with Skinner H. on his pony Babs. The children went inside and found seats, relieved to have missed only the newsreel, now dominated by war dispatches, especially depressing for the youngsters.

Peter would certainly have seen Shakespeare performed by the best in Stratford-upon-Avon, where the Royal Shakespeare Company resides at the Royal Shakespeare Theatre. The plays of the Bard have been offered there since 1769. His Granny H., who had come to live with the family some while after she was widowed, was particularly fond of the historical plays. She was steeped in the history of the Midlands, the Forest of Arden as it was known in centuries past, and its longbow archers. She loved to relate to her grandson the true tales of their heroic exploits in the defense of England, always sure to mention her pride in him, his father and brothers—Woodmen of Arden all.

It was the day before Easter in 1943, a blustery cold day, 24 April, when she and Peter set out for Stratford, just the two of them, leaving the rest of the family to holiday preparations. Lou W. drove them, no more than thirty kilometers. Granny was eager for her grandson to see her favorite play, *Henry V*, with Balliol Holloway, then age 60, as the king.[40] Perhaps she suspected that Peter might be artistic like his brother Michael.

Arriving at the theatre, they had to hold onto their hats against a strong north wind, belying the warm spring sunshine. The building itself had been replaced over the years; the current one was opened in

1932 by the Prince of Wales, six years after the old one burned down. As much as Peter loved the movies, he found the intimacy of live theatre very exciting; and he reveled in the sound of Shakespearean English, even though he did not really understand it yet. He knew the story of King Henry; Granny made sure of that: the Battle of Agincourt, when the English with their longbows won the day against legions of French troops on their own territory. He knew it took place on Saint Crispin's Day, 24 October, in 1415, and he could recite the famous Saint Crispin's Day speech, at least the last part beginning from, "This story shall the good man teach his son . . ." and including, "We few, we happy few, we band of brothers . . ." But holding "their manhoods cheap" went right over his head, and who on earth was "Saint Crispin Crispian"?[41]

It was a matinee performance and a quite large audience; many stood outside before curtain time enjoying the garden beds where tulips and hyacinths bloomed in profusion. With the wind blowing a gale though, Peter and his grandmother did not linger, but went straight inside and took their places. Finally the hall filled, the lights dimmed, and the curtain rose. Peter, settling expectantly into his seat, leaned toward his beloved companion and whispered, "Thank you, Granny!" She smiled, squeezing his arm, and they sat in rapt attention, applauding vigorously at the end till the last curtain call.

A beautiful twilight greeted them as they emerged, the wind having lessened a bit; the setting sun lit up the clouds on the western horizon with a radiant pinkish orange. They arrived home at suppertime, and Cook had baked hot cross buns, the wonderful smell of which Peter detected as soon as he came through the door.

"Mmmmm . . . just in time for dinner!" he announced, throwing off his coat and hat. Aside from the buns, it was a simple supper compared with the Easter feast next day. In spite of rationing and shortages, Cook had managed to trade soap coupons for a leg of lamb. The whole family was home, even the Colonel, whose military obligations had become less pressing.

With that cold north wind raging again, there was a fire lit in the drawing room; and after supper Granny H. took the closest chair to it. She was exhausted from the afternoon in Stratford, enjoyable though it was, and wondered how she would hold up to Easter's festivities: church service, visitors, food and drink. Her left arm was aching all the way to her shoulder, and she doubled her woolen shawl over it. "Are you all right, Mother?" the Colonel asked. He sat with Elizabeth on the settee facing the fire.

"Oh yes, Bill, just tired. The play was worth it though. Holloway makes a splendid King Henry."

"How did Peter like it?"

"Enthralled!"

"You'd better turn in early tonight, Granny," Elizabeth joined in, looking concerned. "In fact we all should. Tomorrow will be busy."

"Don't worry, Betty, I was on the point of suggesting it!"

The Colonel's mother was then age 79, and if she was at all like others of her generation not one to run to the doctor with an ache or a pain, the accumulation of which in their view was only to be expected with advancing age. Her arm was fine the next morning, and she thoroughly enjoyed Easter Sunday, reveling especially in the sound of the church bells, silenced since the outbreak of war, once again allowed to peal.

* * *

Before entering Eton in 1947, at the age of thirteen, Peter may well have attended one of the old and well-regarded preparatory schools in the area, for example, Bilton Grange, just twenty-four kilometers from the village. One source puts him at Abberley Hall, which is a distance of eighty kilometers, at least an hour from home, where he would have been a boarder. But this seems unlikely. His own accounts of the Eton years imply that he had no previous experience with boarding school. We cannot but believe, moreover, that his wonderful mother would have kept him jealously close to her bosom for as long as possible.

And indeed those years were halcyon at the Grange: Parish Sunday in June; Archery Week in August; the Hunt Breakfast in the autumn. Peter was becoming an excellent equestrian and a champion archer, while also participating in plays in school and at church, where he often graced the congregation with his singing voice. He took in every new movie at the Cameo, with or without Daphne, enjoying each and every one, though his greater love was still the horses. Not yet having had the growth spurt typical for boys upon reaching adolescence, he still held out hope of becoming a jockey, though he also considered that he might fulfill his father's dream and follow the Colonel into the military.

The summer of 1944 was very hot, and by August crickets of all kinds were sawing noisily, wasps were in a frenzy, and a green frog by the pond bellowed in a hoarse basso. The roses were still prolific, but wild Michaelmass daisies had begun going to seed. The countryside took on that spent look, as though nature tired of the growing season. But there was no rest for the weary at the Grange; it was Archery Week, and its doors opened in hospitality to the Woodmen of Arden for the yearly Wardmote, a four-day competition.

Starting on Tuesday, with a welcome breakfast, the archers could practice, using targets set up in the back field, with all safety precautions observed of course, and emphasized with the children. There were certainly events as well at the club itself in Meriden, which had Forest Hall, a large, high-ceilinged room where elegant dinner dances were held. But after the competition when winners were declared on Saturday, the final buffet dinner and ball to fete the champions took place at the Grange.

John was then in college, preparing for seminary; Michael had graduated from Eton, while Patrick was still there with two years left. But that year they all came home for this event. Peter was eleven, and no doubt eager to show off his skill with the bow. Neither can there be doubt that he loved the parties: the house full of people in formal dress, the wonderful food, Uncle Leslie at the grand piano, and everyone dancing!

"Waltz with me, Gwanny," Peter beckoned his Granny H. Uncle Leslie had enlisted students from the school where he was Director of Music[42]—two violins and a cello—and along with his piano, they were playing a medley of Strauss Waltzes.

"Thank you, kind sir, I'd be delighted!" she replied.

"You look beautiful, m'lady," Peter continued gallantly as they took to the floor. She was wearing a long green gown with a white jacket, matching the colors of the club's uniform, and in her hair an unusual feathered tiara suggestive of the fletching of arrows. Having turned eighty that year, she was indeed handsome for her age; but she had slowed down quite noticeably, and Peter, now the only grandson left at home, made a point of looking after her.

This boy did not need dancing lessons. Being an excellent mimic, he would just watch the other dancers and easily imitate them. He came up to his grandmother's shoulder, and with him in his new summer white suit from Brett's they made an elegant couple, gliding gracefully round the room.

"Isn't it wonderful that Daddy placed this year?" The Colonel, then in his fifties, had taken a prize. He was as fit as any of the younger participants, thanks to his army service.

"Oh, yes, Peter!" she exclaimed. "I am very proud of him, and of you too. I saw you hit those targets. You will be one of the best. Well, speak of the Devil!"

"Excuse me, Peter, my boy." At that moment, the Colonel cut in; and by the time the musicians had repeated their waltz medley twice, Granny H. had danced with him and all her grandsons.

She returned to her chair, breathless, and Peter came with a glass of champagne from the tray circulating in the practiced hand of Jenny V., who looked crisp in her white apron and maid's cap. She would get no sleep that night. A bartender had been engaged, and as it was the final festivity of the event, everyone, including the archers, felt free to make merry into the wee hours. In fact, by the time the stragglers came to leave, it was incumbent to offer them breakfast. Granny H. kept up with the hardiest of them, though she did not return to the dance floor.

Two weeks later, she was hospitalized with severe shortness of breath and chest pain. She went in on a Wednesday, and Elizabeth spent Thursday there with her, while also telephoning her other children to alert them. The Colonel visited with her that evening, and she seemed comfortable. But in the early morning hours the next day, the first of September, the hospital called with the news that she had passed. It was not unexpected. The boys were still at home, and their mother explained that, sadly, Granny had died peacefully in the night. She and the Colonel then set out for the hospital in nearby Meriden.

As soon as the car had disappeared down the lane, Peter headed for the stable and his beloved Babs. He buried his face in her white mane so that no one would hear his sobs; then recovering a bit, he led her out, put her saddle on, and took out across the field at top speed, fleeing from the angel of death. The pony was no longer young, but she knew the topography well enough to be sure-footed, and she could jump over hedgerows into the neighboring fields. This they did that morning, galloping over the lawn of Miss R.,[43] who fortunately was not at home to shout at them.

Finally, the blaze of his anger having cooled, his mount winded and sweating, he got down and walked her home. Waiting for him was his brother John, leaning on the fence smoking his pipe, which he had long since been allowed to light of course. He was trying not to show his concern.

"She was a sweet old lady, wasn't she?" he said simply.

"What kind of God lets people die, John, takes them away from the ones who love them?"

Somehow John, a sophomore at Cambridge, had enough sensitivity to his brother's mood not to respond. Instead, taking the pipe from his mouth, he put an arm around Peter's shoulder. Peter stiffened at first; but then, his own arm hugging John's waist, the boys walked back to the house together, leaving Babs in the field to rest and graze.

* * *

"Peter, darling," called his mother, "please hurry or we'll be late for church."

Though it was a Tuesday, a national holiday had been declared to celebrate the unconditional surrender of Germany. As this outcome had been foreseen, plans had been made for rejoicing and giving thanks for the Victory in Europe. News of Hitler's death came on 2 May, 1945, and VE Day was 8 May. The village church was holding a thanksgiving service at eleven that morning.

"Coming, Mum!" Peter came down the stairs, deftly pulling on his suit jacket on the way. The Colonel was in uniform, of course, and as he followed his wife and son out the door, he grabbed the largest umbrella from the hall tree.

"Better take this—those clouds are darkening."

The church was overflowing, with the British Legion in attendance. There was a din of excited voices, punctuated with peals of laughter from a joyous, exuberant congregation, until at last Arthur G. struck the first loud chords of the organ prelude. The Reverend W. had obviously been working on his sermon and prayers for some time in anticipation of this very day; he held forth most eloquently, and when he offered prayers for the fallen, military and civilian of all nationalities, handkerchiefs came out of purses and sleeves and vest pockets. Some wept audibly. Even Colonel H. reached into the inside pocket of his jacket, surely thinking not only of the young soldiers he had trained, some of whom never came home, but also of his mother's death just months earlier. If only she could have lived to see this day! But then the victory had been forecast even then.

As the service drew to a close, rumbles of thunder grew louder outside, and just when people came pouring out of the church, there was a loud clap ahead of a torrential shower. Neighbors chatted in the vestibule, hoping it would pass.

"Will you be going down to London, Bill?" It was Mrs. W., widow of Colonel Charles W., who had passed away suddenly two years earlier at the age of fifty-five.[44]

"No, Christobel, up to Birmingham. There will be speeches."

"Come over when you get back. Bring the family. Sir Charles has promised to open his oldest bottle of single malt."

"That is thanksgiving indeed! We'll be there."

Peter had been quiet all the morning. He also thought of his Granny H., missing her terribly. But like most of the village children, he was delighted to have not one but two days off from school. They knew about the war, though it had not touched their lives so much since the bombing had subsided. Later that day, when the sun came out, he was free to ride his pony over the greening fields and hedges. Nanny and Cook would have something special for this tea, perhaps the cinnamon scones, hot of course, with the seedless raspberry jam from last season. They would listen to Mr. Churchill over the wireless, and the kitchen would fill with the heavy scent of lilac drifting in on the warm damp air.

Though his mother was leery, having heard about the Scotch, she relented and brought Peter along that evening. The older boys were away at school, where they would have their own celebrations. From the parapets of the Hall, they could watch the fireworks. The unofficial village diarist, Mrs. M., remarked in her lengthy entry for that day, "As if there hadn't been enough bangs in this war!" She went on to describe the day's weather as allegorical: "It was as if in the thunder one heard Nature's roll of drums for the fallen, then the loud salvo of salute over our heads, and the tears of the rain pouring for the sorrow and suffering of the War. And then the end of the orgy of killing and the victory, symbolized as the sun came out and shed its brightness and warmth on the earth." Two days later her only son, held prisoner for most of the war, returned home.

The war's end, however, did not bring an immediate return to normalcy. Rationing and shortages continued. The impact of two major conflicts in the span of barely more than a generation was enormous and lingered over the British economy and society for some years. But at least the factories could now return to civilian purposes, and the young men who did make it home could resume their jobs and lives. Peter's oldest brother John would graduate from college and go on to seminary that year, and Michael would be starting the second year of college, while Patrick would be a senior classman at Eton.

When another May came around, late in the month, all the boys were home, with Patrick getting ready to take his leave of the Head Master. Once again the house filled with the perfume of lilacs and roses from their mother's garden, bunches of each displayed in fine porcelain throughout the house. Elizabeth entered the drawing room with a vase of red roses for the mantle, and there her four sons had gathered at teatime, each in a cool, crisp white shirt. They sprawled on the chairs and the settee, their long limbs seeming disproportionate. Except for Peter, they were all taller than their mother.

"You are lucky, John; you have a calling," Michael was saying. "I don't know why I need to go to college to be an artist, and what is Patrick going to do with himself?"

A light spring breeze came through the window as Jenny V. brought the tea tray, and John lit his pipe. "Patrick loves the country life. He could be a farmer," he said.

Patrick did indeed share his mother's love of gardening, and he had grown up in the country at a time when the corn harvest and the hay making would require the labor of nearly every man in the village. He also loved the old, historical buildings, the architecture of the old church.

"I would love to be a farmer," he said, "and forget all about Latin Grammar. What about you, Peter?"

The youngest was feeling very grown up taking part in this discussion. "I want to be . . ."

"A jockey!" The three older boys finished his sentence in unison, they knew him so well.

"You're still growing," John felt called upon to observe. "You will probably be too tall."

"Then I will join the army."

"Why not become a singer?" Michael suggested, holding out hope that someone else in the family might have artistic leanings.

"I don't think I could earn a living," Peter answered. His mother handed him a cup of tea as the maid passed around a plate with slices of strawberry tea bread.

"Listen to your mother, boys," she interjected. "I do not want any of you to commit yourselves to a lifelong career until you know deep in your heart that it is something you *must* do, something you have a passion for."

"Hear, hear!" came their approving response.

During their conversation, the Colonel had come in, returning from work in Birmingham. He entered the drawing room, loosening his tie and unbuttoning his jacket, and headed straight for a crystal decanter of port, which sat on a round silver tray on the secretary. Pouring himself a glass, he turned to his wife.

"You are filling their heads with foolish notions, Betty! They are young men now, and they need to think about how they will support a wife and family. They need to prepare themselves for good steady jobs, go into business, just as generations—in both our families—have done."

"And they did so, Bill, in order that some of their descendants might one day flower!" Elizabeth was not one to let such a contention go unanswered, but this outburst had surely dampened the mood. Each of the boys felt the sting of it, and none more than Peter, always the most sensitive of the brothers. He recalled later in life having a strong sense of his father's disappointment in them, and a very personal obligation to do well to compensate both his parents.

The following Friday, Patrick took the train back to Eton, where he would be taking leave of the Head Master, in a traditional ritual peculiar to the school. He would meet privately with Head Master Elliott[45], sign the Leaving Book, and receive a book in return; for example, it might be a special edition of the poems of Thomas Gray, the eighteenth century Etonian. Then on Saturday, he and a few of his classmates also taking leave at this time were having a breakfast to celebrate, and on Sunday his parents were coming down. They would attend Chapel together, collect Patrick's belongings and bring him home. Peter came along for the ride. He especially loved the Chapel, where light streamed in through centuries old stained glass, refracting it like a prism into all the colors of the spectrum. But he must have been apprehensive to say the least at the prospect of being the next in line to enter such an august institution.

It was a fine spring day, the Thames glistening gold in the sun, its banks lined with an opulence of purple wildflowers, and Windsor Castle rising in the background, as in Gray's famous "Ode" to the College. Trees were in bloom on the campus, and the fields of Eton were greening. The dark stone buildings, like tall old men gazing down, seemed too solemn for the season.

After the service, the family, including Patrick, climbed back into the car heading for Bracknell, the town just sixteen kilometers to the south, where they were meeting Elizabeth's brother Richard and his wife for lunch. They had been in London on a shopping trip, and most particularly wanted to see their godchild Peter.

"Peter my boy, you are looking so grown-up!" his uncle greeted him. Peter was indeed the little man in his green tweed suit, the Brett's label from Leamington Spa. Ironically, he was very soon to shoot up to over six feet tall, but at that time Uncle Richard could still take him by the shoulders and muss his hair.

"Congratulations are in order for you, Patrick—what an honor! What will you do now?"

"I might study architecture, or agriculture," he replied.

"I think he means horticulture, Richard," the Colonel added in clarification, horticulture at least sounding more dignified.

They had chosen the lunchroom of a small inn, and enjoyed a substantial meal, with appetizers, soup, fish and salad. Dessert and coffee had arrived when Uncle Richard asked, "Are you looking forward to entering Eton yourself, Peter? You are almost old enough you know."

There was a long pause as Peter lowered his head and peered from under his brow, as he had a way of doing, first at his mother, then averting his eyes from his father and brother. "I suppose so," he said without much conviction. He was already well accustomed to saying what he thought others wanted to hear.

"Of course he is!" the Colonel declared.

"He is not thirteen until November, Bill. There is time to think about it," his mother interceded gently. But the group could feel that the Colonel was already starting to lose his patience.

"Time?" he nearly shouted, startling diners at the next table. "There is nothing to think about!"

"Surely Peter will love Eton as much as his brothers have," came a clever bit of diplomacy uttered softly by Uncle Richard's wife, Aunt Anne. She was a sweet, thoughtful person, who adored her sister-in-law and the godson she considered to be very special. Her remark was of course a dodge. Peter and Patrick knew well that the blissful life at Eton was not unalloyed. But Colonel H. was placated. While he was an engineering graduate of Trinity College, Cambridge, he had not attended Eton.

By the time they had departed the inn and returned to Eton, the hour was too late to pack up all of Patrick's things, so he decided to stay another night and bring the remainder home on the train next day. It was just Peter with his parents then on the two hour journey home in the twilight, after a long, tiring day. They were very quiet in the car. Peter rolled his window down part way to feel the cool, soothing air on his face, his mind awash with an unsettling mixture of excitement and sadness. Like any child, he was eager to grow up, and the next step in his education was the symbol of that. But also like any other child, the evidence of serious discord between his parents filled him with anxiety. The worry on the face of his beloved mother was for him a dreadful hurt at this precarious age.

That summer a pall hung over the Grange, for Peter at least. Oh, he took his riding lessons with Skinner H.; he practiced his archery; he and Babs flew across the fields like the wind; and he saw his idol, Sir Laurence in *Henry V* at the Cameo, agonizing that his late Granny H. wasn't there with him to enjoy the play she loved. But his parents dispute over the question of his going to Eton hung heavily over all the usual pleasures. They tried to keep the argument behind closed doors, but voices were raised in the heat of it. Often in the hours before midnight, as Peter tried to sleep, he would hear his name, and catch some phrases: "Eton will make a man of him," his father would say, then exclaiming, "You have spoiled him rotten, Betty!"

Worst of all his mother would be heard at times nearly sobbing. "He is different, Bill. The other boys will tease him because of how he speaks, and he is not a scholar. He still reads very slowly!"

"You're exaggerating!" would be the rebuttal.

"Please! They still practice caning there—I cannot even think of it!"

"He will learn to behave himself."

So it went. They had quarreled over the older boys as well, not John so much since he took the highly respected path of holy orders, but certainly the artist Michael. At least they all had gone to Eton, that much for their father was a given.

Peter would finally bury his head in his pillow, which would be damp with tears before he slept, shaking with anxious rage. He wanted to prove himself to his father, but not at the cost of hurting his mother. The conflict was rending his adolescent psyche.

By the time his thirteenth birthday came around in November, it was decided: he would enter Eton in the second term, January 1947.

* * *

Chapter 2

What can be said of an institution which has stood for more than five hundred years that has not already been said? About Eton, "the place by the water," all has been written that one might seek to know of its long history, its preeminent alumni; and this prestigious school for elite English boys has turned out many great British leaders, from the second Earl Grey to Anthony Eden. In keeping with the character of its founder, Eton is a place of academic rigor and high religion. King Henry VI, who also started King's College, Cambridge, was a very studious and pious man, but unfortunate as a monarch for being out of step with the bellicose tenor of his times. Still worse, he was given to fits of catalepsy. Across the Thames in the shade of his Windsor Castle, is Eton a place of madness?

Surely it would seem mad to board away from their homes a large number of pubescent boys in close quarters, expecting the study of Latin, daily chapel attendance, even any number of rugby games to sublimate their nascent drives. The resultant atmosphere would resemble nothing so much as a prison, especially considering the stubborn adherence, until the 1980s, to corporal punishment. Then there was the practice of "fagging," a tradition allowing upper classmen to call upon lower classmen to do errands or chores. At some point in the early twentieth century, the servile term "fag" became an epithet for a male homosexual.

We may assert with confidence at least that Eton is an unusual school. The ritual for taking leave, which was just described, is an example. The students live in a number of houses, each governed by a House Master, and many of which with their own dining facilities. The boys' bedrooms are private, and a good deal of their studying goes on in the house. In each house there is also a room called the "Library" for boys in their last year to study, and one known as "Debate" for boys in their penultimate year. Every evening at about eight o'clock they all congregate for "Prayers," a time that may also be used for other mutual activities, announcements, or entertainments. These terms and many others peculiar to Eton are of course historical, to the extent that its website has a glossary. Eton provides a secondary education, but it has always been known as Eton College and originally, as established by the founder, had just seventy scholars. These elite boys are still known as "Collegers," but many more students are admitted as "Oppidans," after the Latin word for *town*; and the twenty-four houses now provided for this majority of the enrollment board dozens of boys each.

On the one hand, we may observe that Eton offers an atmosphere of independence in which young men learn responsibility and self-discipline. A team spirit is very much emphasized in any number of ways, whether on the rugby field, sculling on the Thames, or serving one's house mates as a house captain or captain of games. But at the same time it is a place notorious for formality and conformity, exemplified most certainly by its uniform: black with the stiff white collar and black tie folded under.

We have a photograph of Peter H. in so-called "Eton dress" taken not long after he entered. He stands unsmiling with his hands in his trouser pockets, hair combed back, shoes polished. He is gangly as boys may be in that difficult metamorphosis into manhood, a callow, awkward phase. Yet the most striking thing about this picture to anyone with knowledge of the boy he was and of the man he became is his face, because it is uncharacteristically without expression—utterly.

* * *

She had pulled the car off the road, lain her forehead on the steering wheel, and sobbed. The thought going through Elizabeth's mind was that it must be a cold day in hell for her to have left her baby at such a place.⁴⁶ But no, it was only a cold day in January 1947, and she had just dropped off her youngest boy, Peter, at Eton. The school had been perfect for John; Michael and Patrick had managed, but this one, well, he was vulnerable. Like many women, she had learned to drive a car during the war. Now as she sat by the roadside alone, a constable pulled up and got out of his vehicle.

"Is everything all right, madam? Do you need help?" he asked.

"Thank you, Officer, no. There was something in my eye, but I can go on now. I'm fine, really." He could see she had been crying, but took her at her word and left, though watching in his mirror to be sure. When she did collect herself, she said a prayer and continued down Eton Road toward home in the gathering dusk.

The day had begun with a hot and wholesome breakfast. The January chill was clear and calm, scarcely abated by a wan sun, still low at its southerly angle. Peter's trunk was packed, and they loaded it into the car for the two-hour journey. At the last minute, Nanny came running out with a basket of sandwiches Cook had prepared for them; there were also homemade shortbreads and a thermos of tea. Nanny, obviously at pains to conceal her emotion, gave Peter a hug and hurried back inside.

As they drove, Elizabeth drew upon the Irish in her nature; she had determined for her son's sake to be strong, stalwart, plucky.

"You will have so much fun, Peter, making friends, joining teams, and just wait until they hear you sing! You mustn't be afraid. If you have trouble with your studies, the House Master and the Tutor will help you, the senior boys also. Everyone wants you to succeed. And whatever you do, behave yourself, follow the rules!" The pitch and the pace of this lecture unfortunately betrayed her, especially to the most sensitive of her children.

"I will be all wight, Mother. Please don't worry," he said, unwittingly emphasizing his susceptibility. "I will make you and Father pwoud of me." He had never called her Mother.

"Oh, Peter darling." Now it was taking all her will not to break down. "I *am* proud of you. I could not be more proud of you! All I ask is for you to be happy!"

Peter, for his part, drew upon the strength of his love not to show his mother how really terrified he was. How would he keep up academically? Would the other boys tease him? What if he couldn't learn all the rules and violated one unknowingly? His brother John had never felt the cane, but he had heard of it from the younger two and could only hope that their descriptions had been exaggerated. No one ever spoke of this to parents; that was an unwritten rule.

They rode awhile in silence. Then about midway, Elizabeth pulled over and reached for the hamper with lunch. There was chicken salad on biscuits and grilled cheese sandwiches, wrapped in towels and still warm. Food rationing continued, especially meat, but in the country, there was always a chicken and a milk cow. After some hot tea with cream and sugar, strong as Peter always liked it, the mood lifted, and they finished the trip singing together: folk songs, hymns, rounds.

Reaching the school, Elizabeth went straight to Hawtrey House,[47] where Peter had been assigned. By now she surely knew her way around. The houses were also known to the boys by the surname or initials of the current House Master, who at that time for Hawtrey House was Francis Julian Alford Cruso, so it was FJAC House. The building itself, of the red brick Tudor style characteristic of Eton, was across from College Chapel. The house captain, a senior student, was on hand to greet them and help carry Peter's trunk to his room. He told them there were other new boys checking in for the Lent Half[48] that day, whom Peter would have the chance to meet at Prayers after dinner, which would be at Bekynton, the dining hall, as Hawtrey did not have a kitchen.

Then mother and son had much to do unpacking the trunk and setting up the room: a picture for his desk, of Mum and Granny B. with Jasper and himself; an afghan for the bed, hand-knitted by Nanny Ellen; a calendar for the bulletin board, with all his holidays marked in red.

"See, Peter, you will be home again before you know it!" Mum remarked brightly as she tacked it up, "and look out your window. You will be able to watch the early sunsets." The room did have a southwesterly exposure, and the January sun was streaming in, reassuring to them both. But finally they were done, and it was time for her to leave.

She had her coat, hat, and gloves back on, and they stood outside by the car, he with just his navy blazer and the long green muffler Nanny had made for him years before, its wool now even softer. They held each other for a long time, and he buried his face in the fur trim of her collar, the lump in his throat fairly choking him. Not wanting the tears to run down her face, she daubed them with her gloves, careless that they were leather. Damn the gloves! Simply the fact that he was the last fledgling to leave the nest would have been hard enough, but this child at this place, with its strict traditions, made her sadness and anxiety all the more acute.

"Be good, Peter. Write me as soon as you can. I left paper and stamps in your desk. I love you, darling . . ."

"Yes, Mummy, I love you too."

In an interview published in The Independent three years before he died, Peter recalled his time at Eton, and of this moment, the desolation: "As Mummy's car pulled away, I felt marooned."[49]

* * *

He did meet the other new boys in the house that evening and was surprised and relieved to find that they were as frightened and self-conscious as he was, far too much to notice him or his speech problem. There was immediate camaraderie among them, and the House Master and house captain were very helpful and concerned to have them fully and quickly oriented. But that night alone in his private room, he closed the door and cried.

The next night at Prayers, the house captain of games enumerated what teams might be joined, asking each boy to choose at least one. Peter was delighted that he could keep up his archery, and decided to add swimming at which he thought he could also do well. As they adjourned to go to their rooms, Mr. Cruso approached. "I hear, Peter, that you enjoy singing and are very good at it."

"Yes sir, I do love to sing."

"I will set up an audition for you with the Chapel choir director and let you know."

"Thank you, sir. I would like that vewy much."

The House Master smiled at Peter's pronunciation, which still sounded childish. From what he understood about the boy's angelic voice though, he felt the choir should take advantage before it changed. So by the third day, Peter was feeling much better about his new school, though still extremely homesick. Formal classes soon began, and there was plenty of school work to fill the cold days and long nights of winter. Latin was the hardest, chiefly because he recognized no earthly relevance in it for him personally; but Mr. Cruso, who was himself a scholar of classical Greek,[50] helped him. English Literature should have been his best subject, but still unable to read fast enough, he had trouble keeping up. To make matters worse, the class began the term reading Milton's *Paradise Lost*.

It was the middle of March, and Peter had been at Eton about two months. Of course he had made the choir and was already learning one or two solos to sing in Chapel during Holy Week. Easter would fall on 6 April. When the English Lit teacher called his name in class, his stomach turned into a knot. "Peter! Can you tell the class what Book II of *Paradise Lost* is all about?" There was anxious silence. "Well, Peter where is Satan going in Book II?"

"To hell?" came a tenuous response, setting off suppressed giggling.

"No, Peter, he was driven out of heaven in Book I. You did not do the assignment, did you?"

"No sir, I had choir practice, and I haven't finished . . ."

"Excuses? At Eton, boy, we do not make excuses; we make statesmen!" The teacher scribbled on a piece of paper and handed it to his assistant, an upper classman. "Show Peter to the Head Master."

Was this teacher ex-military, or was he making an example of Peter for the other new students? In fairness we must aver that Eton was by no means alone in its belief in the corporal punishment of children in those days. It was a practice accepted by nearly everyone, parents included. There was the biblical injunction after all, albeit Old Testament.

On their way to the office of Head Master Elliott, the older boy explained the ritual. "Your first beating,[51] isn't it, fag? Sure. He's going to smack your bare bum with a switch. When he's done, he says, 'Do you have anything to say?' This is not an invitation to debate; you say no. Then when you're dismissed you say, 'Thank you.'"

So Michael and Patrick had not been exaggerating. Far worse, in fact, when they got to the Head Master came the horrible shock that this ritual was not private. There were other people in the room. Peter could not imagine who they could be nor why they needed to witness his humiliation. The pain of the whipping was bad, and to keep from crying out he gritted his teeth and counted the strokes to himself. When it was finished, he was so rattled that he forgot the protocol and, without waiting, blurted out, "Thank you." All present broke into laughter.

"He likes it! Bend over," and Mr. Elliott gave him five more.

Released into the cold, late afternoon, Peter wanted only to run and hide. He headed straight for the riverbank, though he wasn't wearing boots, and the patches of remaining snow made for soft, muddy ground. On the down side of a knoll he could sit unseen, and there he let loose his hurt and rage. The injustice and helplessness were terrible enough, but worse was the sense that these people took pleasure in his suffering. Such a thing was incomprehensible to Peter, vile and outrageous. He had the nonviolent sensibility of his Quaker heritage, having taken it in with his mother's milk.

The sun setting behind him lit up Windsor Castle and other buildings across the Thames. Though shielded from the March wind by the hill, he was reminded of that day in Stratford-upon-Avon with his Granny H., and the tears came. He missed his Granny, his mother, everyone at home. How would he possibly endure this cold and cruel place? But he was growing up; defenses kicked in. He thought of his father—a veteran, a war hero—of his three older brothers; they were all strong men, and so would he be henceforth.

He had no supper that night, but went immediately to his room. Just before Prayers, he heard an older boy's loud summons, "Boy up!" This was the signal for all the first year boys to queue up for a command, which would be given to the last boy in line.

He dragged himself down the hallway, wondering if this awful day would ever end, and of course he got the job. To his surprise though, the older boy invited him into his room. "I heard you were having some trouble with *Paradise Lost* in English Lit. I took that class two years ago, and I still have my notes. Here they are," he said, handing Peter a large envelope. "Don't be shy about asking for help, Peter."

Once more Peter's eyes welled with tears. "Thank you, sir, so kind of you!"

"I'm not a beak,[52] Peter. It's Geoffrey." He put his arm around Peter's shoulder, and they walked down to Prayers together. But it was most unusual for a senior at Eton in those days to be so informal with an underclassman.

The next morning not surprisingly Peter awoke with a bad cold. He had to miss classes and choir practice, but luckily thanks to the resilience of youth, he recovered in a few days and was in good voice for Holy Week. His mother and Granny B. were coming down by train for morning service on Good Friday to hear him sing, and he would return home with them for Easter. The Chapel choir sang Mendelssohn's "Hear My Prayer," based on Psalm 55, which began with Peter's solo. We can be sure he sang the words with sincere emotion: "O for the wings, for the wings of a dove! Far away, far away would I rove!" There had never been such a hush in that august and ancient sanctuary. The assemblage was aghast at the beauty of his voice; the choir director was in ecstasy; Mum and Granny were nearly bursting with pride. "An angel! Didn't I tell you when he was born, Mother?" Elizabeth whispered, and Granny squeezed her hand.

At times careless of rules, defiant of authority, moody, this angel was beaten many more times in the coming years, often without really knowing why. He undoubtedly learned many things at Eton. Was it there that he took up smoking, having discovered the calming effects of nicotine? Perhaps that was a punishable offense. In the aforementioned interview from later in life, he revealed that he had received "158 strokes" altogether. So he had continued to keep count. And he confessed to learning something else: bitterness.

* * *

According to a good friend[53] of Peter's, he was known as "the tart of Eton" because of his voice and good looks. Boys were known to faint away in Chapel whenever he sang, though we should consider that the tight collars may have contributed to that. Peter himself noted as an adult that he was "the nearest thing to a girl" in that all-male environment, adding that he tried hard to play down his good looks, and was very much relieved when *girls* found him attractive. Before the word "gay" became the acceptable term, homosexuals were *queers* or *fags*; and Eton must have had its share, given the fact that in the male population at large a substantial minority will naturally fall into this category. Until 1967, when the law was changed based on the Wolfenden Report, homosexuality was illegal in Great Britain. It was a crime, a sin, and a shameful disgrace upon one's family. For an adolescent boy just maturing sexually to face any uncertainty as to sexual orientation would have been a special torture in those times.

Peter was far too modest his whole life to talk openly about so private a subject, assuming as a lad that he would someday fall in love and marry—a woman. He found women attractive, and men as well. There was his idol, Sir Laurence, who was terribly handsome in *Wuthering Heights*, but also his beautiful costar, Merle Oberon. He loved the masculine smell of his leather riding boots, the way they gripped his calves, and he adored the luscious scent of his mother's wardrobe, blending lilac and rose and lavender. He was an unusual boy, growing fast into a man. He turned fourteen that year and seemed to be shooting up inches overnight. When he came home for the Michaelmas holiday that autumn, he had the odd experience of standing at eye level with his mother, and she was keenly aware that her baby was maturing quickly, his face being molded by this process into a classical, manly beauty. But then he was all the more apt to be preyed upon.

The very next time that his hero Geoffrey called "Boy up!" Peter was happy to oblige in reciprocation for the fellow's kindness. But once again he was surprised at the request.

"I have a friend, Peter, in Durnford House, just down the lane, who needs a favor, and I owe him one. Would you go across and see what he wants? His name is Colin." Why, Peter wondered, did this Colin not call for his own fag? But of course he got his coat and went in search of a senior named Colin at Durnford House.[54]

Colin was in his room, and Peter knocked gently, announcing that he was on an assignment from Geoffrey. Colin ushered him in and took his coat, coming so close to him as he did so that his face touched Peter's ear. His breath smelled of gin. "Geoffrey is a good friend, Peter, and you are so obliging!" Colin looked him over as though he were livestock. "Won't you take off your blazer and be comfortable?" To the contrary, Peter was growing more and more uncomfortable with this person's informality.

"Geoffrey said you had a favor to ask."

"I want to take your picture, Peter, just take your picture." Peter had edged backwards toward the door. He opened it, grabbing his coat from the chair just as Colin was grabbing for him.

"I'm sorry," he said, "I can't help you." He felt sick that night, and did in fact throw up his dinner in an ashcan on the way back from the dining hall. How to conceive of such treachery, disloyalty, in someone from his own house, someone who had been so friendly to set him up! He was so disturbed that he could not possibly do his literature homework, and he knew now what that would mean. He was lonelier than ever as he fought for sleep, curled in a ball under Nanny's wool afghan. Finally clutching the pillow over his head, he drifted off.

But he had made other friends from among his classmates and fellow choir members, and often on weekends they would go into London to films and plays, especially in winter when the playing fields were covered with snow, and depressing, thick fogs rolled in over Eton from the riverbanks. The theaters and movie houses continued to be a refuge for Peter, when it seemed that every week brought some reprimand and a visit to the Head Master for a beating.

"Who wants to go into London with me this afternoon?" Peter asked his mates at breakfast one Saturday morning. "Olivier's *Hamlet* is opening at the cinema." He had several takers, and later that day they met to catch the bus. Their first stop however was the pub, since there was time before the show would start. Peter was a year short of drinking age, but managed to slip through with the other boys. The Lamb and Flag on Rose Street, once frequented by Dickens, was a favorite.[55] They took a table near the bar and ordered a round of beer. Surrounded by the dark Georgian paneling, the smells of tobacco and spirits, the lads settled in. Presently a group of older boys came in, Colin among them.

"Peter," said Colin, "aren't you afraid a beak will see you here?" Peter took out a cigarette and lit up.

"No, I'm sure none of the Masters would come to this place for fear of hell fire," and everyone laughed. "By the way, Colin, shouldn't you be around the corner at the Salisbury?" This was an awfully bold thing to say to an upper classman; the Salisbury pub was what is now referred to as a "gay bar." The boys fell silent; the tension was palpable.

Then one of the boys who was soon to take leave of Eton, changed the subject. "I will be going to Cambridge, Trinity College," he said.

"That's where my father went," Peter offered, taking a slow drag on the cigarette. "He wants me to go there too, and study something useful, or follow his example into military service."

"And what does Mum want?" one of his friends inquired. Everyone who came to know Peter knew also of his wonderful mother.

"She wants me to be happy."

"Good woman!" his friend continued. "You should go into acting then."

"He's right, Peter, look what you did yesterday in Chapel." Another of their companions was a choir member. "When that ray of sun came through the window, hitting you as you sang your solo, you nearly pushed me onto the altar trying to keep in the spotlight as the sun moved!" The group roared with laughter.

"I did not, you're exaggerating!" Peter protested, but he knew it was true. As uncomfortable as it made him to be the object of boy crushes, he did love the spotlight, and with it the knowledge that he could move a crowd of people, bring them happiness, stir their hearts; and indeed years later it was this incident with the sunbeam spotlighting him in Eton's beautiful Chapel that he cited as the moment he had decided to be an actor.[56]

Finally Peter and his friends left the pub and headed for the movie house. Parts of London still lay in ruins from the war. Piccadilly had been badly bombed. The Old Vic was under repairs and did not reopen until 1950; but the repertory company held together, performing at the New Theatre[57] on St. Martin's Lane. A sign in the pub window announced that company's production of Marlowe's *Tamburlaine*, opening the coming week.

"Shall we go next Saturday?" Peter suggested, hoping cousin Daphne could get tickets. She was then twenty years old and had gone to secretarial school, planning to find work in the West End. She would at least be close to theatre people if not on the stage. She was only able to get two tickets, and she wanted to go also; so she and Peter met on St. Martin's Lane for the Saturday matinee performance. They enjoyed the play enormously—high Elizabethan drama concerning a brutal and despotic Persian emperor—and afterwards they applauded until their hands were even more red than the cold of winter had made them. "Let's go backstage!" Peter suggested impulsively. Daphne needed no encouragement, and soon they found themselves standing with many other fans waiting to have programs autographed.

As they stood, a good looking, imposing man came into the hallway, and someone whispered, "That's Tyrone Guthrie, the director." Peter, still energized from the play, stepped brazenly into Mr. Guthrie's path and introduced himself. The director recognized his Eton jacket and cap, and took a pen to sign their programs, at the same time graciously accepting their profuse compliments.

Before the man could continue on his way, Peter declared with all the exuberance of his youth, "I want to be an actor vewy, vewy much!"[58]

Guthrie tried hard not to laugh at the poor lad, yet he could not suppress a wide smile at the irony of a youngster with a speech impediment seeking an acting career. "In that case, young man, my advice is to take that 'r' sound to the Central School of Speech and Drama." This institution, founded in 1906 by Elsie Fogarty, had by then become the premier training ground for British actors, including among its alumni Sir Laurence. In due course, Peter would find his way there, but first he had to survive Eton.

* * *

Peter did not excel academically, though he tried hard and managed well enough. As he quickly attained his full height of over six feet however—his childhood fantasy of being a jockey fading equally fast—his body grew lean and muscular. He stood out as an athlete in whatever arena he chose: archery, of course, born in the Forest of Arden; and equestrian skills, with his early training. Indeed we need only have mentioned that his father was a Woodman of Arden and a major in the Royal Horse Artillery. He was also an excellent swimmer, and while at Eton became a valuable member of the swimming team.

Eton did not have a swimming pool until 1956, but it is surrounded by water. The River Thames, wending its way eastward, collects in places forming pools that amount to lakes; and there is the Jubilee River and Colenorton Brook, which are tributaries. There was no lack of good swimming, and in fact the excellent coach was training some boys in diving, Peter among them.

It may have been in the spring of his senior year that there was a diving competition, a wet spring with heavy rains causing much runoff. The match took place in a backwater of the Jubilee, and Peter could do no wrong. His performance was flawless, resulting in a win for the team and a first place prize for him. But a few days later he developed an earache and sought the attention of the Dame of the house.

The Oppidan Houses were originally known as Dames' Houses and were governed by the wives of the Masters. The term is preserved in the residual female role of the Dame, who serves in part as a nurse for each house. Peter's earache was attributed to his diving and treated with aspirin and warm compresses. Penicillin had come into use in 1942 but, apparently, did not seem warranted. An earache could be expected to clear up on its own. Instead it got worse. In a week or two, Peter's ear was dreadfully painful, and he had a fever that was escalating alarmingly. The Dame sent him home.

Mrs. H. met her son at the train station, and when she saw him, strong though she was, she nearly fainted. Peter's face was ashen, his red eyes standing out in contrast. He leaned against her weakly, too sick to speak, as she helped him into the car. Nanny Ellen, with her decades of experience, was a hand at caring for the sick, and she had been alerted. She had Peter's bed ready, an extra pillow with a hot water bottle under the slip for his ear, and blankets, even though it was almost summer by then. The bedside table was supplied with a pitcher of water, towels, a thermometer, and the aspirin bottle. But when she saw how poorly Peter really was, she went pale herself.

"Don't look so worried, Nanny." Her expression inspired Peter to speak as she and his mother helped him up the stairs to his room.

"Your pony's too old to give you a ride up, lad," Ellen joked, attempting to allay the anxiety hanging over them.

As soon as the Colonel came home that evening, he went to check on his youngest son. The boy's athletic prowess had filled him with pride, and with visions of him as an army officer rising in the ranks. But when he saw Peter's condition that night, he knew this was not the simple earache it had seemed. His fantasies of Peter's future aside, it was the thought of losing him or of having him damaged seriously that made even this old soldier quake.

"Peter, dear boy," he said, sitting on the edge of the bed, "don't speak. Try to sleep. I will have the doctor come first thing tomorrow." He left the room, wiping his eyes with his handkerchief. Elizabeth was standing in the hall, and a current of fear passed between them as they looked at each other. "I'll call Dr. Oliver," he said.[59]

"I did already. He will be here early. He was very concerned, but said not to worry, to try to keep the fever down."

"My god, Betty! What can it be?"

"We can only wait and pray, Bill. Now come downstairs. Cook has kept dinner for you."

The family doctor did indeed arrive early; it was not even eight o'clock. By then Peter had a fever of 102° F, and every joint in his body was aching terribly.

"What's going on with you, Peter? A championship diving event and now this?" The doctor tried to put his patient at ease as he examined his ears, his throat, and listened to his heart and lungs. But the history and symptoms alone were enough in this case for a diagnosis. Mum and Dad and Nanny were all in the room waiting anxiously. "I feel quite certain," the doctor declared, "that this is rheumatic fever, precipitated by the ear infection. I am starting Peter on a course of penicillin, which will help his symptoms, and he is to stay on aspirin. We must get his fever down to prevent any brain damage."

"Should he be in hospital, Dr. Oliver?" Elizabeth asked.

"No, Betty, I think he will do better here, unless his condition worsens. I will come every morning to check on him." Then turning to his patient, "We will get you better, Peter, rest assured of that."

"Thank you, Doctor," the Colonel said. "We are most grateful." He was visibly relieved. Having lived through the flu pandemic, that was among the terrible possibilities he had entertained, another being polio. He and the doctor walked out together, leaving Mum and Nanny with Peter. "Is there anything else I should know, Doctor?"

"Peter will live, Bill. He is young and strong, but he could have some heart damage from this." The Colonel took the doctor's hand, speechless with mixed emotion, among which gratitude was foremost.

It was another week before the fever was reliably controlled. Elizabeth and Ellen monitored Peter's temperature and gave him his medications, sponging him off with damp towels and changing his pajama when he became drenched in sweat. Edna V., who had worked at the Grange in years past as under-nurse, was able to return; she was the maid Jenny's sister-in-law, and very helpful.

But Elizabeth's heart broke to see her boy suffer this way, and she barely slept. Her father, Grandpa Arnold B., had died just the year before, leaving her mother a widow after a marriage of over fifty years. As soon as Granny B. heard from her daughter what was going on, she appeared at the Grange with a suitcase.

"I couldn't stay away, Betty. You will need help." Elizabeth collapsed in her arms, breaking down in tears, which at last released some of the enormous strain.

"Thank you, Mother!"

After two weeks, Peter's temperature finally went down to normal and the aching began to subside. "As much as I enjoy seeing you, Peter," said Dr. Oliver, reading the thermometer he had just taken out of the boy's mouth, "I think I can now safely wait a few days."

"I am feeling much better, Doctor, but very weak."

"That is to be expected, I'm afraid, son. But be patient, don't overdo. Promise?"

"Yes sir."

In fact, Peter spent the rest of that summer convalescing. If it was indeed his senior year when this illness occurred, he would miss his last Fourth of June festivity, another tradition peculiar to Eton, which celebrates the birthday of George III, the king most supportive of the institution. The comical sight of the "wet bobs," as they are called, standing in their sculls wearing straw boaters adorned with spring flowers is just the kind of spectacle that would have appealed to Peter. But he rested, reading and studying in preparation for his final term.

His constant companion was "Gramps," a small terrier who had belonged to his late grandfather, and was ironically named because he did appear to have a fuzzy white beard. The poor dog had grieved terribly for his master, and Granny B. brought him to the Grange in hope that he and Peter could help each other, which indeed they did. There had been no dog in the house since the old Airedale, Jasper, died years before. Gramps took to Peter right away, and seemed to sense that his presence was needed, whether lying on the bed when Peter was too tired to get out of it, or in his lap whenever he sat reading a book. As the patient improved, Gramps would follow him outside, and the two would lie together in the grass, Peter dozing off with Gramps asleep on his chest.

His mother of course loved having him home, and kept his room filled with fragrant flowers the summer long. One afternoon later in the season, Peter was reading in the garden room, sheer white curtains billowing at the open windows, and Gramps perched on his knees, when his mother came in with a large vase of red roses. Setting them on the table, she said, "I've told Jenny to bring our tea in here, darling," and she took the chair next to him.

He was reading *Hamlet*, but was happy to put it down. Presently, Jenny came carrying the tea tray, and Peter sat up, moving Gramps beside him. When the maid had left, he said, "I have made a decision, Mother. May I tell you?"

"Of course, Peter, by all means," she replied, a bit taken aback by his seriousness. She fixed his tea and handed it to him, with several tea sandwiches on the saucer.

"I want to be an actor," he announced. Elizabeth was not surprised; she had herself often thought theatre would become his career, from the time he played a shepherd in church at Christmas. Still, she demurred.

"Are you sure, dear? You know your father expects you to go on to Cambridge."

Suddenly he became energized, and raised his voice. "I can't do it, Mother, I won't! I would simply waste those years on things of no interest to me!" Then he told her about meeting Tyrone Guthrie backstage with Daphne after *Tamburlaine* at the Old Vic. "He recommended the Central School of Speech and Drama. It's at Royal Albert Hall, Laurence Olivier trained there, and it's where I want to go."

"Will you want the surgery then?" His mother was referring to the surgical procedure they both knew was available to correct his pronunciation.

"Yes, just as soon as I am fully recovered."

"I will ask Dr. Oliver for a referral."

"What about Daddy?"

"Leave him to me. You are a grown man now, Peter, and you must listen to your heart."

She waited until Peter was back at Eton. It was October; a cold rain came on toward evening, and the housekeeper Joyce had a warm fire going in the drawing room after dinner. With Peter's birthday approaching, the Colonel brought up the subject himself. "Has Peter thought about what he wants to study at Trinity College?"

Elizabeth braced herself for the inevitable. "He doesn't want to go there. He wants to be an actor." The Colonel blanched; he got up and poured himself a Scotch from a decanter on the sideboard. For an old man, now sixty, this was an unpleasant shock.

"Pure foolishness, Betty! Acting is a terribly unstable, insecure life. A person must be very good to make a go of it."

"His passion will ensure that he is good."

"What about the way he talks?"

"A simple procedure will correct it. Dr. Oliver has recommended someone."

"He will become associated with a different class of people . . . well, you know what actors are."

"They are creative, Bill, and so is Peter."

"And that is another concern. Peter is a sensitive, sweet-natured young man. How will he handle 'the slings and arrows of outrageous fortune'?"

"By being a good Hamlet!"

Bill stood warming his back by the fire, and the Scotch having already taken the edge off his temper, he could not help smiling at this last rejoinder. "Where will he study then?"

"The Central School at Royal Albert Hall. Lord Olivier attended there; it is well regarded."

"Well I won't have him using the family name!"

"That can be arranged. Of course."

Perhaps the Colonel was thinking that since his son was turning just seventeen, there was plenty of time for him to come to his senses, that a taste of drama school would change his mind. He was still keenly grateful, to God and to medicine, that Peter had survived rheumatic fever. He had accepted the presumption that his son would as a result not qualify for military service. With an air of resignation he turned toward the fire, a foot resting on the brass fender and a hand on the mantle, and finished his Scotch. There were no more words that night.

* * *

By the end of that winter, Peter was ready to take leave of Eton, a ritual which must have been especially awkward in his case, considering the many instances of that other, humiliating ritual he had endured in the office of the Head Master. But Mr. Birley, who replaced Mr. Elliott in 1950, was civil and dignified, enquiring as to Peter's future plans. When he learned that Peter would be studying drama, he of course enumerated several Etonians who had flourished in the arts, including but certainly not ending with the poet Thomas Gray, whose collected works he then bestowed, in keeping with tradition and inscribed "To Peter H. from the Provost, Fellows, and Head Master of Eton College, with our blessings for his future success." Peter then signed the Leaving Book, his face impassive, inscrutable, but for the anger flaring in his eyes as he thought, "158 strokes."

Still it was bittersweet as all such rites of passage are at that tender age. He walked out onto the lanes of Eton a last time and down to the banks of the Thames, steel grey under the winter sky. A heron in the shallows, straight as the reeds he stood among, was barely noticeable, while a group of ducks swam by quacking noisily. It was March again, but Peter found the chill invigorating. He skipped a stone over the water, then turned and headed back to Hawtrey House, the sun making a brief appearance on the horizon as it set at the end of Keates Lane. Somehow he felt his breath came easier and deeper than it ever had before.

The next morning he would have a last breakfast with some other boys who were also taking leave around the same time; then he would pack up his few remaining belongings in a suitcase. Most of his things had already been taken to London, where he would be sharing a flat on Queen's Gate Road near Royal Albert Hall with other drama students. Later in the day the plan was to meet his parents and Granny B. at the Savoy for high tea with Uncle Richard and Aunt Anne. This nephew after all was their particular favorite, so Richard was treating. His wife Anne was delighted that Peter was going to drama school, giving him a proper outlet for what she had always recognized as his outstanding aesthetic qualities. She knew that Elizabeth was happy about it, but everyone was aware of the Colonel's opposition. When the subject came up that afternoon,

Richard simply winked at Peter and quipped, "Here I thought you would go into business with me, young man!"

Everyone laughed, and Granny adroitly changed the subject. "Richard, you remember your father's little terrier, the one we call Gramps?" It had been two years since Arnold B. had passed on.

"I do indeed, Mother. Does he continue to grieve?"

"Well, you wouldn't believe how that sweet dog looked after Peter when he was so ill last summer. They took to each other right away!"

Further tense moments were thus avoided, and the group concentrated on the fine offerings provided at the Savoy for high tea, including the tea itself; and if there was one thing that Elizabeth's clan knew, it was tea.

* * *

Perhaps the most curious thing about acting is why anyone chooses to do it. Even actors themselves often wonder, and come to assume they are merely extroverts who love the attention; or they may acknowledge that they enjoy the power to move people, to give them pleasure, to make them laugh. The more profound psychological reasons for the choice may thus elude many individuals who make it.

By the middle of the twentieth century, the old style of acting was being left behind, replaced by what was being called "method acting," based on the ideas of Russian actor and director Constantin Stanislavsky. Where formerly an actor was trained to mimic the voice, the expressions, the gestures and movements of whatever character he played, Stanislavsky's approach was to step into the mind of a character, thereby as a performer arousing the appropriate emotion within himself. The actor would then unconsciously portray every subtle nuance, giving a far more convincing performance.

Stanislavsky did not claim to have a "method," and did not like the word, but he wrote a good deal on the subject of acting. Peter's idol, Laurence Olivier,[60] confessed to being strongly influenced by his book, *My Life in Art*. In a later work, *Building a Character*,

Stanislavsky wrote, "An actor takes his dream of a character, realized through his subconscious, his inner creative state . . . and brings it to life by means of his voice, his movements, his emotional power directed by his intelligence."

He goes on to observe in the same book that acting enables the individual to express feelings too personal to reveal, by disguising them as those of his character. We may infer therefore that while an actor of this school may channel the personality of a character, he does not necessarily escape his own. Yet that very hope could be a secret motivation for many actors: the chance to become another person, to leave aside their own angst however briefly, or at least to air it. The Central School of Speech and Drama was doubtless up to date in embracing this new method.

Directly upon leaving Eton in the winter of 1951, Peter had oral surgery to correct his ankyloglossia, performed by a surgeon in London who had been recommended by Dr. Oliver, his family physician. The mouth heals quickly, so it was not long before he could speak again, if somewhat awkwardly as he became accustomed to the alteration. Forever after he reveled in the ability to trill his "*r*'s." At the Central School in fact, he began in speech therapy, and was given vocal exercises, which he continued to use throughout his life.

But the hope and the gladness of that year were not unmixed. It was early June when Peter got a phone call at the London flat; the sound of his father's voice was concerning.

"Peter, I'm sorry to break this news to you like this . . ." and he paused, Peter becoming increasingly alarmed. "Your Granny B. has passed away." Then he related the details: a brief illness, a quiet death without struggle. "Your mother, of course, is taking it terribly hard. The funeral will be Saturday, here at St. John the Baptist. I know you were planning to come up for Parish Sunday; you will need to come a few days early."

"Yes, of course, Father. Tell Mum I will be there as soon as I can." Peter too was very sad though not surprised. Edith B. was 78, and the strain of her husband's death, followed by Peter's long illness, had taken a toll. Considerable anxiety had accompanied the possibility of losing a grandson, especially one as dear as Peter. She may have been the first of her sisters to die, though at that time Jessie would have been eighty-five. Helen and Margaret were then seventy-four and seventy-two, respectively. We can be sure that any of the "elegant old darlings" still living would be on hand to see their sister off, dressed in appropriate mourning.

There was a black wreath on the door of the Grange, but inside, the house was full of roses in all colors imaginable, their mingled scents the essence of the season. Peter found his mother in the drawing room when he arrived and took her in his arms without a word. He was now taller than her, causing him an admixture of feelings in being able to console the person to whom he had always turned as a child; and for her the great joy she had in seeing what a beautiful, strong man he had grown to be mitigated the grief of the occasion. Then too as a religious person, she truly believed her mother's spirit was still there sharing that joy.

The funeral of Edith B. was the next day, and the church was full, with family taking up several front pews. Her four children were there with their families, her sisters, and many friends from all over Warwickshire. Her grandson John, oldest of Peter's brothers, was in his last term of seminary, and did readings from Psalms and the Gospels. Uncle Richard, her oldest son, gave a eulogy. Elizabeth had supplied all the flowers from her garden, which cascaded on either side of the steps to the altar and blanketed the casket. By this time, she was calmer, resigned to the loss of her aging mother; but she was glad nonetheless that she had worn a hat with a heavy veil. Conducting the service was the new rector, Rev. Henry B.[61] Reverend W., who had retired the year before, nevertheless attended the funeral as a family friend.

Peter never left his mother's side that day except to help carry the casket to the churchyard, along with his brothers and two uncles serving as the pall bearers. There was a short graveside service with prayers, following which many of the mourners gathered at the Grange. So many had brought food that Cook scarcely needed to add anything but tea and coffee. There was hard liquor for the men— Jameson's, Beefeater's, Glenfiddich—but this was not an Irish wake, such as the one two years previous for Grandpa Arnold. Edith was more of a Quaker, so the mood was calm though by no means somber. Relatives drew closer in their common loss, glad to be together if even for a sad occasion.

Colonel H. stood at the window in the drawing room looking out over the pasture, where his horses grazed on the lush spring grass. The two reverends were with him, along with his oldest son John and brother-in-law Richard. But for the clink of ice in their glasses they were quiet. Then Reverend W. broke the silence.

"Your youngest has grown up to be a fine looking man, Bill. What does he want to do with himself?" The Colonel took a chair and lit a cigar as he responded.

"He will be going to drama school in London."

"What a splendid idea! With his voice and good looks"—the reverend paused, catching the glances exchanged between Uncle Richard and John, then continued—"he is sure to succeed."

"Maybe," said Colonel Bill, taking a swig of his Scotch. "But it's a hard road. I worry for him."

"The young people have to find their own way," the new rector offered. "They are quite independent these days."

Then John said, "Surely God guides each of us onto the path he has chosen for us."

"Yes son, if we listen," his father concluded.

"Like the Quakers?" came John's riposte.

"A fine old single malt, Bill!" Richard abruptly changed the subject, seeing how uncomfortable the Colonel was becoming. "Too bad Sir Charles could not be here. Remember how he loved his Scotch? Don't you miss him?" Sir Charles H. had passed in 1942 at age 66. The men proceeded to reminisce, at the same time acquainting the newcomer with local lore; and John excused himself, having noticed Peter outside from the window. Their mother was in the garden room with her Aunt Helen. When visitors began to leave, they came to pay respects, so Peter took the opportunity to step out for a cigarette, the habit slowly becoming an addiction. His mother knew he smoked, but he was not proud of it and did not like to smoke in the house. He was leaning on the fence rail when his brother came out. John lit up his pipe. They stood for a while without speaking, watching the horses, one of which was a new chestnut gelding named Darjeeling.

"He's beautiful, isn't he?" said Peter. "I'm eager to ride him!"

"Yes indeed, Mum says he's a dream horse. She may ride him in the Hunt this autumn."

"Have you taken an assignment yet, John?" John had received calls from two parishes that he was considering.

"Not yet. I will go where I feel most needed."

"Of course. You have such a strong faith; I thought of it during the funeral. I envy that. Death just makes me angry. It seems unfair, a meaningless ending."

"The way I see it, Peter, life cannot possibly be meaningless, therefore it must have a meaning we cannot understand. As Sherlock Holmes learned from his father . . ."

"'When you eliminate the impossible, whatever is left, however improbable, must be the truth,'" Peter quoted, and they both laughed.

"How is it going in London?" John continued.

"I'm settling in, ready to start at the Central School."

"I am very excited for you, brother. I think it's a good decision. You will be excellent!"

"Kind of you, John, thanks." He put out his cigarette. "Shall we go back?"

The next morning at the break of dawn, by prearrangement the night before, Peter and his mother met at the stable. They saddled their mounts and took off over the fields, Peter on Darjeeling of course. There was something about the feel of a horse between his knees, as though the animal's power entered him and in exchange discharged his own rage at fate. They galloped over the tract known as Carol Green, jumping hedgerows, walked awhile down Spencer's Lane to rest Elizabeth's horse, who was some years older than the new one, then galloped back toward the Grange, the rising sun dazzling them as it cleared the trees.

* * *

As much as he loved being home with his dear mother and family, Peter was glad to get back to London this time. Wearing black gave him nightmares of Eton, which he admitted to having long after he had left it. And this was a heady time in London, which like all of the nation yearned to recover from the hardships of the war. Theaters in the West End began importing American musicals: *Oklahoma!*, *Carousel*, *South Pacific*, and *My Fair Lady*, an extravaganza produced by Hugh Beaumont. "Binkie" as he was called was a driving force behind much going on in the theatre district. But there were others, like Sir Laurence Olivier, and a rebellious young playwright by the name of John Osborne.

It was an exhilarating time for Peter as well. At last to be studying something he truly loved, surrounded by others who also loved it, was bliss. What could be better than to attend class in Royal Albert Hall, to hear the sound of his own voice resonate in its magnificent auditorium? Add to all this the opportunity to see the greatest British actors, including his idol Sir Laurence, in person and Peter was surely the happiest of young men.

He stood out in drama classes, naturally. His memory was excellent, and in fact he already could recite various Shakespearean soliloquies. He had no stage fright, being self-confident and outgoing, and he was surpassingly handsome, with his dark hair, limpid eyes, high cheek bones and aquiline nose. His height we might observe was emphasized by a rather sinuous gait. The girls all swooned over him. Yet for a person in whom one might expect to find it, Peter had a most engaging lack of conceit, and was thus popular even with the boys, who found him kind and supportive. He was his mother's heir, inwardly as well as outwardly.

One day the Shakespeare class was given the assignment to pair off, boy and girl, to try their skills in the balcony scene from *Romeo and Juliet*, no great challenge to their imagination at their age. A student named Wendy,[62] a slip of a girl and somewhat homely for an aspiring actress in those days, was teamed with a boy she detested. She sat next to Peter as they waited their turns.

"I can't do it, Peter," she whispered, leaning close to him. "You know how I hate him. I won't be able to do this." Peter thought quickly for some way to help.

"I will go behind the others, Wendy, and move to where you can see me from the stage." He too whispered. "Ignore Romeo and look at me. Be my Juliet, no one will notice." We have seen his penchant for the waif. She did as he said and pulled it off ably, though the instructor, not having noticed Peter in the back, did comment that her eyes seemed somewhat averted.

It should be noted that Peter's good looks were "boyish," and in fact remained so until he was in his late thirties; that fact may have limited him to some extent in his early career, though not remarkably by any measure. Unusual for a boy his age, he was not interested in romance, but was absorbed in learning and practicing this wonderful profession of acting.

Each morning he would walk from his flat up Queen's Gate to Royal Albert Hall, across the Kensington Road from Hyde Park. Midday, he might take lunch at a neighboring pub: the Queen's Arms in Queen's Gate Mews perhaps, or the Gloucester Arms, a Georgian pub a bit farther. In good weather, he could buy something from a street vendor and take it to the Park. East Albert Lawn was close, or else he could sit by Round Pond or the Serpentine and feed the water fowl from his sandwich. Then back to the Hall for classes.

He and his mates would certainly have availed themselves of plays at the Old Vic and the Globe, or any one of the thirty-six West End theaters, as well as films, both American and British, at the cinema. *Desert Fox, High Treason, The Lady Says No, Showboat*, all came out in 1951; it was the heyday of film stars like Humphrey Bogart, David Niven, Claudette Colbert, Vivien Leigh. There was no lack of exposure to excellent professional acting, and Peter soaked it all in with much enthusiasm. His cousin Daphne, who was secretary to Orson Welles, was back in town too, her boss having run out of money filming *Othello* on the Continent.

Personally, for himself, Peter loved doing Shakespeare. He savored the poetry of it, tending to a slower, more articulate delivery, which was becoming the old fashioned way, the manner of Sir John

Gielgud. The trend taking hold, embraced even by Sir Laurence, was and remains to speak lines very fast, like street language, with the unfortunate effect that much may be lost on the audience.

As for the Stanislavsky method, however, it seemed to Peter the obvious way to approach acting, the natural way, so he fell right in line with the drama teachers at the Central School. Some older actors, the Canadian Raymond Massey for example, were critical of it, viewing it as lazy, even cheating. What art was there, they thought, in portraying an emotion that one actually felt? But the deeper realism achieved was appreciated by performers and audiences alike. Peter very much enjoyed his increasing knack for entering the psyche of a character. From one role to another he was developing an uncanny ability to change his appearance simply by the most subtle changes in facial expression. Even in the same performance, from one scene to another, he could transmute and seem another person, though certain personal gestures became hallmarks: one was the quick smile, mouth turning up but briefly; another was the way he had of peering out from beneath his lowered brow; and there was the pointed index finger pressed against his lips.

By 1953 he was becoming quite accomplished. It was the year he would turn twenty, and the year that England would crown a new queen. King George VI, who had reigned since before the Second World War when his brother Edward VIII abdicated, died in 1952. His daughter was crowned Elizabeth II on 2 June, 1953, and the coronation in London was an enormous spectacle. What better occasion for the city and the nation to shake off the lingering misery of post-war than the grand celebration of a new and beautiful young monarch? An estimated three million people lined the streets and eight thousand packed into Westminster Abbey on a rainy Tuesday.

These were the early days of television as well, and this historic event was broadcast, leading countless families to acquire the small sets with the flickering screens. Even the ceremony inside the Abbey was televised by order of Her Majesty. With Peter still in town though, we can imagine his parents would have had all the more reason to see it in person. Colonel H. had friends in Birmingham who were peers, and arranged invitations for him and Elizabeth to the Coronation

Ball at the Savoy on the night of the event.[63] The Colonel also managed to procure seats in the Oxford Street viewing platform, where Peter could join them to watch the parade that afternoon. They came on Sunday and stayed for three nights at the Dorchester, east of Hyde Park, as the Savoy was completely full. Peter met them at the hotel soon after they arrived, and surprised his mother with a bunch of red roses he bought from a flower seller on the way. She was delighted, as the one rose she had pinned to the lapel of her spring suit had not survived the trip. They ordered tea brought up for the three of them to the very spacious room. It was a happy reunion, though for Peter, having been the independent young man for some time, it felt oddly regressive to be with his parents.

The tea came and was poured by the uniformed porter. The Colonel gave him a tip and made himself comfortable in one of the easy chairs. "Tell us about school, Peter," he began.

"It is going very well. I especially enjoy the Shakespeare class."

"Any thoughts about what comes next?" his mother asked.

"Oh, yes!" Peter exclaimed with much enthusiasm. "The Shakespeare instructor has told me that the library in Manchester has just started a theatre company, and he thinks I should audition." The reputation of the Central School was such that it was naturally considered as a source for young talent by theaters in London and beyond. "They are using a small auditorium in the basement, 312 seats," Peter continued.

"That's a wonderful idea, darling! Manchester is an exciting place," his mother offered genuinely. The Colonel heaved a sigh of apparent disappointment.

"Well, at least it is in the Midlands," he said wearily. Elizabeth poured him more tea.

"Have a shortbread with that, dear."

"I hope you're not taking up with any of these city girls, son."

"Oh Dad! I'm too busy for that."

"Well, your brothers have started their own young families now. And there are several decent young women at church this year—beautiful too, in my opinion."

"Really, Bill!" Mum came to the rescue.

The next day, Monday, they were getting together with the Colonel's sister Margaret, who was in town staying with daughter Daphne. They would all take in a matinee at St. James Theatre, where Olivier was starring in a comedy, *The Sleeping Prince*, with his second wife, Vivian Leigh; then back to the hotel for dinner.

The day of the coronation, trench coats were in order to watch the parade, perched above Oxford Street in the drizzle. There were dignitaries and military bands from every corner of the Empire, and whenever he heard a certain march, Peter would joke with his mother. "That's 'The British Gwenadiers,' Mummy," he would say, in self-mockery.

The Coronation Ball at the Savoy would certainly have had appeal for Elizabeth; it was a dinner dance to benefit charity, with fourteen hundred guests paying twelve guineas apiece. The lobby was hung with heraldic banners in primary colors, against a backdrop of dove grey fabric. Peter was not attending the ball that night, going instead to a party with friends, but before he and his parents parted ways, his mother had dressed for the affair. Her long formal gown was a royal purple with a matching stole and long white gloves. Her black hair, curled from the rain, was piled on her head, some soft grey now framing her face. She was then fifty-three.

"You look positively regal, Mum!" said Peter, giving her a careful hug.

"Thank you, darling. Well after all, the new queen is my namesake. Enjoy your party, and I want to hear about your success in Manchester!"

He did indeed audition for the new theatre company at the Manchester Library, and was easily accepted. In the following two years, he had roles in eight plays, three of which were Shakespeare.

* * *

At this point in the story of Peter H. it is time to reveal that he had always been known by his second name, Jeremy. As he began his professional career, he kept that name, and for a surname he hit upon the label of one of his suits. It was from Brett's of Leamington.

His father had banned his use of the family name, Huggins, which Jeremy thought unglamorous in any case, while *Jeremy Brett* had a certain panache as a stage name.

The Manchester Central Library was and is an impressive round building. It could be easily mistaken for the Globe Theatre, but it is a library. The theatre was in the reference section, in the basement, an intimate setting, and the young talent joining the Manchester Library Theatre Company assured its reputation.

One of the first plays Jeremy appeared in was *Othello* in 1954. He was Cassio, and a young man just two years older played Iago. His name was Robert Stephens, and they were destined to become close friends thereafter, though their backgrounds could not have been more dissimilar. Stephens was the son of a laborer and a factory worker; his parents abused him, particularly his mother, who made it clear in no uncertain terms that he had not been wanted. Doubtless he was one of those who went into acting for the chance to assume other identities. In his memoir, *Knight Errant*, characteristically self-deprecating, he writes of meeting Jeremy Brett: "Being a country bumpkin, I had never before met anyone so elegant, so charming, so Etonian." Jeremy admired Robert as a man whose commitment to the profession had enabled him to overcome humble beginnings and to become a first rate actor. He also appreciated his supportiveness and lack of jealousy, an unusual absence of the vanity and arrogance that typify too many who take to the stage; and Robert was fun. He loved people, women in particular, though given his four marriages, his seemingly compulsive infidelity, and his childhood history, the context might suggest an unconscious misogyny, a Don Juan syndrome. He also loved to drink.

Robert Stephens at the age of twenty-three, had already been married and had a son. When he and Jeremy met in Manchester, he had his eye on an actress by the name of Tarn Bassett, who would become his second wife in 1956, with Jeremy as his best man.

But first *Othello*. The staging of this production was Edwardian, the idea of such anachronism becoming popular even then, we presume as a way to make Shakespeare seem more immediate to contemporary audiences. The Manchester group allowed a full month of rehearsal, which the actors loved. Soon after the play began its run, Robert popped into Jeremy's dressing room following the performance.

"Splendid job, my friend, but you threw me with that impromptu cigarette business." Cassio had said to Iago, "Have a cigarette."

"Sorry, Robert, but I was craving a smoke." Jeremy became notorious for exploiting such opportunities. "Not Shakespearean, but neither are the costumes."

"Come for a drink?" Jeremy grabbed his jacket, and they were off to the pub. After a couple of glasses of the cask ale at the Abercrombie, and exchanging life stories, they felt like old chums, joking, laughing, sharing their hopes and their fears. "You'll have an easy go of it in this business, with your good looks," Robert observed.

"That's what most people think, Robert, but it's possible to be too pretty. You understand?"

Robert did indeed; in fact in that instant he realized that Jeremy was attractive to everyone irrespective of gender, and in the next he felt a sense of protectiveness. He would stand between Jeremy and "the heavy old queers in the company," as he wrote in his memoir. His love for Jeremy was deep from the start, and it was chaste. As hard as it may be to associate that word with Stephens, in this case—perhaps the only case—it surely applies.

Othello at the Manchester Library was reviewed in the Daily Telegraph, where it was dubbed the "Have a Cigarette Othello." By the end of its run, Jeremy and Robert were rooming together and having a helluva good time, as only two young men, loving their freedom, loving their work, loving one another's company, may be seen to have.

The next Shakespearean role Jeremy took on was Mark Antony in *Julius Caesar*, and it may have been the one which required him to borrow his father's army boots.[64] The Colonel handed them over, joking that he would have to come to the play just to see his boots; and one day, a week into the run, Jeremy got a call from his mother to say that his father would be in Manchester on business and might well be at the performance that evening. Naturally, Jeremy was a bit anxious, given his father's strongly negative attitude toward his career choice, but his training stood him in good stead. On the stage he would become Mark Antony.

Failing to see the Colonel in the audience that night, he was disappointed, and when Dad was not backstage either, he grew not a little dejected. "You're awfully quiet tonight," Robert noted, passing by the open door of Jeremy's dressing room. "Everything all right?"

"I was just hoping to see my father here, that's all."

"Well, his loss I'd say. I'm off to meet Tarn. See you tomorrow."

Slowly Jeremy took the short walk back to their flat, glad for the crispness of the autumn night, but wrapping his woolen muffler around his neck. The smell of wood smoke from the chimneys, the dry leaves blowing down around the street lights and scraping along the walk, seemed a bracing comfort. But nearing the flat, he saw someone on the steps, a most untoward occurrence.

"Jeremy, my boy, I have succeeded in surprising you." That was putting it mildly! There stood the Colonel holding a bottle of champagne.

Jeremy was speechless, finally managing to say, "Were you at the play? I didn't see you."

"Of course, son, and I didn't recognize you either, not until I heard my boots squeak," and they burst into laughter. "But truthfully, lad, in all sincerity, you were brilliant, just brilliant!"

"Thank you, Dad . . . thank you," and Jeremy flashed that quick smile, formerly reserved for his mother. Such a pronouncement was the last thing he expected ever to hear from his father. A gust of wind came up, catching the brim of the Colonel's hat. "Let's go inside," and Jeremy put a hand on his father's shoulder, holding the door for him. They popped the cork of the Dom Peringnon, and Jeremy fetched his best glasses, absent of stemware. They toasted one another, the play, the Manchester Library, the Queen, and then they talked: of Shakespeare, of Granny Huggins, of horses, of home and family, the archery club. Jeremy had not felt as close to his father since that Parish Sunday, perched on his shoulders by the campfire, singing.

* * *

The third Shakespeare play Jeremy did in Manchester was *Richard II*, taking the role of the Duke of Aumerle in 1955. He was gaining a reputation as a classical Shakespearean actor, helped perhaps by the rich baritone of his speaking voice, his physical stature, and his slower delivery. In fact by the very next year he was at the Old Vic, where director Michael Benthall was staging the entire First Folio of Shakespeare's plays, a second time. Jeremy not only reprised his Duke of Aumerle, he also played Malcolm in *Macbeth*, Paris in *Romeo and Juliet*, and Patroclus in *Troilus and Cressida*.

We are duty bound to point out that this was the same year that British theatre in general began to become decidedly less traditional. Over at the Royal Court Theatre in Sloane Square actor and playwright John Osborne was starting the English Theatre Company. His play, *Look Back in Anger*, about the troubled marriage of an upper class woman to a working class man, in spite of its success, drew critical opprobrium for its crude realism. Even Jeremy's friend Robert, who had joined the new company, found it "monstrously offensive." It gave rise to the phrase "angry young man," which became emblematic of the new era. Noel Coward, very much old-school, said of it, "I wish I knew why the hero is so dreadfully cross and what about." But in 1957, Laurence Olivier, who had left the Old Vic in 1949, lent his prestige to the company in Osborne's play *The Entertainer*, and Robert Stephens burnished his own reputation in another Osborne success, *Epitaph for George Dillon*, in 1958. All these works share the leitmotif of thwarted ambitions in the failure of a male protagonist.

The Old Vic Company, meanwhile, took three plays across the pond to the Winter Garden on Broadway, where Jeremy again played Malcolm in the Scottish play and Paris in *Romeo and Juliet*. In *Troilus and Cressida*, though, he was Troilus; and the production was directed by none other than Tyrone Guthrie, to whom Jeremy trilled, "As trrrrue as Trrrroilus!," reminding him of their long ago meeting.

While in New York, Jeremy met a young actress, not yet twenty years of age, who was appearing along with her mother in *The Reluctant Debutante*, her first acting job. Her name was Anna Massey, daughter of Raymond Massey. She was born into the theatre world, with both parents actors, though they had divorced shortly after she was born. Her older brother Daniel was also an actor. She had taken this propitious opportunity to meet the Old Vic cast backstage, though she lived in London with her mother, Adrianne Allen, stepfather, and loyal nanny. She fell immediately under Jeremy's spell, as all the young women were wont to do, but she had special qualities that set her apart. She was a slip of a girl, a will-o-the-wisp, with dark bangs above a heart-shaped, chinless face. She was a waif, and this impression was only reinforced when they met again back in London.

Anna's mother was not only an actress, but also a prominent and gracious hostess. Her second husband, Bill Whitney, stepfather to Anna and Daniel, was an American attorney, who manned the London office of his New York law firm. They lived at the Grove, an area of historic houses in Highgate, a prestigious suburb of London bordering Hampstead Heath. Their house was three-story brick, semi-detached, with a long garden in the back facing the Heath to the west and overlooked by a conservatory. It was ideal for the parties Adrianne was fond of throwing, and with the family's connections, her guest list would have had not only old friends and prominent attorneys, but many celebrated theatre people. To one such party in 1957, she invited their new acquaintance, the young and very promising actor, Jeremy Brett.

It was a dinner party of an evening in late spring, and Jeremy arrived in a proper white dinner jacket with a red rose boutonniere. The tall house, behind a low brick wall topped by a wrought iron fence, looked down on a tree-lined street. Jeremy was greeted by the maid and ushered back to the conservatory, where guests were having pre-dinner cocktails. The view was truly spectacular, with the sun approaching the horizon and in the distance the seventeenth century Kenwood mansion.

He spotted Anna, and she approached, adorable in a pink satin sheath and a soft silk scarf tied in a bow under her chin. She was partial to soft things. With difficulty she suppressed her excitement, a challenge to her nascent acting skills. "Jeremy, how good to see you again! Won't you have a drink? The bartender is filling orders."

"Thank you, Anna. You look charming this evening." Indeed he was impressed with her sweetness, unusually shy and modest for an actress, and so unlike her mother. He had a gin and tonic with a twist of lime, which he nursed slowly knowing there would be wine with dinner. Shortly, the hostess saw them together, and sprang, interrupting her conversation with Noel Coward, with whom she had been friends since appearing in his *Private Lives*.

"Jeremy! May I call you Jeremy?" He appeared such a boy to her, even at twenty-four.

"Of course, Mrs. Whitney."

"Please, Jeremy, we are theatre people; call me Adrianne. You were outstanding on Broadway, you know."

"Why thank you, Adrianne."

"And we loved you in *War and Peace*." Between Manchester Library and the Old Vic Company, Jeremy had hopped over to Rome, where he played Count Nicolai Rostov in the film, directed by King Vidor. It was his first experience with the medium.

"Well, the best part of it for me," he responded, "was being on location with all those horses," and they laughed. The battle scene had Napoleon's huge army on horseback.

"You are so photogenic, Jeremy, clearly," Adrianne continued. "I predict you will make a go of it in this upstart new television business that has the rest of us old hands so worried."

"Perhaps, but I love the stage. Film is so very different."

"Yes, of course, and you appear to have no stage fright. You must tell my daughter your secret; she is petrified of drying." She used the theatre slang for forgetting one's lines.

"Mother!" Anna finally chimed in, abashed, though she was obviously long accustomed to mute forbearance.

"Well, it's true. Excuse me, dears. Dinner will be soon." The party was small enough for a sit-down dinner in the oak paneled dining room, and the guests were very congenial. As they waited after the soup course for the cordon bleu, the hostess announced, "I regret that the Oliviers were not available tonight, especially for your sake, Jeremy, knowing you are a fan; but on the other hand, it allows us to talk about them," and a ripple of laughter went round the table. "What do we think of his going over to this English Theatre Company to do Osborne's new play?"

"My dear friend Robert Stephens is his understudy," Jeremy volunteered, not shy about speaking up, "and in his opinion it is only thanks to Sir Laurence that the play is any good."

They were speaking of *The Entertainer*, which concerned a washed-up music hall performer, exemplifying the gritty sensibility of the new playwrights.

"It's certainly a far cry from *Henry V*," remarked Anna, who was seated next to Jeremy. On that they could all agree. Dinner was served, conversation continued; and following dessert there was more drinking in the conservatory, while those inclined gathered around a grand piano in the living room. Naturally Noel Coward was called upon to sing something from his cabaret act, his own songs, with which he had lately wowed Las Vegas. Jeremy requested "Mad Dogs and Englishmen," then Anna, clever girl that she was, asked for "I've Been to a Marvelous Party," a perfectly hilarious send-up of London society, which had Coward winking as he sang at each guest hanging over the soundboard: "Poor Grace started singing at midnight, and she didn't stop singing till four . . . Maureen disappeared and came back in a beard . . . I couldn't have liked it more!"

The evening wore on; there was moonlight over Hampstead Heath. Before paying his compliments to the hosts, Jeremy found Anna. He came up behind her, and putting an arm over her shoulders, spoke close to her ear to be heard above the laughter and singing. Her perfume had the sweetness of a rose, or of the wisteria when in bloom at the Grange. "Meet me for tea tomorrow after the matinee, the cafe around the corner from the Westminster." Anna had taken on another substantial role in an insubstantial play called *Dear Delinquent*, at the Westminster Theatre, about a lady burglar.[65] Then he slipped away, sensing that of course she would be there.

And she was. Following her matinee performance, she walked over to Whittard's,[66] and Jeremy was waiting, having started on a pot of good strong English tea. They picked up their conversation, which had been scant at the party, and exchanged their life stories, talking about their parents, childhood, then about acting, their plans and ambitions. But Jeremy had something he wanted to express, having observed her, if only briefly. He liked her awfully well, and she was bowled over by his attention. Such a beautiful man, so gifted, so well bred. "Anna, if I may be so bold, I could not help noticing last night how forceful your mother is, imperious even, especially in contrast to you. I really think you should break away, find a place to live on your own. You are old enough." He had that earnest expression, his head lowered, brow knitted, in a way that anyone could see his intentions were innocent.

"Will you help me?" she heard herself ask. Before long she had made the move, to a room on Ebury Street—with her nanny.

* * *

Adrianne Allen loved her two children, but she was not motherly; that role was left to the nanny. Her life was centered on the theatre and filled by the society it availed her. Anna had a good relationship with her mother but never felt close. Her father, Raymond Massey, who lived in Los Angeles, seemed to be simply uninterested and totally self-centered. The adult with the most positive influence during her childhood, aside from the nanny, was her stepfather, whom she recalled in her memoir as a quiet, thoughtful man. Nevertheless, with her pedigree she was inevitably destined to be an actress, in spite of the fact that she did indeed have considerable stage fright. Not only did she fear forgetting her lines in front of an audience, she also was anxious about continuing to find work, though she was a good actress, very professional, and appears never to have lacked for appropriate roles. For a good many years, she was in therapy for these problems. She thought of her life in terms of the theatre, linking every personal incident with what play she was in, at which playhouse, and together with whatever celebrity actor. While not unusual for an actress, her memoir reads like just such a catalog.

Jeremy appreciated her commitment to acting and was beguiled by her girlishness, her vulnerability. They began seeing each other very often that summer, their friendship deepening into romance, despite Anna's occasional embarrassment at Jeremy's exuberance.

They would be sitting in a pub with Robert and Tarn, who had been married for a year, and Jeremy would break into song—Rodgers and Hart, or Cole Porter—with Robert gamely joining in, though he was no singer. Or she and Jeremy would be walking through Piccadilly Circus, and he would swing around a lamppost like Fred Astaire, serenading her with "Bewitched, Bothered and Bewildered" from *Pal Joey*. The British of course are stereotypically stuffy; but if such audacious behavior was atypical, Anna could overlook it. She was head over heels for Jeremy Brett.

Before summer's end, he had decided to propose. He wanted to do things properly though, so at the next party in Highgate, he took Bill Whitney aside to ask his approval, which he received, easily and enthusiastically. But he also was eager for Anna to meet his family; and when they both got a break from their respective jobs for the Michaelmas holiday, they were off to Berkswell. His oldest brother John, looking avuncular at the ripe old age of thirty-four in his clericals and smoking his ever-present pipe, met their train. He was delighted when he saw Anna, in her navy blue linen suit over a white silk shirt. She was exactly the type of girl he envisioned his baby brother with: diminutive, dark haired, with alabaster skin and large, dark eyes.

"Welcome to Berkswell, Anna. We're honored to have you at the Grange."

"Why thank you, Reverend, I'm happy to be here. A pleasure to meet you," and she offered her hand, clinging with the other to Jeremy's arm.

"Our parents would have been here to greet you, but Mum has planned a party for you tonight and is busy arranging flowers."

"Did she cut the late roses?" Jeremy asked. The sacrifice of late blooming roses was the ultimate gesture of hospitality.

"There won't be a one left on the bushes!" his brother exclaimed.

Elizabeth had rounded up as many of their friends and family as she could to meet Anna that evening, but of course her table would not have theatrical celebrities. There would be: her brother Richard with Anne; the rector and his wife; the widow Wheatley; son John and his wife; the Colonel's sister Aunt Margaret, Daphne's mother;

Uncle Leslie, along with other neighbors conversant with London theatre.

Being a city girl, Anna must have been very well impressed with the Grange. Fifteen acres would seem a sizable property, and the house itself, with its many spacious rooms, so unlike a London flat or even a suburban town home. Autumn color had begun to tinge the lime trees and the wisteria vines, and chrysanthemums in all shades of orange, yellow, and red were in bloom in the garden beds. Elizabeth saw the car pull up from the kitchen window, and walked out to the drive to meet her visitor.

"Anna, my dear, I'm so glad you could be with us! Welcome to the Grange," and she took Anna's hand in hers, while Anna continued holding onto Jeremy.

"Jeremy speaks so glowingly of you, Mrs. Huggins. I'm delighted to make your acquaintance." The maid came out and took Anna's overnight case.

"Jeremy will show you to the guest room. Please make yourself at home. We will be having drinks in the drawing room."

As Anna and Jeremy went inside, his Mum and brother John exchanged smiles, her raised eyebrows conveying her concurrence with his happy but as yet unspoken impression. Anna was also an immediate hit with Dad, who held forth over dinner on the historical plays of Shakespeare. With all the leaves in the table, the guests were able to sit down to dinner, a very special effort by Cook, who served medallions of beef in a Burgundy sauce, with a Grand Marniere soufflé for dessert. Aunt Margaret was sitting near Elizabeth's end of the table and across from Jeremy. "You know, Jeremy, your cousin Daphne was very sorry she could not be here with us."

"And why is that, Auntie?"

"You haven't heard? She's being courted by Alec Clunes and dares not leave London." A sudden but brief hush came over the table at the name Clunes, and everyone glanced furtively at the Colonel, who was indeed scowling. Alec Clunes had been a conscientious objector during the war, and his reputation suffered for it, though by then it was quite redeemed. But Daphne's strategy of taking work in the theatre district had, in fact, paid off, and the following year, she married the actor.[67] "As usual, the two of you would seem to be running neck and neck," Aunt Margaret continued, looking at Anna, who blushed a radiant pink.

"We've always been kindred spirits, that's a fact," he retorted, also looking at Anna, who sat next to him, and turned a still deeper shade.

In self-defense she was moved to declare, "Oh my, I really have had a bit too much wine tonight!"

After dinner, Uncle Leslie took to the piano, and Jeremy had to sing, show tunes of course. Then he beckoned to Anna, very chic in her black cocktail dress, a triple strand of pearls at her neck, and they danced out into the grand foyer, followed by a few of the other couples. But if she was intoxicated that night, it was with him: tall and strong and so commanding. He was all she had ever dreamed of in a beau, even dare she think it, a husband.

The next morning Jeremy awoke early, and as soon as he heard his mother go down to breakfast, he went also. He had an agenda. She was sitting at the table waiting for Cook to bring two eggs, once over, with bacon and toast. Coffee was on the sideboard, and he poured them both a cup. "Well?" he began. It was unnecessary even to introduce the topic.

"She is enchanting, Jeremy, just the type of girl for you—warm, unpretentious, modest. Do you love her?"

"Very much, Mum. I want to propose marriage."

"I anticipated this, given what you've been telling me." She reached into the pocket of her dress and took out a small box. "If you have not yet bought a ring, I want you to have this." It was a two-carat diamond solitaire in an antique gold setting. "Aunt Jessie left it to me in her will. It has been in the family for generations."

"Oh, Mother, this means so much to me! Thank you!"

"It means a good deal to me too, darling, and to Aunt Jessie up in heaven. I love you, son." She wanted to add "best," but would never have burdened him with that information.

"And you will always be my first love, Mummy!" So he already knew.

Later that day as she was going out to the greenhouse to begin potting some mint and other herbs, she saw Jeremy on Darjeeling, just as he was reaching down to help Anna climb on the horse's back behind his saddle, and off they rode across the field with the city girl hanging on for dear life. Elizabeth smiled. For any parent, it is bittersweet, the sight of one's child going off into a life for which one prays he is prepared. But for Elizabeth, any sadness was eclipsed by the joy she felt at the happiness of this very special son.

Jeremy became more rather than less impetuous as he grew older. He simply could not wait for their return to London to pop the question—after dinner, for example, or on the steps of her flat. Instead, on the train going back, with twilight coming, the car darkened, and just a handful of other passengers, he quietly put his arm around Anna and pulled her close to him. Her heart began racing so fast she thought he must be able to hear it. Without a word, he handed her the jewel box, and when she opened it to find Aunt Jessie's gorgeous diamond, he said, "Marry me, Anna."

"Oh god, yes!" she answered, melting into his arms.

* * *

Though not keen on sharing the attentions of her only daughter with anyone, Anna's mother could offer no overt objections to Mr. Brett as a fiancé, except perhaps that he seemed so young. She could not have been happy that he had already encouraged Anna's independence, yet being the planner *sin par* she launched right into wedding preparations upon hearing of the engagement, which was forthwith announced in the London and Birmingham papers. St. Michael's Church across from the Grove in Highgate was reserved for a Saturday in May,[68] with a lavish reception to be held in the Whitney's garden. Anna would be done with *Dear Delinquent* by then and could focus on being *the bride!* Invitations were engraved and sent out to at least a hundred people, among them many of the most illustrious in British theatre at that time.

It would of course be a very traditional wedding. Anna's bridal gown covered her from head to toe, the veil long and white, the bouquet of spring flowers large and trailing. Jeremy wore white tie and tails with the pinstriped trousers and a white carnation in the lapel. Another tradition though proved to be unfortunately contentious.

Like so many young brides from broken homes, Anna faced the dilemma of choosing which man would have the honor of giving her away, father or stepfather. She much preferred the latter having lived with him from early childhood. Sadly her father vindicated her low opinion of him by acting the insensitive obstreperous old fool. But both were intransigent; and in the end, after her father Raymond had come all the way from the west coast of America with his second wife Dorothy, he was denied the walk down the aisle with his only daughter. She chose her stepfather, no compromise being acceptable to anyone, and Raymond and Dorothy went home before the event. It was Anna's fate it would seem to be buffeted from pillar to post by older and stronger people, but she carried on to her credit.

Jeremy's one disappointment came when they received a negative response from his friends Robert and Tarn, in whose wedding he had been best man. They would not attend.[69] Since February of that year, Stephens was making a name for himself at the Royal Court Theatre starring in John Osborne's play *Epitaph for George Dillon*, another example of what was being called "kitchen sink realism." With Robert's background he could easily identify with these truculent roles, but they would not have been to Jeremy's taste, who would have inclined more than likely to the opinions of the older generation, for example, Noel Coward and John Gielgud. So he and Robert must have drifted apart. Over the years Stephens's reprehensible behavior—his heavy drinking, his knavish love affairs—would add to the distance, though they managed to remain friends. He was jolly good fun.

In spite of it all, the bride recalled the day as happy, filled with children, laughter and hope. The service was performed by the bishop of Coventry, probably arranged for by the Huggins family, and the photographer was Anthony Armstrong Jones, the same who later married Princess Margaret. Perhaps Patrick stood up as his brother's best man, and his son as the ring bearer. One of the brothers must have had a daughter by then who could be the flower girl. Jeremy had to leave the festivities early because he was performing in a Terence Rattigan play, *Variation on a Theme*, at the Globe. He was to meet Anna afterward at a suite they had taken at the Savoy.

As such parties will, this evening of eating and drinking, dancing and singing, talking and laughing, went on and on. We should wonder what the guests from Warwickshire thought of those flamboyant theatrical people. But eventually the bride slipped away to change her clothes. Her voice teacher,[70] with whom she was quite close, drove her to the hotel. The suite was large of course and very well appointed. There was a writing desk in front of a large window overlooking Waterloo Bridge, a dressing table, two easy chairs, and a chaise. The bed was in another room, with a spacious bath adjoining. On a table next to the chaise, she found an ice bucket with a bottle of champagne from the American playwright Moss Hart and his wife, who had recommended this particular room.

Exhausted, Anna quickly got into her nightgown, a long white satin, and a chiffon robe that was trimmed with white fur. She kicked off her slippers and stretched out on the chaise to wait for Jeremy. Naturally, she nodded off; then like Snow White, she was awakened with a kiss. He had come in quietly and was sitting beside her. His face still smelling faintly of stage makeup, his breath sweet with desire, he lingered on her lips before taking her in his arms into the bedroom. She was light, a slip of a thing, a waif, and he reveled in his youthful power to give pleasure. Allaying any skepticism, we have but to quote Anna's own memoir: "The bride was radiantly content."

* * *

The body has its own agenda, which, as we pass through the phases of life, it has a way of fulfilling. Thus we may remark for example that conception can be the ready result of passion in young lovers. After a brief stint in T. S. Eliot's *The Elder Statesman*, Anna learned that she was pregnant, and for a few months she became the stay-at-home wife. They were living at Jeremy's house in Chelsea, her nanny Gertrude Burbidge included. She remained heavily dependent on his woman until Gertrude died some ten years later. But this was a quiet, happy time for the young couple, and they looked forward eagerly to having a child.

Brett had enough to keep him busy. He played Eugene Marchbanks in the comedy *Candida* by George Bernard Shaw at The Playhouse in Oxford. The heroine, Candida, is the wife of a clergyman, and Marchbanks a youthful poet who attempts to woo her away. Then at the Piccadilly Theatre he appeared in *Mr. Fox of Venice* as William MacFly, a struggling actor hired by Fox to pretend to be his secretary for the purpose of a practical joke. This was written by Frederick Knott, known for complex, crime-related plots. Finally, Brett took a role in the musical *Marigold* at the Savoy Theatre; he was Archie Forsyth, a young soldier who courts the girl of the title, ward of a wealthy Scots woman. We should note with interest how often he played a soldier, but none of this drama could hold a candle to that going on in his personal life.

It was August 1959, and Jeremy was appearing in *The Edwardians* as Sebastian, heir to the country estate known as Chevron, where his widowed mother Lucy gives lavish parties. A suitable part to be sure. At home he and Anna had just celebrated her twenty-second birthday three days earlier with her parents in Highgate. The phone rang in his dressing room at the Saville Theatre after the play, and it was Gertrude, sounding unusually agitated. "Mr. Huggins, I have been trying to reach you. Anna went into labor three hours ago. We are at the hospital. You'd better come."

Jeremy spoke no further. He dropped the phone, and quickly changing to street clothes, but still in makeup, set out for Charing Cross. When he arrived at the waiting room of the delivery suite, it was Nanny who was pacing the floor. "How is she, Gertrude? Is Anna all right?"

"I think so, sir, but being her first she may have a time of it." Then he took over the pacing. After at least another hour, a nurse came out.

"Mr. Huggins? Your wife is coming out of delivery. She did have some light sedation. If you come with me you can see your son from the nursery window."

"A boy!" he exclaimed following the nurse. They had chosen the name "David" in this event, and there he was behind the viewing glass as newborns were then displayed, alphabetically in rows of bassinets, labeled, "Huggins, David." The baby was brought to his mother, and finally Jeremy was allowed to see her.

"I came as soon as I heard, darling. How are you?" He sat by her bedside, stroking her hair and marveling at their new son, who lay between them wrapped in the same blue receiving blanket that had swathed Jeremy twenty-five years earlier.

"Just a little groggy, dear, and very tired. Isn't he beautiful? And wasn't your mother prescient sending this blanket?"

"Of course. But then she wouldn't have anything else *except* blue! Now rest sweetheart. I will be back tomorrow, and Nanny will have things ready when you come home." He kissed her, and very gently the baby. She put a hand on his.

"Will we be good parents, Jeremy?"

"We will do our best Anna, like most parents do. Don't you worry."

But then most parents default to the familiar template of their own childhood, so when Anna faced the dilemma of many professional women, she followed in her mother's footsteps, if reluctantly. Nanny was there to care for little David, while acting was her priority, as she confessed in her memoir. Very soon she was at work, a starring role in *Peeping Tom*, a horror movie about a serial killer, and yet another example of the iconoclasm that was shaking British mores. Its themes of terror and graphic torture earned opprobrium and destroyed the career of director Michael Powell.

Nevertheless, a christening was planned for mid-September, before another Michaelmas could come round, at the church in Highgate were they had been married.[71] The Reverend Huggins, Jeremy's brother John, would assist with the service, and Patrick and his wife would be godparents. The day before this event the Colonel and Elizabeth checked into the Dorchester, where they had stayed six years before on the occasion of the coronation, and immediately set out to meet their newest grandson in Chelsea. Jeremy was eager to introduce them.

"Mum, Dad! Welcome to our humble home," he greeted them at the door, and there were hugs and handshakes all around. The baby had started crying at the sound of the doorbell, so Nanny went to fetch him, while Anna put a kettle on for tea.

"Bring that child to me!" Elizabeth exclaimed, and Nanny handed him over. "Oh, Jeremy! Isn't he 'beloved'!" This being the meaning of the name David. "And unmistakably a Huggins," she went on, showing the baby to her husband. "He looks like you, Bill."

"Now Betty, you can't tell that yet." Granddad seemed a little embarrassed.

"No, no, Mum's right, Dad, I agree. Tell me, how are you enjoying retirement so far?" The Colonel was then sixty-nine and had recently cut back on his work in the family business.

"I love it, son, more time for archery and for the horses, though I'm still kept busy with activities in Birmingham."

Anna entered with a large tea tray, and Nanny helped her to serve. "And what is happening in Berkswell Parish?" Anna asked Elizabeth, still uncertain how to address her mother-in-law.

"We had an illustrious visitor for Parish Sunday this year, the bishop of Swansea."

"From Wales," Jeremy observed. "Isn't he the second of the six bishops in their chain of command?"

"That's right, just below the Archbishop. His name is John Thomas, and he just took over from Glyn Simon about a year ago. He is a friend of the rector. He was most interesting, a few years younger than me, and he suggested we get together to compare notes on the history and administration of endowed parish charities. Perhaps I'll go before winter sets in."

"Oh, Swansea will be beautiful!" Anna spoke up as she cradled the baby, who was becoming fussy. "I think he wants a bottle, Nan," and she handed him to Nanny.

"Was it hard going to work, Anna, so soon after the delivery?" Elizabeth enquired.

"Indeed yes, I must say, but Nanny is so very experienced, and I had a chance to work in film. I am learning a lot, although the story is so macabre. I don't know that it will be well received." And it was not. Critics and movie goers were morally outraged at the brazen portrayal of sadism, worried that all restraints of decency and good taste were collapsing.

"You know, Jeremy," said his father, changing the subject, "your Aunt Margaret will attend the christening tomorrow, her second this year."

"Ah, yes, Daphne's baby, Amanda, and Auntie will doubtless chide me again about being in step with my favorite cousin!" They all smiled. "Now set me straight, Mum, is Daphne's child my second cousin?"

"No, no, darling, she is still a first cousin, removed by one generation. She is a second cousin in relation to your son. We will go round to see her before we leave."

The service next day went smoothly; the baby was well behaved, and at Elizabeth's request one of the hymns sung was "O Holy Jesus, Lord Divine," which had been sung at Jeremy's christening. Those attending were mostly family, and afterwards they crossed the street for high tea at the Grove. Adrianne had planned everything with her customary care: the food, the beverages, the best china and silver, the flowers. It was a more decorous occasion than her usual parties, a nod to Jeremy's family, who were a tolerant lot, though class distinctions still prevailed in England.

The Colonel got into a lively conversation with Anna's stepfather upon learning that Mount Whitney in the Sierra Nevada had been named for a relative of his who had been a mountaineer; and Bill Whitney was curious to hear about the Royal Horse Artillery and the Colonel's exploits in the Great War. While the two Bills were in this tête-à-tête, the grandmothers walked out into the garden, Adrianne eager to show it off knowing of Elizabeth's keen interest and long experience.

Anna and the baby were the stars of the show inside, so Jeremy stepped out onto the veranda for a smoke. When he saw Adrianne excuse herself, he put out the cigarette and went to talk to his mother. "How do you like the garden?" he began.

"It's lovely, very elegant and formal, the perfect city garden!" They reached one of the iron benches and sat down.

"You've been so quiet today, Mummy, so pensive. Are you all right?"

"Oh son, I'm fine; your mother is just getting old."

"Nonsense, you are still young and healthy!"

"You know I am happy for you, very much so, you and Anna having such wonderful success in careers that you love, and now a beautiful baby . . ."

"Yes?" It was unlike his mother not to complete a sentence.

"As I watched you today at the baptismal font, thinking of your own baptism twenty-five years ago—God forgive me—I had the strongest sense of being left behind."

"No, Mother, no . . ."

"Let me finish, Jeremy. I guess it's only natural to be a little sad about it, and yet it's God's plan for us, and we must accept it."

He was quiet, his feelings more of defiance than acceptance. He took her hand, kissed it, and held it. "But how, Mum, how?"

"For myself, darling, I lean on the teachings of George Fox." She cited the founder of Quakerism. "Like him, we must feel God's overwhelming love for us, all the greater in our worst trials, and reflect it in our compassion for others." Her eyes misting over, she withdrew her hand to reach for a hankie in the pocket of her suit. Then she mussed his wonderful soft hair as of old and kissed him on the temple. "Come on, let's go back inside." Reaching the veranda she stopped. "By the way, remember your grandmother's little dog, Gramps? Of course you do. You loved him so."

"Yes, he died of old age."

"Well, the breeder has a litter of puppies. She's over towards Meriden. Next time you're home you should go have a look."

"Thank you, Mum, I will."

* * *

Reverend Bursell was sitting in his study in the rectory on a grey November afternoon, a Saturday, the day before Remembrance Day, when the phone rang. Janet, his assistant Parish Administrator, answered it. "Reverend, the bishop of Swansea is on the phone for you."

"Thank you, Janet." This was unexpected, though he knew Bishop Thomas from Oxford, and he had heard that Mrs. Huggins was to pay him a visit that week. "Good afternoon, John, so good to hear from you!"

"Henry, I have just had the most awful news from the Chief Constable of Merioneth. Are you sitting down?" The bishop's tone was alarming, and Henry gripped the arm of his desk chair defensively.

"Yes?"

"On her way to see me this morning, Elizabeth Huggins encountered a sudden hailstorm along the coast. Her car went off the road, and she was killed."[72] The rector let out a loud gasp as though the wind had been knocked out of him, bringing Janet to the door of the room, where she continued to listen. "Her appointment book was beside her in the car, so they called me first, and I prevailed upon the officer to let me call you before they went further. I thought you should be the one to notify the family. The Colonel will need to go to Merioneth to claim her body."

"My god, John, I am stunned! This will be such an enormous shock to everyone. I will go to the Grange immediately."

"Let me give you the Constable's name and number for Colonel Huggins to contact." When the rector put down the phone, he turned to Janet, who had inferred something of the disaster.

"Janet, Mrs. Huggins has died in a road accident in Wales." His assistant reeled at this information, falling against the door jam. "Call the Grange and speak with the housekeeper. Do not give her the news yet; just make sure the Colonel is there, and tell her I am coming right over. Oh, and have her check to see that there is Scotch and two glasses in the drawing room."

The Colonel was upstairs when he saw the rector's car drive up, and he went down to answer the door himself. "Rector, what a pleasant surprise! Come in," he said, taking his visitor's overcoat, damp from the chilly drizzle. "Let us go to the drawing room."

"Please sit down, Bill. I have had a call from Bishop Thomas," and the rector opened the decanter of Scotch. "May I?" Bill Huggins started to feel uneasy; it was uncharacteristic of the reverend to presume upon his Scotch.

"Yes, of course, Henry." The rector poured two glasses, neat, no ice, and handed one to the Colonel.

"There has been a terrible accident on the coast at Swansea. Betty's car was driven off the road in a hailstorm." He paused to take the measure of the old fellow's reaction. "She has been killed."

Colonel Huggins was an old soldier, by no means unfamiliar with the gravest miseries of humankind, yet his first response in this case was of unreality, disbelief. His beautiful wife, just fifty-nine? How was it possible? He too gasped audibly, sunk back into his chair, and emptied the snifter of Scotch in one gulp, handing it to Henry, who refilled it.

"You will need to call the Constable in Merioneth right away to let him know I have told you. I will help you, Bill."

The Colonel had begun to shake, and his eyes were welling up. "Good Lord, Henry, how will I tell the boys?"

A fire had been laid, and the rector took the liberty of lighting it as the room was cold. The two sat near it in silence watching it blaze. Then the reverend spoke up. "I would tell John first and have him gather his brothers together. What do you think?"

"Of course, yes, John is a church man, and the oldest. I have to tell you, Henry, I am a tough old soul, but my heart breaks for Jeremy."

By nightfall, the Constable had been called and the oldest son had been reached. John came immediately, arriving by supper time to be with his father. The rector stayed until then, and the three of them prayed together before he left. The plan was that he and the Colonel would drive to Merioneth next day to claim the body. It was a long trip in those days and John begged his father to let him go instead, but the Colonel wanted him to get Patrick and Michael and go down to London to break the awful news to Jeremy. So in the morning, after the rector and Colonel Huggins had left for Wales, John went to find Patrick, and they continued on to Coventry, where Michael was then a struggling artist.[73] Shaken by this sudden and terrible loss, but trying to be strong for each other, the young men set out for

London, knowing that their dreadful mission would be as an arrow to the heart of their baby brother.

He was not at home when they arrived at the house in Chelsea. In fact only the nanny was there. Jeremy was having lunch with his agent to talk about possible work in television in the coming year, and Anna was occupied with a play called *The Last Joke*. The brothers told Nanny of the tragedy, and came inside to wait. She was horrified of course, though she had not known Mrs. Huggins well or for long. She provided them with a bottle of Courvoisier and four glasses. Patrick paced in front of the window; John poured the brandy. Soon enough Jeremy arrived.

Seeing John's car parked in front, he could not imagine a reason. It was a week past his twenty-sixth birthday, upon which occasion John had called with greetings and all his brothers had sent cards. When he found the three of them in the living room, he was still more perplexed. Patrick took him by the shoulders and sat him down on the sofa.

"Jeremy," John began softly, "there was a terrible car accident in Wales yesterday. Mother was killed." It took several seconds for the awful meaning of this to penetrate, and when it did Jeremy leapt up, grabbing John by the lapels as if he would kill the messenger. Patrick stepped between them and sat Jeremy back down, handing him a glass of brandy as he did so. The truth sank in with the alcohol, and the earsplitting, bloodcurdling wail that erupted from Jeremy terrified his brothers, and likely all the neighbors. The baby was awakened of course, and screamed in echo of his father—their wonderful son, just three months old, whom Jeremy had dreamed of growing up to love his grandmother and bring her joy! Patrick sat beside him then, and they leaned against each other sobbing. The older two exchanged somber glances in silence, glad of the brandy.

When poor Anna arrived home to this awful scene, the men stood up, well-mannered as they of course were, and John gave her the news. "Oh Jeremy, Jeremy!" she gasped, "This is horrible," and she too cried as they hugged. She invited the brothers to stay for supper, but they declined.

"We must get back home," explained John, still the spokesman. "Family must be called. A story like this will be in the newspapers. And when Dad returns we will need to make arrangements. I will let you know about the funeral." His words were indeed like a rain of arrows, each one piercing Jeremy mortally. But what could be done? He was thrown by an inexorable fate into the mire of grief.

* * *

The body of Elizabeth Cadbury Huggins, *nee* Butler, was brought by train to a funeral home in Meriden, and then in a hearse to St. John the Baptist Church in Berkswell on the next Sunday for the funeral. On that day the Church was filled to the rafters with every soul in the village; even with folding chairs in the vestibule, there was standing room only. An additional memorial service would be held later at Woodbrooke[74] in Birmingham so that more of the Cadbury clan and family friends might attend. Bishop Thomas of Swansea would speak at that one, but Reverend Bursell performed the funeral service and spoke movingly. He recounted a Buddhist legend in which a mother whose infant has died brings his body to the Buddha, begging him to use his powers to restore the child to life. Buddha gives her a jar, instructing her to go to every house in the village and collect a mustard seed from all those who have known no grief. This she does and of course returns to him with an empty jar, having learned that this human condition is universal and that she is far from alone. Thus as sad and unexpected as the death of Mrs. Huggins was, the rector assured the congregation that their shared grief would uphold them in God's compassion.

Her husband and sons, good Englishmen all, Woodmen of Arden in fact, were stoical, even Jeremy, aside from the chain smoking. They walked behind her casket to the churchyard where the couple had a double plot, the Colonel's side awaiting him. Following the service, Mrs. Wheatley opened the Hall for mourners to gather and pay their respects. The Grange would not have been large enough. Jeremy stood with the family, receiving the sincere condolences of people he barely knew, and growing increasingly numb. Their words, the pat phrases, well intended as they surely were, became overwhelming: "Freak accident . . . killed instantly . . . so sudden . . . family devastated . . . she didn't suffer . . . sorry for your loss . . ."

Surrounded by this sea of people, he felt nonetheless alone, isolated, marooned just as he had the day his mother brought him to Eton and he watched her drive off without him. After a while, Mrs. Wheatley pulled him aside. "Well-wishers can be so tiring, so insipid," she said softly, putting an arm around him. Christobel always knew what to say,[75] and after all she had lost her husband, Colonel Charles, in 1943, also unexpectedly and in his fifties. "If you want to leave," she continued, "I will explain to your father. You go back to the Grange and sleep. What does Macbeth say about it?"

"'Sleep that knits up the raveled sleeve of care.' Thank you, Mrs. Wheatley, for your kindness, for everything."

"Your mother was my dear friend, Jeremy. She loved you the best, you know that. It will be hard, but please, for the sake of her memory, do not allow yourself to be drowned in the sorrow of this tragedy. Now, go."

He left, but did not go to the Grange. He went straight back to London, arriving home after midnight. Nanny and the baby were asleep. Anna was away, touring with *The Last Joke* prior to the London opening. She could not pass up the opportunity to work with Noel Coward, a pillar of British theatre. Jeremy went quietly to look in on his beautiful infant son sleeping in his crib, the warm sweet smell of his breath mingling with that of baby powder, his peaceful innocence a balm to his young father, in whose mind echoed the wise words of the widow Wheatley.

When the Colonel and his other sons got back to the Grange that night exhausted and drained, they expected to find Jeremy there. "He must have gone back to London," John suggested, taken aback.

"Without telling us? But he was going to stay over," the Colonel protested, looking surprised and worried. John would have understood Jeremy's seeming ungraciousness; as a pastor he already knew the rawness and anger of grief, but Patrick was very hurt. Of all of them, it may have been Michael, the artistic soul, who alone intuited something unnatural, dark and dangerous, in his brother's mood.

The next day, however, Jeremy called to apologize for his unceremonious departure. His father was relieved to hear from him. "Christobel told me you had left, but we presumed you were coming here for the night. It was a hard day for all of us. I'm just glad you're all right, son."

"And you, Dad, how are you?"

"Your brothers are leaving today; they must get back with their families, but Uncle Leslie and Aunt Margaret will stay to help sort things. I'll survive. When will I see you?"

"At Woodbrooke."

"And Christmas?"

"We'll be there."

Returning to the Grange in the absence of his dear, dear mother would certainly have been exceedingly fraught for her youngest, each of its rooms haunted with her memory, her beloved roses seeming to pine for her, his footsteps on the wood floors echoing his own unspeakable loneliness. But he did go for Christmas, bringing Anna and the baby and the indispensable nanny. They came on Christmas Eve, and there had already been a light snowfall, turning the village of Berkswell into a Christmas card. But to no one's surprise, a black wreath still hung on the door of the Grange. The family gathered in the drawing room, where a fire was blazing, for drinks preceding a light supper. Jeremy leaned on the mantel with one foot on the fender, a habit he was acquiring, and Michael handed him a glass of sherry.

"How are you, young brother?" He got no answer, just a heavy sigh, then a question.

"What's wrong with Patrick?" Jeremy had sensed an unusual coolness.

"The night of the funeral, when you left us. You'd better patch it up with him while you're here."

The mood around the dinner table was subdued if not somber. The wives tried gently to lighten the atmosphere, talking of their children and of course the new baby. Following supper, the men adjourned for a game of snooker; the table was in the game room, which had once been the nursery.

With his cigarette in one hand, Jeremy took Patrick's arm with the other. "Let me apologize, brother, for leaving so suddenly the night of the funeral. I should have stayed."

"No, no . . ." Patrick answered, dismissing the matter. But Jeremy continued.

"I just needed to get home, to be with my son." Patrick also had a son, not much older. "Our boys will never know Mum."

"I know, I know!" Beginning to choke up, the two exchanged a brotherly hug.

"Your break," said Jeremy, and Patrick began the game.

The next day would bring more extended family for Christmas dinner, and visits from neighbors intent upon continued support of the Colonel and his sons in their untoward bereavement. But after an early breakfast, his father had a surprise for Jeremy.

"Come to the stable with me," he said, pushing back from the table. "I have something to show you."

Jeremy got up, folded his napkin, and followed his father as instructed. On their way to the stable he could not help thinking of his sixth birthday, when Nanny led him blindfolded on the same path, and the surprise was a pony. As they approached though, he heard barking. Had his father acquired a new dog? In one of the stalls, frolicking boisterously in their pen, there were indeed two Jack Russell puppies.

"These are a pair from the litter your mother told you about, Jeremy," the Colonel said. "If you want one, it's yours for Christmas, and I'll keep the other."

The notion that a soldier cannot be sentimental is far from true, since the opposite is often the case. As his father watched a slow smile come to Jeremy's face, he thought to himself how his wife lived on in this beautiful man, body and soul, and he coughed to clear the lump in his throat.

Jeremy had squatted by the pen, and the male puppy jumped on him, licking his face. "This will be the one then. Thanks, Dad."

"I knew you'd leave me the bitch!" Dad joked.

Thus on the way back to London that night, the young family had a new member. Making conversation as she held the puppy on her lap, Anna was telling Jeremy about seeing Binkie Beaumont at the Grove recently, and how she thought the stress of his latest musical was aging him. The show was *My Fair Lady*, which opened with much fanfare in 1958 and ran for five years.

"His hair, what's left of it, is as wiry as this little dog's." Then she added, "Shall we call the dog 'Binkie'?"

"Too obvious," came Jeremy's response. "How about 'Mr. Binks'?"[76] He could be so fanciful!

Elizabeth Huggins, nee Butler—mother of Jeremy Huggins.

Colonel Henry William Huggins, decorated for his service
with the Royal Horse Artillery in World War I.

The Grange, Berkswell, Warwickshire, England—Jeremy's boyhood home.*

The Huggins brothers in order of birth—John, Michael, Patrick, and Jeremy.*

Tea in the garden. Jeremy is on the far right beside Nanny;
Patrick in the foreground, and maid Jenny Vines on the far left.*

Young Jeremy stands in front of brother Michael, flanked by his mother, Nanny Clifford, and behind his mother, grandmother Butler. Other staff members include the cook Lily Knight, far left, and next to her the under-nurse Edna Vines.*

The Berkswell Boy Scout troop in front of the Grange on Parish Sunday—compliments of Mr. John Webb.

Jeremy is mounted on one of the family's donkeys, his mother in the middle, brothers Michael (left) and Patrick (right).*

Ann Gay and friends at her birthday party in the garden of Nailcote Hall, where she lived with her parents. Jeremy peeks around on her left.*

Young Jeremy in costume for the Christmas play at church.*

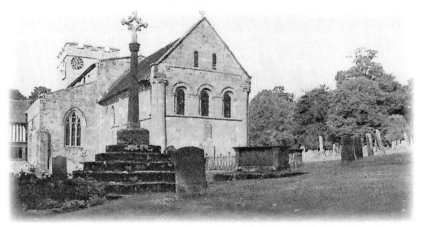

St. John the Baptist Church of England, and the adjoining churchyard.

An older Jeremy, holding the family dog, with mother and maternal grandmother, Edith Cadbury Butler.*

Eton portrait of Peter Jeremy William Huggins, age 13.

Wedding of Anna Massey and Jeremy Brett, in May 1958.

Anna and Jeremy with newborn son David, in August 1959.

The lych-gate in the churchyard of St. John the Baptist, provided by the Huggins brothers and dedicated in 1979 to the memory of their parents, compliments of Wendy Burns, curator of the Berkswell museum.

Plaque on the lych-gate in memory of Col. and Mrs. Huggins, also provided by Wendy Burns.

Farewell party at the Grange in 1966, with family, neighbors, and former staff. Jeremy, in the far right corner, holds Mr. Binks, his son David sitting on the ground in front of him. Standing in the back row in a white shirt is brother Patrick, to whose right is the Earl of Aylesford, and next to him the family's former driver Lou Wilcox. Other former staff members stand in the second row, third, fourth and fifth from the left: Jenny Vines, Joyce Jakeman, and Bob Creber. Mrs. vines was a maid, Mrs. Jakeman, the housekeeper, and Mr. Creber took over the garden from Tom Houghton.*

Jeremy Brett and Joan Wilson.

Jeremy Brett as Dracula, onstage in LosAngeles, 1978.

Jeremy at his desk in the apartment on Clapham Common, London.

Jeremy Brett and Linda Pritchard.

Grayshott Hall in snow, compliments of Grayshott Spa.

* These photographs appeared in the *Berkswell Miscellany, Volume 5*.

Chapter 3

Early in the New Year, 1960, Jeremy had returned home from a screen test for a role in *Tess of the d'Urbervilles* for Independent Television, and he and Anna were relaxing together before dinner. He was bent over putting a record on the turntable when she threw a pillow playfully in his direction, hitting him on his backside. He wheeled around in a rage and snapped at her. "Never do that to me again! It is insulting, humiliating!" She was dumbfounded, and cites this incident as the first sign the marriage could fail.

If nothing else, it raises a question as to the degree of their intimacy, since a knowledge of his years at Eton would have made her more sympathetic. Jeremy was naturally in a dark mood for some time following the shock of his mother's horrible death, but the sudden angry outburst was more troubling. It is not unusual for mental problems to surface in young adulthood. Later in life, he was diagnosed with bipolar disorder, also known as manic-depression, a mental dysfunction that may well be more misunderstood than any other. Everyone has moods. At any given time, most people could find some reason to be sad or happy; in fact we now know that moods are largely controlled by neurochemicals in the brain irrespective of circumstances. So a person with a mood disorder seems only different from others as a matter of degree. He is not just sad, he is depressed; not merely happy, but ecstatic. Often it is only the depressive phase of this illness that is recognized and treated. The manic mood brings energy and creativity that can lead to great success in life. It is seen as the normal personality.

What is not common knowledge is that this disorder involves not only these two extremes but also, notably and most destructively, irrational anger, often directed at those closest, who slowly become alienated. The angry tirade may be uncharacteristic of the individual, and he may even repent and apologize soon after. A further aspect that is not widely known is that bipolar disorder can become more serious with age, in some cases causing psychotic episodes.

But at this point, Jeremy Brett was at the start of a brilliant career, still young, loving his profession, thrilled to have a son. His mother was gone, his rock and his refuge, yet as his father noted, she lived on in him, her strength, her vitality, her generosity. He did not turn to drink, as do so many who suffer depression, but with his friend Robert Stephens back in London, after *George Dillon* got bad reviews on Broadway, they were bound to meet up at a pub.

On a winter afternoon, Jeremy had just had another screen test, this one with the BBC for an episode of their Saturday Playhouse, and he was walking down St. Martin's Lane, bundled against the cold, his long green muffler, just like the one Nanny Ellen had knitted him years ago, doubled around his neck. By chance here came Stephens headed for the Salisbury.

"Robert, my good man, back from New York so soon?" Jeremy teased him, smiling.

"Jeremy, good to see you. It was John, got on the wrong side of the critics.[77] But I had a taste of Chesapeake oysters in Baltimore—the best! Come inside, let's have a drink," and he put a hand on Jeremy's shoulder as they walked in and sat at the bar. Over a couple of pints, Robert was going on about his current part in a Noel Coward play that was not to his taste, called *Look After Lulu*, and noticed that his friend was unusually quiet. He stopped talking. Jeremy lit a cigarette; he was very tired, not sleeping well. After a while Robert said, "Heard about it, man, bloody awful," and of course they knew what was referred to. "How old was she?"

"Fifty-nine." They ordered another round, Stephens using his as a chaser for his Haig's. With his working class sensibility, he had a certain perspective on life.

"The way I look at it, that's a lot of years, a good life. You don't live forever," he said. "We're just getting our chance, my friend. We've got to make the most of it," and he raised his mug as if to ratify the sentiment. Jeremy flashed that quick, brief smile and followed suit. He finished that second beer slowly, then left Robert in the pub to get soused, his second favorite pursuit after women. Jeremy continued on his way to the Strand and caught a bus home. It was beginning to get dark when he arrived, stars coming out in the crystal clear chill, and Mr. Binks met him at the door, wagging and jumping and barking his joy. There was nothing for it but to pick him up, put on his leash and take him for a walk before dark. They did not go far, just to the river, the Chelsea Embankment, and back, but this little ritual brought them both such happiness. They would be close companions for many years to come.

* * *

No observer ever really knows what goes on between married people, because there are always two versions of questionable validity. But we have no reason to doubt Anna when she writes that before the London run of *The Last Joke* ended, Jeremy had left her. We can only remark how ironically titled the play was for them personally. She makes it amply clear that she was deeply in love with him and continued always to care about him. They both wanted sincerely for the marriage to work, but we have only her account, and must therefore read between the lines.

She was very young, and we are given the impression, younger than her years: dominated by her mother, dependent on her nanny. Her view of life was her mother's script, to which she hewed faithfully, even neurotically. She followed the same profession, admired the same people. Looking back she reflects that her "emotional demands" were too much for Jeremy. What we do not read is any reference to his needs, which at that time were overwhelming.

Yet apparently seeing the wisdom of Robert's advice, he got on with his career. He was selected for both of the television roles he tried for. He was the romantic lead, Angel Clare, suitor and true love of the tragic Tess in *Tess of the d'Urbervilles* for ITV, based on the novel by Thomas Hardy, written in 1891 and set in the 1870s. Then he was Nigel Lorraine in "The Guinea Pig," an episode of the BBC's

Saturday Playhouse. He was also in three plays that year: Malcolm in *Macbeth* at Royal Festival Hall; a role in *All Good Children* at the Bromley Little Theatre, a venue southeast of London; and the Reverend Highfield in *Johnny the Priest*, also in London. The latter was a musical, presented by Don Gemmell and Reginald Woolley, on the sensitive subject of juvenile delinquency. It was withdrawn after fourteen performances.

With the rise of the "kitchen sink" style in British play writing, not to mention the influence of American movies with the likes of James Dean and Marlon Brando, the actors in demand were the craggy faced men like Robert Stephens, the angry young men, the rebels without a cause, and not as much the handsome, genteel, old-school kind. But Jeremy Brett was loved by the camera, and would be increasingly sought after for television, though in years ahead there was still much work on stage in classical drama upon which to perfect his art.

By the late autumn of 1960, Anna was between jobs, and she and Jeremy got back together in hope of saving the marriage. They planned a trip to Tenerife, one of the Spanish Canary Islands off the coast of North Africa, where they could relax together and work on their relationship. Before they left, Anna had auditioned for the part of Annie Sullivan in *The Miracle Worker*. She presumed she would not get it, so she left with Jeremy on holiday.

They checked into a suite at the Gran Hotel Bahia on the south end of the island, with a balcony overlooking the ocean and a long stretch of gleaming white sand beach. Their bags were brought up, and Jeremy tipped the porter. He lit a cigarette and went out on the porch. In the distance, sailboats large and small dotted the water, taking happy advantage of the ocean breezes that were also whipping up little whitecaps here and there. Anna was starting to unpack their dinner clothes when the phone rang.

"Long distance? For me? Of course, put it through." She sounded concerned, puzzled. "Hello? Yes, this is she. Really? Are you serious? But I thought . . . I am away on holiday with my husband. We're in Tenerife. This is so awkward. I will have to get back to you," and she hung up the phone.

"Don't tell me," said Jeremy, coming back into the room, and reading her chagrin.

"They want me for *The Miracle Worker* after all."

"What a stunning dilemma for you," Jeremy remarked calmly. Then putting out his cigarette, he left the room.

Oh, how she wanted to stay in this beautiful place with the man she loved! But for an actress at age 23, such a role in an important, serious play could make her career. She wanted to scream at the bad timing of this good fortune, and tears came to her eyes. From the balcony she saw Jeremy on the shore, then putting on her sandals, ran outside to join him. Catching up, she grabbed his arm and hung on tight.

"I'm sorry, Jeremy." So she had decided.

"No, darling, it's a marvelous opportunity." He was ever the gentleman, and courtly at that, but in the moment he was missing Mr. Binks, awfully.

"I will surely work it out with them so that I can stay at least a week here," she suggested as a compromise. And that she did, though her priority couldn't be denied. We may appreciate the conflicting demands of a professional woman with a family, but in this case there seems a taint of compulsion to her acting career, since it is hard to detect in her accounts any real zest for it. She loved theatre people—her parents were theatre people—and it was the family business, that's all.

They returned home after a week, and she went right into rehearsals. When the play opened on tour in Stratford, it was an instant success, and it then ran for nine months in London, during which time Jeremy left her once again.

It was 1961, and he was quite busy himself that year. He had two more roles on television for BBC, playing the Prince in two episodes of *Beauty and the Beast*, based on the fairytale, and Julian Bennett in *A Kind of Strength*, by the prolific British writer, N. J. Crisp. Then he reprised his Malcolm for the American audience in an NBC production of *Macbeth*. He was also in two stage plays at the Royal Court Theatre. First *The Changeling*, a Jacobean tragedy in which he was Alsemero, the lover of Beatrice, who is inconveniently betrothed to Alonzo. Beatrice has Alonzo killed, thereby leaving herself exposed to blackmail. Second was *The Kitchen*, a play from 1957 by Arnold Wesker, which follows the kitchen staff of a cafe on one busy morning. But most importantly it was the year he played the Dane. He was in *Hamlet* on stage at the Strand Theatre. Reflecting on it years later, he concluded that he had been too young, and at the same time disclosed something very insightful: that he brought to that role an intense personal anger, surprising even himself. In the scene where Hamlet vilifies his mother the Queen, he had been extremely rough with her physically. Surely he thought, this had been his rage over the death of his own mother suddenly bursting from his subconscious. In the wider perspective of Brett's life, specifically his bipolar disorder, this instance is indicative and disturbing.

Sir John Gielgud used to say that an actor can only submerge 10 percent of his own personality in a performance, and we have previously quoted Stanislavsky on the subject. His idea that an actor may more easily vent some personal emotion disguised as that of his character was perhaps exemplified by Jeremy Brett's Hamlet.

He was disappointed in his performance, but the part is notoriously problematic. When *Hamlet* had completed its run at the Strand, he decided to take a break. Anna was still preoccupied with *The Miracle Worker* at Wyndham's, so he set out on his own for Switzerland, booking a room at the Hotel Grand Palace on Lake Geneva in Montreux. He could be back by Christmas.

* * *

Montreux sits on the eastern side of what the French call the lac Leman, with commanding views of the Alps across the water. Taking advantage of this natural beauty, the town has a promenade along the lake, lined with a low stone wall, and thanks to a mild climate, landscaped with trees, flowering shrubs, and seasonal flowers. Enjoying the prime spot in this prime location is the Montreux Palace Hotel, where spacious green lawns spill down to the promenade and the lake beyond. It was late October when Jeremy came; there was autumn color in the surrounding hills, and gardens were still in bloom.

Checking in before dinner, he went right to the hotel bar to have a drink before eating. He ordered a gin and tonic, and the gentleman sitting next to him, upon hearing the accent of a countryman, struck up a conversation.

"I say, a fellow Englishman! Welcome to the Palace, sir," he said cheerily.

"Why thank you," and Jeremy took out his cigarette case.

"Allow me." The man quickly deployed a lighter. His name was Victor, from Yorkshire, and he also was traveling alone, so they decided to dine together, thus to continue talking. He was nattily dressed for dinner in a continental style, with a grey paisley ascot, and grey sweater vest under his blazer, complimenting his salt-and-pepper hair that receded at the temples. He was easily as tall as Jeremy, but a bit heftier.

They joked and laughed over dinner, which of course was sumptuous, and learned that they had much in common. Both were born and raised in the English countryside, and both their fathers were army officers. Though he seldom went to London, Victor had an interest in theatre, but his passion was opera. He was a musician—organist and choir director at a church in Harrogate. After dessert and coffee, Victor suggested they walk outside to the promenade. Jeremy claimed his ever-present muffler on the way, wrapping it around himself against the evening chill. A full moon was rising over the Alps, casting a shimmering path on the lake, which also reflected the stars and the lights on the shoreline.

Coming to a bench, the two men stopped for a smoke. Somewhat fatigued from his journey, Jeremy was feeling the added effects of the gin and the dinner wine. The faint musky scent of Victor's cologne was further intoxicating, and he had a strong impulse to stroke his companion's cheek, which was showing the stubble of a very dark beard. He resisted.

"Jeremy," Victor began, "why don't you come with me tomorrow. I'm going to Morzine to ski, just for the day. It is only an hour and a half by train. We could be back by dinner time."

"I don't ski."

"Well, I am only a beginner, and the slopes there are perfect, long and gentle. Even if you don't ski, the place is just gorgeous, really. It would be great fun. What do you say?" What could he say? "Meet me after breakfast then, in the lobby."

So next day early, off they went to Chalet Nicolas in Morzine, France, an altitude of more than 1,100 meters. Jeremy was a quick study on the skis, being an excellent athlete with the coordination of a very good dancer. Victor had but to demonstrate the rudiments. When his student took a spill trying to stop, they both roared with laughter, and Victor hauled him up with one hand. He was very strong. Then he himself spun into a drift avoiding a little girl with her father, and they howled again. It was a glorious day, and Victor had not exaggerated about the stunning Alpine views. Craggy, snow-capped peaks surround the place, the wind whipping up the powder, the sunlight blinding from snow-covered rooftops.

Back in Montreux that night they were too exhausted for a walk on the promenade, but they continued to keep company for the rest of Jeremy's stay. Victor had visited before and so enjoyed showing his new young friend the sights. They strolled through town in the mornings, looking in shops and galleries, went to Les Mosses-La Lecherette, a closer place to ski, took boat rides on the lake, one such to see the Chateau Chillon, a thirteenth century castle situated on an offshore island. This popular attraction has ramparts, a moat, a chapel, and centuries old murals.

They sailed through a chilly mist to reach this latter sight one morning, and so sat awhile in the chapel, which provided some warmth in spite of the damp stone walls. Jeremy shared with Victor the story of his mother's death two years previous. His gaze fixed on the chapel altar, he concluded, "I simply cannot forgive a God who could take away that wonderful woman's life in such a way."

"I understand, truly," Victor returned, clearly moved, "but I have always reasoned that if there is a God, there must be a Devil." Jeremy shuddered visibly, doubling the muffler around his neck, and they moved on.

Afternoons found them lounging on the wide lawns of the hotel, where tea was served, engaged in lively conversation, punctuated by their laughter. They spoke of their fathers, their hometowns, old churches, choirs and choir music, Shakespeare, opera. They discovered that among the several things they shared was a taste for strong English tea, and singing. Every evening they would take to the promenade arm in arm. One night when the moon was lending its considerable magic, they stopped and Victor began a Noel Coward song, "Someday I'll find you, moonlight behind you . . ." and Jeremy joined in, surprised to be blushing. Then he kept the medley going with a Rodgers and Hart song from *Pal Joey*, "If they ask me I could write a book about the way you walk and whisper and look. I could write a preface on how we met," Victor sang along, and reaching the end began to harmonize, "And the world discovers as my book ends, how to make two lovers of friends!" By that time they had drawn an audience. They were gratified by the applause, but more so by the closeness they had begun to feel.

Next day at tea Victor asked, "When are you leaving, Jeremy?" Jeremy was spooning crème fraiche on a petite croissant.

"The eleventh, Remembrance Day." It was then November.

"Splendid!" Victor exclaimed, sitting up as the waiter replenished his cup. "I want to take you to the Opera House in Lausanne on the tenth. They are doing Puccini's *Turandot* with an Italian tenor, Giuseppe diStefano.[78] No one sings opera like an Italian."

Thus on the evening of the tenth, a Friday, dressed formally for the opera, white gloves included, Victor and Jeremy took the short ferry ride over the lake and thence to the Opera de Lausanne. Sensitive that Jeremy's mother had died on this date, Victor had provided a red rose boutonniere for each of them. The Opera House is an opulent, ornate building dating to the nineteenth century, where three tiers of balconies wrap around the orchestra below in the colorful auditorium.

Opera is indeed a preeminently Italian medium, a somewhat ungainly marriage of music and drama at which they are uniquely adept. Puccini embodied the high Romanticism that spanned the turn of the twentieth century. His music is incomparably evocative, the language of emotion, at times more expressive of his own stormy and tangled love life than of the storyline. He was haunted, for example, by the suicide of his wife's maid, with whom he was suspected of having an affair. "Nessun Dorma," among the best loved tenor arias of all time, is from *Turandot*, the composer's last opera; and the plot involves palace intrigue in imperial China. The aria is sung by the hero, a stranger who has won the hand of the Princess by solving three riddles. She pronounces that no one shall sleep—"nessun dorma"—until someone tells her the stranger's name, and the aria ends as he sings, "Vincero!" ("I shall win!"). Puccini died in 1924 before the opera was finished. His publishers chose composer Franco Alfano to complete the final act from Puccini's sketches, and the opera premiered in 1926.

Jeremy had been emotional all day, considering the anniversary it marked, but he was enjoying the performance. As Act 3 begins, the tenor starts the aria "Nessun Dorma" softly, the orchestra subdued in the background. Victor put his hand over Jeremy's, knowing as a musician that the near magical reflex upon hearing this sound is for every hair on a person's body to stand up. But then the rich melody comes in, the voice slowly builds, the orchestra crescendoes then soars, wrenching uncontrollable tears from a listener's eyes. By the time Stefano hit that last long high note, both men had tears streaming down their faces. They looked at each other and smiled ironically at their synchronous response.

As they left the hall Victor remarked, "Cathartic isn't it?"

"I think I just became an opera buff!" declared Jeremy. When they got back to the hotel, this being Jeremy's last night, Victor proposed that they go to his room for a nightcap. He stopped at the desk and requested room service, ordering a bottle of Madeira. It was late and they were tired, but still wound up from the performance.

"Please, be comfortable, my friend," and Victor poured two glasses from the decanter that had been brought up. Jeremy obeyed, taking off his jacket, loosening his tie. Victor also removed his jacket. He was terribly attractive in a tux. With the jacket off, the white shirt was fitted enough to show the lean muscle of his physique. Jeremy tossed back the wine quickly, then walked onto the balcony. The cool air was welcome, and as he leaned against the railing, Victor could see his profile lit by the full moon. The classic lines of his jaw, his brow and cheekbones, might have been carved in marble. Victor followed him out and slowly turned him around by the shoulders, embracing him. "Jeremy!" he cried, in a hoarse, pleading whisper. They could resist no longer. Their lips met in a hungry kiss.

* * *

In any time or place where homosexuality is regarded as a heinous aberration there will be some men who marry to hide their true orientation; and certainly some of these, perhaps most, may themselves be unable to admit their own natural proclivity. Bisexuality is seen as a ruse and met with widespread skepticism, although it is a fact that an individual can have the capacity for romantic feelings toward either gender. Adding to the persistent burden of intolerance is the simple reality that homosexuals are not readily identifiable. Certain professions then become stereotyped as associated with gay men; every hairdresser, florist, any man involved in the arts, all are assumed to be gay until proven otherwise. If they are successful, they will be tolerated, provided their truth remains hidden. In the theatre district of London, the West End, gossip seems to have plagued every man in the business, particularly if he typified the dandy. In his memoir, Robert Stephens refutes many such assumptions. Laurence Olivier was prone to call everyone "darling," but he was far from gay; neither was John Osborne gay. Stephens knew these men well. Noel Coward was known to be homosexual, but he was an enormous talent and he did not advertise it, considering in fact that "any sexual activities when over-advertised" are tasteless.

Jeremy Brett was said to be bisexual, but we must reiterate that he was not one to talk about such personal matters. When he returned from Switzerland late in 1961, he told Anna that he was leaving her, that he had met a man in Montreux, that they were in love. Looking back from the distance of years, she writes that she was shocked, but had suspected it all along. In the recollection of their wedding night, she claims to have felt they were playacting. We have no wish to cast aspersion on her recounting, but surely it is sexual naiveté to think that a young man could leave his virgin bride "radiantly content," and impregnate her into the bargain, without feeling some attraction. No man is *that* skillful an actor.

Even more suggestive, she says that following the sudden death of Jeremy's mother their marriage was never the same. Taken together with her other remarks, there is the intimation that this loss freed him to come out of the closet. In the context of Jeremy Brett's life story and a knowledge of his character, such an idea is ill-conceived foolishness. If anything was loosed by the death of his mother it was the instability of an emergent mood disorder. Reliable sources do not link Brett with a gay partner until 1969, and that was fellow actor Gary Bond. Who then was the man in Montreux? What became of him? For all we know he might have been Victor from Yorkshire, an older man introducing Jeremy to his unexplored potential.[79]

Fortunately for Jeremy, his flourishing career kept him very busy. In 1962, he was in three more television productions for the BBC: *The Ghost Sonata*, in which he played the student; two episodes of *The Bacchae*, playing Dionysus; and *Dinner with the Family*, as Jacques. The latter was based on the 1958 farce written by Jean Anouilh, Jacques being a young man who rents a grand country house and hires actors to play his parents and servants in order to impress a girl. For ITV he played Pascal in *The Typewriter*, a drama written by Frenchman Jean Cocteau in 1941 during the Nazi occupation.

Brett also had a role that year in the British film, *The Wild and the Willing*, about the boys of an elite, fictional "Kilminster University," uncomfortably reminiscent of Eton: the old brick and stone buildings, the uniforms, the playing fields, the classrooms. The plot involved a *wild* student and his behavior with *willing* women, including the wife of a professor. Brett played Gilbey, a smart, ambitious student, who had preceded the wild protagonist, played by Ian McShane, in that lady's affections.

He was in growing demand for film and television roles. The following year, 1963, there were two British films: *Girl in the Headlines*, a murder mystery; and *The Very Edge*, in which he played a psychopathic stalker. He was also Dorian Gray in *The Picture of Dorian Gray* for BBC television, and he appeared as Tonino in *Three Roads to Rome* for the ITV Play of the Week, a trilogy of short stories set in Rome. In this last, Deborah Kerr made her debut on British television.

In the meantime, he and Mr. Binks had moved out of the house in Chelsea, having found a town home in Notting Hill just a few miles away, northwest of Hyde Park. This area of Greater London, which had been rundown in the first half of the century, was finally experiencing redevelopment. They settled in Ladbroke Square[80] across from Ladbroke Gardens. A dog needs a park, and this dog was very spoiled. Lining the streets are neat rows of homes faced with white stucco. They have four stories, and Jeremy's provided a studio flat on the upper floor, later to be occupied by his son in his adolescence.

His work was across the Waterloo Bridge at the television and movie studios. He found film to be an interesting medium, and the roles were good, though he may have been dismayed that after *Peeping Tom* broke barriers for the horror genre, with his wife playing the victim, he was too often cast as the ironically handsome psychopath. But busy as he was, he needed to be home each day to walk Mr. Binks, who came to be nicknamed "Bonkers" for his rambunctious terrier nature, chewing on slippers and pillows and chair legs, and jumping with irrepressible glee at the sight of his master. One story Jeremy told about this naughty pup was how he somehow managed to sire a litter with a greyhound named Gladys. "What emerged," he reported, "were the most improbable, simply adorable, but *different* puppies!"[81]

After a walk in the park with Mr. Binks he might go to the Ladbroke Arms for pub fare, or meet with friends at the Prince Albert, also nearby. He and Anna remained on good terms, and little David was nearly four. They may have met on a fine spring day at a tea shop, like Candella, near Kensington Palace midway between Chelsea and Notting Hill, with David in a stroller.

"Daddy! Daddy!" The lad jumped out of the stroller and into Jeremy's lap as he sat outside Candella's at a sidewalk table with Mr. Binks. His son hugged him tightly around the neck, and Jeremy kissed his head. His happiest moments were those spent with the boy. David then got down and kissed Mr. Binks, who was equally effervescent.

"David, be careful, come sit. Your father has tea for us," his mother said. She and Jeremy exchanged polite kisses.

"How are you, darling?" he asked.

"Busy as usual, and you?" He poured the two of them tea from an old fashioned china pot.

"It's vanilla flavored," he commented on the tea, "quite nice. Oh, I am well, also busy. David, do you want a scone with jam? They're still warm. How about you, Anna?" Anna helped herself, while Jeremy fixed a scone for their son, who proceeded to get jam all over his hands and face. "We'll be needing finger bowls!" and Jeremy smiled broadly at the boy's plump baby cheeks. "I hear you got a part in *The School for Scandal*."

"Yes, along with my brother Daniel. That will be interesting. John Gielgud is directing. But when are you getting back on the stage? It's what you love!"

"Very soon, dear. I am joining the new National Theatre Company. They will do their first productions at the Chichester Festival this summer."

"That's wonderful news! You'll be working with Olivier." She so envied his self-confidence.

"I will indeed. But I enjoy film too, the more I learn." He had taken a cloth napkin and was cleaning David's face. "Do you remember the song I taught you, Master David?"

And his son began to sing, "The grand old Duke of York, he had one hundred men—"

"—ten *thousand* men," Jeremy chimed in with emphasis, and they sang together, "He marched them up to the top of the hill and marched them down again. And when they were up . . ."

Anna sat shaking her head, "Like father, like son," among the adages that came to her mind. No sooner had they ended that ditty than the sound of piano music was heard from within the tea shop, unusual surely, but the proprietor loved to play. He was doing a medley of tunes from *My Fair Lady*, which was finishing its long run in the West End that year. Jeremy of course could not resist.

"The rain in Spain falls mainly in the plain . . . I could have danced all night . . ." David was delighted, Mr. Binks started barking along, and listeners were gathering on the sidewalk. Anna wanted to duck under the table. "I'm sorry, darling." Jeremy spoke after the music was interrupted by an influx of customers. "So, you won't be going to Glion this summer, what with the play."

Not one to gather moss, Anna's mother had pulled up stakes and moved with stepfather Bill to a chalet overlooking Lake Geneva, and close to that of her friend Noel Coward. "No, I'm afraid not. The show must go on, but I like being busy."

"You might come down to Chichester then, or send David down with Nanny; we could take the ferry to the Isle of Wight, relax on the beach," and turning to his son, "Sandcastles, David!"

"What fun, Daddy! Mr. Binks, too?"

"Of course!" The teapot now empty, he picked up the dog under his arm, and they rose to leave. As they did so, a very proper, elderly woman sitting at the next table with her granddaughter, caught Jeremy's eye.

"I must say," she declared, "if I may be so bold, it warms my heart to see such a happy young family!"

"How very kind of you," he replied, with a wry smile. Their divorce was soon to be finalized, most amicably.

* * *

After years of dithering, it was in fact 1963 when the British government established the National Theatre Company with the Old Vic as its core, and Sir Laurence Olivier its managing director. The troupe tried its wings at Chichester in July, then opened officially in October at the Old Vic Theatre, recently refurbished. They would remain there until new facilities could be built, also in Southwark, which took another ten years. Jeremy was delighted to be in the annual Chichester Festival, started just the year before by a local man of means, who had been inspired by the summer event in Stratford, Ontario.

A sleepy town on the English Channel, Chichester is the only town in West Sussex. It has the Old Cross pub and Good News tobacconist, one's source for the city papers and of course, cigarettes. In years to come, the newly formed National Company would do summer theatre there on a regular basis, and Brett would stay with his friend Stephens, also a member, and his wife, in a house they had taken. The actors appreciated a break away from the city life.

That first year, Jeremy appeared in two plays, and relished being again before a live audience. He was in *The Workhouse Donkey*, a contemporary musical comedy by John Arden that satirizes the corruption of local politics in a northern English town, and George Bernard Shaw's *Saint Joan*, in which he had the role of Dunois, the Bastard of Orleans. The historical Dunois was inspired by Joan of Arc to rally his troops in her effort to free Orleans from the English. He was called "the Bastard" respectfully, as it was meant to indicate that he was truly a cousin of the king. Written and produced first in 1924, it drew criticism for its less than saintly characterization of the heroine.

The Manor House, as Stephens called their place[82] in the village of Chilcomb, would likely have been large enough so that Jeremy's son could visit with Nanny while Mum was struggling with the role of Lady Teazle in *The School for Scandal*. David had just turned four in August, and his father wanted to take advantage of the serene summer weather, and the warm sand beaches on the Isle of Wight.

For the short ferry ride across the Solent from Portsmouth, Jeremy held his son seated on the railing, the cool sea breeze in their faces, flattening their hair. It was morning, and all manner of seabirds were diving for breakfast.

"Don't let me go, Daddy!"

"I've got you, son, never fear," and indeed his arms held the boy tightly. Nanny was along manning the stroller, which at the moment was holding a picnic hamper, a beach blanket, towels, and Mr. Binks.

"It's a good thing your mother isn't here, lad," she announced. With the influence of her attorney stepfather, Anna had something of a reputation for being risk-averse.

The Isle of Wight has been a summer resort since Victorian times, and some mansions from that era remain, though being located in the Channel it was bombed heavily during the war. The stunning views of cliffs and shoreline are reminiscent of Cornwall. A bus ride to the beach allowed the chance to marvel at the scenery, and when they arrived it was close to lunchtime. They left the stroller on the esplanade, and finding a spot on the sand for the beach blanket, sat down with the hamper.

"What have we for this hungry youngster?" Jeremy asked as Nanny opened it.

"We have peanut butter and jam, chicken salad sandwiches, and then there are shortbread cookies and a thermos of tea." She set about helping David with a plate and a cup and napkins. His father gazed out over the water, lost in reverie. The hamper, the sandwiches, the thermos could not but recall to his mind that ride to Eton on his first day with his mother, a bittersweet memory.

"You found all that in Robert's kitchen?" he wondered, coming back to himself.

"No sir, at the market up the street!"

Jeremy was feeding Mr. Binks the dog biscuits he had in his pants pockets; then he pulled his black knit shirt over his head and, prepared with a swimsuit under them, slipped off the white breeches. "I'm going for a swim, David, and when I get back I expect to see a sandcastle!"

"Yes, Daddy," the boy mumbled, with his mouth full of peanut butter.

It was a calm strand, shallow for many meters. Jeremy waded out to deep water, then slipped into it and swam parallel to the shore, keeping an eye on his son. He was in good form, and fit, easily drawing himself smoothly along with each stroke. The sea was bracingly cool and the exertion exhilarating. He was loving the feel of the water, his mastery in moving through it. Whatever anxious recollection of that long ago ear infection that might have remained in his mind was far back in the recesses.

More people had gathered on the beach, though it was far from busy, and more were coming in to swim. When Jeremy got back to Nanny and David, a sandcastle was taking shape, and David was wading in and out of the water to fill his bucket with wet sand. He was also in his swim suit, which he had worn under his shorts.

"I have never seen a finer castle!" declared his father. "Good job!" The boy's grin exuded pride, but he was done with sand for the day.

"Can I go swimming now, Daddy?"

"You *may* go swimming, and you *can* if I teach you." Daddy hoisted his son up to his shoulders, while Nanny rolled her eyes apprehensively. She of course had no intention of getting wet, and stayed back to watch Mr. Binks. At the point where the water was appropriately deep, Jeremy lifted the boy down and dipped him, eliciting squeals of delight.

"Now David, I will hold onto you. I want you to paddle with your legs, fast like a dog." He followed instructions, kicking furiously. "Good. Now put your arms out to the side. That's it." Briefly he let the boy go, and sure enough he was buoyant. Then he showed David how to float on his back, what is called the "deadman's float."

"That's enough for today, son. Let's see the dog paddle again." Thrilled with his newly acquired skill, the indefatigable child paddled like crazy, with Jeremy pulling him forward to shallow water. Then looking shoreward, David spotted an ice cream vendor.

"Ice cream!" he shouted. "*May* we get some, Daddy?"

Well of course there was nothing for it but to sprint across the hot sand with bare feet, Mr. Binks joining in eager pursuit. There were the customary three flavors: vanilla, the dog's favorite; chocolate; strawberry; plus black cherry and peppermint stick.

"Mmmm, that sounds good!" David said of the last two. "I can't decide. What should I get, Daddy?"

"Why don't we get a black cherry and a peppermint, and we'll share." Could there be any more infectious happiness than that of a blissful child with his ice cream? They walked along the shore back to Nanny, savoring their cold creamy treats, Mr. Binks chasing the sandpipers, then stretched out together on the blanket while their swimsuits dried.

When they got back to Chilcomb, Tarn was there with baby Lucy, then age 2. Robert was still in Chichester, probably at the Old

Cross. "Your agent just called, Jeremy," Tarn said. "He needs to speak with you right away. You had better call him." Jeremy got on the phone without delay.

"Are you sitting down?" his agent asked excitedly. "I wouldn't want you to fall over and hurt yourself."

"Yes, I'm sitting. What is it for heaven's sake?"

"I had a call from Robert Lennard, the casting director in London for Warner Brothers. He wants to know if you would be available to play Freddy Eynsford-Hill in their film of *My Fair Lady*, with Rex Harrison and Audrey Hepburn. He saw you in *The Wild and the Willing* and wants no one but you. You won't even need to test for it." There was stunned silence as Jeremy absorbed this information. To act *and* to sing, in an American musical? A romantic lead with the beautiful, the *waifish* Audrey Hepburn?

"Good God, man, of course I'll do it! The Old Vic will have to wait. Get back to him before he changes his mind."

Tarn had been listening as she fed the baby in her high chair. "What's up?"

"It seems I'm going to Hollywood," came the incredulous reply.

* * *

Indicative of the glory days of American movie studios, the film adaptation of Lerner and Lowe's *My Fair Lady* was produced in its entirety on a back lot in Burbank, California. So large and elaborate were the sets that one has the impression that they reconstructed the whole of London, circa 1907. There were the horse drawn carriages pulling up to Covent Garden to meet the exiting theatre goers—in the rain! There was the Ascot Race Course on opening day, and the amazing ballroom scene where Eliza Doolittle, the transformed cockney lass, meets royalty—and passes muster. The casting of Jeremy Brett as the aristocratic Freddy, who falls under the spell of this genteel and mysterious creature, was inspired. The role was made for him; he had the voice, the accent, the exceptional good looks. He loved every minute of it, especially singing his heart out together with Audrey Hepburn.[83]

This was the year he turned thirty, and in a top hat and tails he at last looked quite mature and extremely dashing. The film was released 9 November of 1964, just after his thirty-first birthday. He may well have been back in Notting Hill by then, thoroughly exhausted, though not so much as to miss a round of celebrations on his triumphal return. Friends and family lavished congratulations, and critics praise. It was a masterpiece of an entertainment that won eight Academy Awards, and for Rex Harrison, who had starred in it since 1956 on the stage in New York and London, Henry Higgins became his signature role.

With Christmas nearing, Jeremy would nevertheless look forward to retreating to the countryside to spend it at the Grange. In any clan, as generations pass, the family tree has a way of branching out, and the *dramatis personae* around the holiday table tends to change. The Colonel might have his sons and their families, but their uncles and aunts on the Butler side would by then have their own children's spouses and grandchildren. Uncle Leslie and Aunt Margaret, the Colonel's siblings, might come and perhaps his niece Daphne with husband Alec Clunes and their two children, Amanda and three your old Martin. Some staff remained to help care for the Grange: the cook, the housekeeper, maid, and a gardener. The latter was Bob Creber, who had taken over from Tom Houghton. Nanny Clifford had retired to Bournemouth. The Colonel himself was 75, and had slowed down considerably.

Jeremy drove up on Christmas Eve, just he and Mr. Binks. He was heartened to see the village of Berkswell as it always had been, and dusted with snow as it often was that time of year. Arriving at the Grange, he found his father and Patrick in the drawing room by a roaring fire. Brother John, the reverend, of course had duties in his own parish, but would be at dinner next day as would Michael. The Colonel rose from his chair to grasp Jeremy's arm.

"Wonderful movie, son, you were absolutely fabulous. I was so proud all the buttons burst off my waistcoat!" There was some back slapping by brother Patrick as well, and good natured ribbing about Hollywood stardom. Jeremy poured himself a sherry, and they all sat back down. Soon, cause for hilarity arose when Mr. Binks and his litter mate, who had been named Princess Margaret but answered either to Princess or Maggie, had sniffed one another out and were enjoying a reunion in the foyer, barking and jumping and tumbling together.

"I had better take Maggie for a walk," said Patrick, going to fetch her. Jeremy and the Colonel stayed, enjoying their drinks and listening to the crackle of good dry wood burning.

"How have you been, Dad?"

"Just getting old, son. The young doctor Oliver has me on water pills for my heart. He took over when his father retired. Trained as an internist." He paused, a little short of breath. "I rattle around in this big house, but I still ride. Couldn't live without the horses."

"Do you still have Darjeeling?"

"Oh yes, an old-timer now, out to pasture. I ride a young dapple grey, a sweet mare."

"And Mother's horse?"

"Gone. Old age. Bad arthritis." The Colonel studied his son's reaction to that news. Jeremy's face as we have noted was uncommonly expressive. "It's a part of life, Jeremy. You wouldn't want to live forever, would you?"

"No, I suppose not, but I hate being left behind." They chuckled at that.

"Believe me, son, the older you get the more friends you have in heaven!"

Patrick returned with Maggie, who being worn out, curled up with Mr. Binks on the hearth rug. The Colonel started to get up, and Patrick helped pull him from the armchair. "The pups have the right idea," said the old man. "I'm turning in. Tomorrow will be a long day. Goodnight, boys." The brothers watched him climb the stairs slowly, showing in a glance their shared concern.

Michael came to church Christmas morning with his family, and Patrick as well; Jeremy, now a hometown celebrity, must have caused a stir in the congregation, though everyone was discreet in true English fashion. After the service, Mrs. Wheatley hosted a brunch at the Hall for a good number of neighbors, including the Huggins clan, which gave everyone a chance to congratulate Jeremy on his wonderful if not surprising success. Of the older generation, all could remember his angelic child's voice coming from the choir loft on many a Sunday.

The Colonel had taken to carrying a cane, harking back perhaps to his youth, when a walking stick was still a common accessory. But now it was something to lean on when he could not sit; and as the day wore on, Jeremy observed he was using it more and more. He suggested they get back to the Grange, where other relatives would be coming to dinner, among them Aunt Margaret with Daphne and the children. Her husband Alec was off in Majorca, his favored retreat from the stresses of acting.

The table talk that year would have been all about *My Fair Lady*, the great score, the incredible sets, and of course Jeremy's superb performance. Aunt Margaret did ask after David, who was spending Christmas in Switzerland with his maternal grandparents. Then Jeremy turned to Daphne's little boy Martin. "Where would you rather be at Christmas, Martin?"

"I'd rather be here!"

"Right answer! Clever boy, and why is that?"

"Because you have horses! And dogs!" At which laughter broke out all round.

"Your son is going to be a comic, Daphne," Jeremy proposed, and little Martin did indeed have the cutest ears, standing out from his head like a leprechaun's.

Meanwhile, the head of the family sat quietly at the head of the table, breathing heavily as he started a second glass of wine, though in fact he was craving a Scotch and a cigar. He must have wondered to himself how his family had become so involved in the theatre world. Was this the future of his country, entertainment? Young people going their separate ways at Christmas, divorcing for no good reason? As everyone rose following dinner, he took his cane and headed for the library and that smoke, too winded for the niceties. Jeremy excused himself and followed.

"Dad, I hope you will see the doctor this week. I'm worried for you." The Colonel poured a Scotch and offered his son a cigar.

Jeremy declined, preferring his cigarettes. He lit one, and his father's cigar.

"What can the doctor do? Nothing! You go to him!" he said, exasperated.

"I will then!" came the retort.

"Please don't worry, son." The old man recovered somewhat. "Let's just enjoy Christmas night together."

And so they did, but Jeremy was able to meet with Dr. Oliver the next day, a personable and knowledgeable man about his own age. He learned that his father was in the advanced stages of congestive heart failure.

"Your dad has made his wishes quite clear," the good doctor explained. "He does not want you boys to worry over him; he has his affairs in order, and he does not want to be hospitalized. I believe though that soon he may require a private duty nurse."

"No, Doctor," Jeremy said, "I will come."

Whenever he was asked about his parents in interviews, Jeremy Brett never failed to express a deep gratitude toward them and a desire to repay them, which he felt for some reason fell upon him as the youngest. He would say simply, "The tail of the crocodile is heaviest."[84]

He knew his father's condition was deteriorating rapidly, and sure enough right around Candlemas,[85] Dr. Oliver phoned to say he had been called to the Grange by Joyce the housekeeper after the Colonel had been too weak to get out of bed for more than a day. Anticipating this eventuality, Jeremy had been turning down work; so he packed a large suitcase and the next morning set out for Berkswell.

* * *

Approaching the vernal equinox, the early morning sun streamed through Colonel Huggins bedroom window, glinting off the handles of an oxygen tank that stood near his bed, ready for him to use as needed. He was awake and sat up just as his son Jeremy nudged the door open and came in carrying a breakfast tray. Setting it down across his father's lap, he lifted the cover and the smell of bacon and eggs filled the room. On the side also were toast and orange juice and a small pot of coffee, adding to the warm delicious aromas.

"You're spoiling me, son," the Colonel protested, "but thank you. This is wonderful."

"I'm just the delivery boy. I'll thank Cook for you. Eat while it's hot now." Jeremy took the chair between the bed and the sun-filled window. It was the same bed his parents shared when his mother was alive. Her dressing table was gone though, to a granddaughter. "The doctor calls today you know."

Dr. Oliver was looking in every Tuesday morning to check on his patient, and each time the Colonel would praise him for maintaining the same high level of dedication as his father. More than once he also heard the story of how the senior Dr. Oliver had pulled young Jeremy through a dangerous bout of rheumatic fever.

After breakfast and the doctor's visit, Jeremy would help his father dress, the elastic stockings being especially tricky; and they would joke that Jeremy was rehearsing for the role of valet. He would then help the Colonel down the stairs, where the old man would stretch out in his chair by the fire in the drawing room with the newspapers, and Princess Maggie at his feet. The maid Jenny would bring him lunch on a tray, a big meal, with supper being a lighter one, again served in his bedroom. Jeremy would field calls from friends and relatives, who always wanted to speak with him first to learn the particulars of this father's condition.

By no means were loved ones keeping vigil though. In fact, when word reached Birmingham that Jeremy Brett was staying at the Grange, the Repertory Theatre there prevailed upon him to accept a role in *A Measure of Cruelty* by a French dramatist, concerning a wealthy older woman who buys the affections of a younger man, the part he took of course. Wendy Hiller, in her early fifties, was the older woman. It was good to have work, particularly on stage.

With April came the occasional day of warm sun, when Jeremy and his dad might have afternoon tea outside in the garden overlooking the pasture, where the grazing horses made a bucolic scene. Cook would outdo herself for them on these occasions, baking her cinnamon scones and cranberry walnut tea bread with raspberry jam from last season's fruit, and all with the very finest English teas.

"Tea always puts me in mind of your Granny Butler," the Colonel said on one such afternoon, "the Cadburys you know." He paused as the maid filled his cup. "Dr. Oliver doesn't want me to drink or smoke, but really . . ."

"I'll be right back, Dad," and Jeremy went into the kitchen by the back door, returning quickly with a bottle of cream sherry he had smuggled out. "Just the thing to sweeten our tea," which he proceeded to do.

"Thank you, son. I won't tell!" The warm rays and hot tea spiked with sherry seemed to give the Colonel more energy, and even in his frail state he was still good looking, in a soft grey woolen cardigan, a full head of grey hair over his chiseled features. "Bob has done a great job with the garden, don't you think?" he continued. Long rows of narcissus bloomed along the garden borders, and clumps had naturalized beside fences and hedgerows. The rose bushes, which had been Elizabeth Huggins's special joy, were leafing out robustly preparing to bud.

"Oh, indeed," Jeremy answered, "it looks gorgeous. Mother would be so pleased."

"That she is," his father added. It seemed an odd comment, in the present tense, though not perhaps to believers in an afterlife. Signs of a growing connection with the deceased, however, may seem portentous.

"Do you dream about her, Dad?"

"Most vividly. We have long discussions, and she expresses her opinions as forcefully as ever." Now he was joking. "And you, son?"

"Sometimes. Very sad dreams."

"When I see her, I'll ask her to ease up on you." At that, Patrick appeared from around the corner of the house with tennis rackets.

"I see I'm too late for tea. Well, I really came to challenge you to a game of tennis, brother."

"I should warn you, Patrick, that I have been playing with Dr. Oliver at least once a week." The doctor was not a golfer, but was quite skilled at tennis, a sport still popular in Berkswell almost a century after Maud Watson. "Excuse us, Dad," and the sons entered the tennis court, which was usable despite cracks in the asphalt where weeds were growing. As they played, the rhythmic volley made a hollow sound in the stillness of the countryside; and with the sun lowering, the light became bronze. The Colonel soaked it in, utterly at peace.

Easter that year, 1965, was 18 April, but with the Colonel's declining health, no celebration was planned. He had become so weak and breathless in fact that he barely left his bed. Rev. John McKie, who had replaced Reverend Bursell as rector of the parish the year after Elizabeth's death, offered to come the night before Easter and perform a private service of Holy Communion at the Grange, which he did, for the Colonel and Jeremy.

Each of the sons visited the next day, trying not to tax their father, who seemed agitated, anxious to ensure his affairs would be properly handled; and each of them begged him not to worry on that account. The Colonel was a man of proven courage, so they would never intimate that he might fear death.

Just four days later at around four in the morning, Jeremy was awakened by a sharp, inarticulate cry from his father's room. He grabbed his robe and hurried across the hall; turning on the light and sitting on the bed, he took his father's hand. The old man began to sit up staring straight ahead, then turned that wide-eyed stare upon his son. Arm in arm the two gripped each other, and as Jeremy watched with alarm, the light went out of his father's eyes.

* * *

Even when a death is anticipated, it gives a shock, and losing a beloved parent brings a lonely sense of abandonment, of being orphaned. We may well imagine that after the weeks of care he had provided and the times of closeness they had shared, Jeremy wept over his father's body that night. We know from the account of a close friend[86] that at some time in his life he became curious about Eastern religions and was persuaded by the doctrine of reincarnation. Might it have been on the occasion of his father's death that he took up the practice of meditation? He himself dated his interest to that terrible brush with rheumatic favor, raising even at a young age the question of mortality.

In any case, in the heavy days that followed, the Grange must have seemed to him very empty indeed, the whole chapter of his happy childhood closing forever; and upon those long sleepless nights before the funeral, we envision him sitting cross-legged before an eastern window where a nearly full moon[87] would be rising, his spine straight and muscles relaxed, allowing all troublesome thought to clear from his mind. As morning would approach, exhausted enough to sleep, he may have dreamed of his father's afterlife experience in the bardo[88] of rebirth.

But then came yet another funeral to attend at St. John the Baptist Church of Berkswell, he and his brothers sitting as stoical as ever in the family pew, where the number of the older members diminished by the year, and yet another slow procession to the churchyard, passing on the way the screen in front of the Lady Chapel dedicated by them to their mother after her death. The Colonel's name would now be added. Following the service, the Grange would receive the mourners; staff had been given leave to arrange it, a thing in which they were certainly well practiced. The house was filled with the season's flowers: bunches of daffodils and tulips, and great branches of lilac filling the rooms with its lush fragrance. Coffee and tea, finger sandwiches, and Cook's best baked goods were served, and of course wine and whiskey. Reverend McKie, himself of Scottish descent, brought the single malt Scotch, and even Jeremy partook, on the rocks with club soda.

"Will you be returning to London now, Jeremy?" the rector enquired. They were in the library along with Dr. Oliver and John.

"Not until next week. There are lawyers to meet with in Birmingham." Scotch was not his accustomed drink, but he was glad of it that day.

"What will happen to the Grange?" the doctor asked.

John responded, "That is one thing we will need to discuss. Until it is decided, the staff will stay on."

"If I may say so," the rector continued in his very slight brogue, "the four of you were wonderful to your father. Most admirable."

"And having you here these past weeks, Jeremy, meant everything to him," the doctor added.

"No, no, Doctor, I stayed on to get your help with my tennis game!" Jeremy quipped, then seriously, "Really it was a pleasure to give back to such a fine man, a great father." Starting to choke up, he lit a cigarette in hopes of concealing it.

John took out his pipe, after offering his father's cigars to the guests. "The service was beautiful, Rector. We are so grateful to you," he said. The doctor did not smoke, and the rector had his own pipe. The rector's given name was also John, so they referred to him by his title. He accepted the praise with diffidence, drawing slowly on his pipe.

"Yes," Jeremy began, "I'm sure Dad was smiling down on the whole proceeding. Do you believe in reincarnation, Rector?"

"Our faith holds that the immortal soul rejoins God, but of course the Empire introduced many Britons to the ancient religions of the East, which do give credence to the concept."

"You must excuse my brother, Rector," John explained. "He has always leaned toward the Quaker side of the family."

"Interesting, that would be their liberal, progressive school I should say."

"No, gentlemen," Jeremy spoke up, "I just try to keep an open mind." He lit another cigarette from the one that was still burning, then leaving both in the ashtray and his drink on the side table, he got up and left the room, passing Patrick and Michael on his way out.

"What did we miss?" Michael asked John. The oldest brother, Reverend Huggins, retained a parental feeling toward his siblings, especially the youngest.

"Patrick, maybe you should stay here with Jeremy until he returns to London," he suggested. "I don't think he should be in the house alone, you know, without one of us."

"If Uncle Leslie is not staying I will, John, certainly." Maggie, the poor bereaved terrier, had followed him in. Picking her up, he added, "I think Princess Margaret needs me too!"

He did stay at the Grange that week, and Uncle Leslie as well, and they all met up with John and Michael at the office of the family solicitor in Birmingham, where the will was read. There were no surprises, the Colonel having made his wishes clear to his family. Apart from several generous bequests to staff members, the bulk of the estate would be divided equally for his four sons. As for the Grange, he had expressed no objection to whatever they might agree to do; and since none of them was in a position to take it on, the simplest solution was to sell it, as much as they grieved at the thought. So as soon as the estate could be settled the property would go on the market, though that would be some months hence. In the meantime, Patrick would adopt Maggie, to his young son's great joy, and neighbors had come forward to take in the two remaining horses.

But not before Jeremy had ample opportunity to ride his father's dapple grey. In the few days he had left before he needed to go back to Notting Hill, he had the unsettling experience of feeling sad and happy at once, and was certain beyond any doubt that Dad's spirit was the cause, lingering, as the Tibetans believe, to cheer him. After breakfast with his brother and uncle, he would saddle his mount and, once again feeling the ripple of horse flesh between his knees, ride off down the lane, breaking into a gallop over the fields and jumping hedgerows. It was then early May, and the weather was perfect, the countryside richly green, the trees leafing out—native hawthorne and hazel, and the ancient small leafed lime.

One afternoon he spent in Meriden practicing his archery with Lord Charles Ian Finch-Knightley, the eleventh Earl of Aylesford,[89] at the lodge of the Woodmen of Arden. The Earl was fifteen years his senior, but their fathers had been old friends in years past. Their target practice may likely have involved a comradely challenge.

On the last day of this long sojourn, he was invited to tea at the Hall with Mrs. Wheatley.[90] The maid showed him out to the garden where the widow was waiting. "How good of you to come, Jeremy!"

"How gracious of you to invite me; it is a pleasure." The maid served them tea, and between them on the table were plates of scones and *petits fours* and tea cakes, together with pots of jam and marmalade.

"Your father will be missed by all of us in the community, of course, but you and your brothers have our deepest sympathy, rest assured." She offered the strawberry jam for his scone, then went on to reminisce about Parish Sunday in the old days, when the festivities would alternate from year to year between the Grange and the Hall.

"Dad and Colonel Charles were such great friends," Jeremy recalled, referring to her late husband.

"They were indeed. What will become of the Grange now, Jeremy?" She had heard of their decision to sell but asked him just to be sure.

"Sadly it will be sold after the estate is settled. The practical thing to do, I suppose. Do you mind if I smoke?" he asked politely, though they were outdoors.

"No, dear, go ahead," and she handed him an ashtray from one of the side tables. "It's the right decision surely, and not a surprise," she continued, "but it breaks my heart, and yours too, I think. What sweet memories you must have of growing up in that beautiful old house!" At the age of 67, Christobel Wheatley might be forgiven a penchant for nostalgia. "The world is changing too fast for me, Jeremy. The new plays for example, so depressing, and the films are so needlessly graphic."

"But at least we still have American musicals," he commented.

"Oh yes, weren't you splendid in *My Fair Lady*. Berkswell is so proud of you! What did you make of Hollywood, though?"

"I had a wonderful time, to be sure, but it showed me how very English I really am."

His companion laughed. "What was it Churchill said? 'Two great nations divided only by a common language.' So tomorrow it's back to London then?"

"Reluctantly, but my agent has arranged for me to play Belyaev in the Russian classic *A Month in the Country* at the Cambridge."

"Turgenev. The title is sheer serendipity."

"I believe my father's spirit had a hand in it. I am gaining friends in heaven."

They went on to talk about the Old Vic and the new National Theatre Company, to which he was also returning, again to do the Shakespeare he so loved. The shadows lengthened, and a cool breeze came up as the sun dipped behind the tall sycamores. Jeremy got up to leave and helped Mrs. Wheatley out of her chair. She would walk with him around to the gravel drive where he had left his horse tied to the fence. He had ridden over on the mare, as Berkswell Hall was some distance from the Grange, on opposite sides of the village green. A last quarter moon was rising over the Meriden Road, but he would cut across the fields and the meadows, skirting Hawkhurst Moor, south of the Coventry Road.

"Take care of yourself, young man," and Mrs. Wheatley took his hand. "Keep in touch. Don't forget us."

"Never," he replied, kissing the hand she offered, a gallant, bygone gesture, but sincere, expressing his heartfelt respect and affection. "I promise."

* * *

The Turgenev play, *A Month in the Country*, concerns the troublous romantic entanglements that may churn beneath the serene facade of a country estate. The role was congenial for Brett. Belyaev is a young man who comes to the manor to tutor the son and becomes involved with the mistress, who is bored in her marriage. Perhaps Mrs. Wheatley came to see it at the Cambridge Theatre in the West End, Eartham Street, brought by her daughter, Ann Christobel, and son-in-law.

Jeremy also took two television jobs that year for ITC Entertainment: an episode of a series called *The Baron*, where he guest starred as the villain, and *Act of Reprisal*, a romance set against the backdrop of the Cypriot uprisings of the 1950s. In this latter, a film shot on location in Greece, he played Harvey Freeman, a British official caught up in the violent struggle of Cypress against British rule.

The small screen had become bread-and-butter for young actors. The next year, 1966, Brett was in three television productions, including *The Lost Stradivarius* for ITV, based on a late Victorian ghost novel by J. Meade Falkner. Jeremy played a college student who finds a Stradivarius violin that carries an evil spell which then possesses him. In *The Three Musketeers*, a serialized version for BBC of the novel by Alexander Dumas, set in 1625, he played d'Artagnan. The third, also for the BBC, was a role in *The Queen and the Welshman*, a television adaption of the contemporary play, concerning an affair between the widow of Henry V and Sir Owen Tudor. This production was part of the drama anthology series, Theatre 625.[91] Brett took the part of Villiers.

He was not in a stage play that year, perhaps because of the sale of the Grange. But before it changed hands there was a big farewell party for all the staff, their families, and anyone in the village who had ever worked for the Huggins family, as well as other friends and neighbors. It seems probable that Jeremy was himself the instigator or, if not, was closely involved in the planning. He was known to love parties, and what more satisfying way to show his gratitude. It was just the type of occasion his late mother would have insisted upon. Invitations went out for a Sunday afternoon in June, somewhat more than a year after Colonel Huggins's passing.

So once more the Grange came alive with people on a perfect spring day, the wisteria still climbing its front, heavy with blooms, and Elizabeth's rose garden, an artist's palette of color. It even seemed possible that one might see her there with a trug on her arm gathering flowers. This party was catered by an establishment in Coventry; the loyal staff members would be honored guests, indicative of a new egalitarian spirit seeping into British society since the war. Cook did not have to bake, and the maid did not have to serve. Tables were set up on the lawn with all manner of food and drink, and when the afternoon became too warm, the house was open to all who might resort to the garden room, the drawing room, the library, the grand foyer.

Jeremy was in fine form and high spirits, circulating among the guests, swapping stories of growing up on Truggist Lane, the address of the Grange. There were neighbors like the Wagstaffes, remembered for their decorative garden gnomes and windmills. Lou Wilcox came, who had so often chauffeured the family in the Daimler. The Earl of Aylesford represented the Woodmen of Arden, and reminisced with Jeremy and his brothers about the annual Wardmote in years past that would culminate with a dinner dance and awards banquet at the Grange. The housekeeper Joyce Jakeman also recalled "Archery Week" as did the maid Jenny Vines. They could laugh now about those late parties and serving breakfast to lingering guests in the wee hours.

Mr. and Mrs. Stan West, who were neighbors when the family still lived at Holly Lodge in Spencer's Lane, also attended. Stan used to take care of the Colonel's parrot when he was away. Did we neglect to mention that Colonel Huggins once had a parrot who startled visitors with his uncanny mimicry of his master's voice?

Several children were at the party that happy afternoon. Jeremy had brought his son David, his baby cheeks as chubby as ever, though he would soon turn seven. Patrick's son was there along with Patrick's wife and mother-in-law. The Earl and his wife brought their little girl Clare, and Jenny Vines had her boy Robert with her. To the delight of the youngsters, Mr. Binks and Maggie, the sibling terriers, were as frisky and playful as ever rolling on the lawn, chasing balls, and jumping for treats, *Mr. Bonkers* living up to his nickname.

We are fortunate that someone came with a camera that day, and twenty-seven of the guests assembled in front of the Grange for one last group photograph which appeared, with legend, in the *Berkswell Miscellany, Volume 5*, published in 1989 by the Offshoot Group of the Berkswell Historical Society. Two rows of adults are pictured standing, with a front row of older ones seated, and the children at their feet. Jeremy crouches to the children's left, smiling broadly with Mr. Binks on his knee.

The festivity waxed into the evening, everyone reluctant to part, each leave taking a sweet torture. But finally when the guests were gone, the caterers had cleaned up, the four brothers settled in the garden room to smoke and talk and finish off the last of the cold beer. It had been a hot, tiring day. They were all staying over, since the caterers would be back next day to claim whatever remained of their equipment. Patrick's wife was staying also, and of course his son and Jeremy's. She was upstairs reading the two cousins a bedtime story. They were so excited about bunking together it would take some doing to get them to sleep.

A humid breeze came through the open windows of the garden room, bearing the lush perfume of wisteria, while from under the front hedges came the somnolent snore of crickets. In the darkness, fireflies floated up from the grass decorating the trees like Christmas lights. The brothers were quiet, Jeremy dragging on his cigarette, John on his pipe, Patrick and Michael chugging beer. Then breaking the stillness, Michael cried, "God, I hate losing this place!" His three brothers nodded in sympathy.

"Life goes on," Jeremy responded.

"Of the four of us, baby brother," Michael continued, "I would've thought you would be saddest about it."

"The happiest years of my life were here in Berkswell, no question," Jeremy said in defense, "but we can't hold onto the past. We each have our own lives."

"How can you be so cheerful?" Patrick asked. "Michael's right, it is unexpected." Were the brothers developing a sense of Jeremy's moods?

"Don't forget," John weighed in with the credential of eldest, "Jeremy missed out on the fights our parents used to have before he was born."

"She *was* half Irish," said Patrick, and they laughed.

"And he was from another century," was Michael's observation.

"We have been lucky, my dears," Jeremy would have the last word, naturally humorous. "Just look at the Earl: his father left him with so much debt on their estate that he has gone into garbage collecting!" They roared with laughter. In fact the eleventh Earl of Aylesford had become hugely successful in the landfill business and influential in recycling policy, saving Packington Hall, the family seat.

But then they went on sharing memories: Parish Sunday; the Hunt Breakfast; Skinner Horn; Sir Charles; Colonel Wheatley; the air raid shelter; the evacuees from Coventry, especially the Western family, all forty of them; the gypsies; their great aunts on the Cadbury side, arriving at church in the Daimler; the churchyard gate that always swung loose, causing Nanny to latch it every time she passed; the look on Nanny's face when Jeremy rode his pony into the house, leaving manure in the foyer. It was midnight before they wearied of this conversation, and even then Jeremy could have continued; but his brothers urged him to get some sleep, so, the beer gone, they retired for the night.

This would hardly have been the last occasion they would be at the Grange. There would be belongings to clear out, furniture, china, heirlooms, disbursing these to family and friends, staff. Whatever remained would likely have been donated, perhaps through the Church, to needy families in the parish. In any case, whenever each of them did leave the homestead a final time, it would surely be an anticlimax to this gladsome day of reluctant farewell.

* * *

Upon returning to London, Jeremy was on a high for at least another week. When his busy thoughts would not allow sleep, Mr. Binks would have the unusual pleasure of a nocturnal walk in Ladbroke Garden across the street. One night he arranged an impromptu dinner for several friends, cooking his favorite pasta and tossing a salad. They ended that evening walking over to Prince Albert pub in search of more beer and cigarettes.

But then he had to settle down. He had not worked with the National Theatre Company since that summer at the Chichester Festival, and he was eager to get back to the troupe, now installed at the Old Vic until its permanent home could be constructed. This was finally accomplished in 1973, an impressive facility with three stages. Sir Laurence Olivier was one of several influential figures whose persistent efforts bore fruit in the creation of a National Theatre, and he assumed its leadership for a decade starting from its birth in 1963. He saw the institution as an incubator for young British actors and playwrights, who would work alongside older accomplished performers and learn from them in the process.

Olivier was the son of a clergyman in the Church of England. Quite apart from the usual case, it was Laurence's father who decided he should become an actor. And so he did, training at the Central School where his natural gift was nurtured and bloomed. His was a great talent, in fact, and like many another personality of superior ability, he was arrogant, egoistic, and intolerant of mediocrity. Nonetheless, his young protégés respected his exacting standards, admired him for his hard work and commitment, and trusted his sincerity in helping them.

Some ninety actors belonged to the National Company, and Olivier divided them into two troupes. He was far from aloof but made himself available, eating in the canteen and rehearsing with the actors. Influenced perhaps by his father's preaching from the pulpit, he emphasized the voice and had a vocal coach always on hand. Seeing as well that a strong voice requires a strong body, he encouraged the young members to use the gym, which he had set up in the building.

Work is often salubrious, and learning the part of Orlando in *As You Like It* was just the thing to focus Jeremy Brett's mind. Once again to have the genial poetry of his beloved Shakespeare rolling from his tongue was comfort and joy. This particular romantic comedy is set in the Forest of Arden, so Brett was right at home. The second scene of Act One takes place on the lawn before the Duke's palace, where Orlando, suitor to the Duke's daughter Rosalind, has challenged Charles the wrestler to a match. All present including Rosalind, attempt to dissuade him, convinced he will be injured by this redoubtable opponent.

Charles taunts, "Come where is this young gallant that is so desirous to lie with his mother earth?"

Orlando replies, "Ready, Sir . . . You mean to mock me . . . but come . . ."

Rehearsing this scene, Sir Larry demonstrated to the two young performers some moves to suggest the action without hurting themselves. Charles must be thrown in the end by the underdog Orlando.

The actors gave it a go a few times, but Sir Larry was not happy with it. Then he said, "Boys, let's make it look real."

On the next try Jeremy Brett was the one thrown, and blood came gushing from his nose. Olivier was horrified. Everyone rushed to help, to stop the bleeding, but it was soon evident that the nose was broken, and Jeremy was carted off to Waterloo Hospital.[92] Sir Laurence was disconcerted in the extreme: one of his very best actors, certainly his best looking, the perfect male lead, with a *scar* on his *face?* This was *unacceptable!* No sooner had Jeremy arrived at the hospital than Olivier was on the phone with hospital staff insisting that a plastic surgeon be called in. He would pay for it himself. He felt a nearly parental responsibility for the young people in the company and perhaps a sense of guilt for this accident, though Jeremy insisted the fault was his own. Sir Laurence Olivier, after all, was an idol to him as to many of the younger generation of actors.

Sidelined in such a painful way, Jeremy was at leisure to fall into a truly dismal funk. He was angry at himself, at the other actor in that wrestling match, and while not letting on, at Olivier. He was angry at fate, a diffuse anger that would not settle on any particular object but that clouded every day with a sour mood. He kept to himself for a time in Notting Hill, he and Mr. Binks. To friends who phoned he was jolly, upbeat, then he would put down the receiver, stretch out on the sofa, and fall asleep, with the dog on his chest. Sleep is conducive to healing.

It would be hard to say exactly how long Brett was idled by this incident, but it could not have been long, since in that same year, 1967, he was in two more plays and four productions for television. There remained a very slight line across the bridge of his nose from the break, but it was hardly conspicuous.

It must have been the year for classic comedies, because the next play was Shakespeare's *Much Ado About Nothing*, concerning the vicissitudes of romance for two couples: Beatrice and Benedick; and Hero and Claudio, the latter played by Jeremy Brett, the scar on his nose notwithstanding. This production was directed by Franco Zeffirelli, who apparently saw it as an *opera buffo*; it was controversial, but audiences loved it. Robert Stephens had the role of Benedick with Maggie Smith his Beatrice.

Smith had made a name for herself in light comedy with Binkie Beaumont in the West End and, now with the National Company, was gaining a reputation as a classical actress. Just two years prior she had played Desdemona on stage and screen with Olivier, who played Othello in black face rather than as a Moor, drawing some criticism. In real life, Robert and Maggie were having an affair, which ended his marriage to Tarn Bassett that very year when Maggie got pregnant.

Much Ado About Nothing was followed by Moliere's *Tartuffe*, for which Brett was Valere, the romantic lead who courts Mariana, daughter of Orgon, the man who is taken in by the pious but unscrupulous Tartuffe.

Television was of course well established by that time, but it was an ephemeral medium. No one thought of preserving these works or of archiving them; so information about them, even in the internet age, is scarce to none.[93] For example, we know that for the BBC Brett played Casanova in a drama called *The Incantation of Casanova* in 1967, and we may presume, if not with certainty, that this was about the legendary eighteenth century rogue who had a keen interest in many things, not only women, one such being the occult. Also for BBC, he appeared in a series entitled *Kenilworth*. If this program concerned the town of that name in Warwickshire, Brett was on home ground. For ITV that year he was in a play for their Armchair Theatre called *Quite an Ordinary Knife*, and in an episode of a series entitled *The Champions*, which involved a group of secret agents who acquire superhuman powers.

The breakup of his friend Robert's marriage would have been upsetting to Jeremy, who was equally fond of Tarn. Her mother was also Irish and her father retired military, so they got on famously. She was devoted to Robert and had given up acting when their daughter was born. During the divorce, wanting to support them both, Jeremy took her frequent calls for advice, so when the phone rang one evening in summer, he assumed it was she. It was not.

"Jeremy? Oh, I'm so glad you're home!"

"Anna, what a surprise! Is everything all right, dear?"

"It's Nan," she said, referring to her Nanny Gertrude, "she's in hospital. The breast cancer has come back."

"My god, that's awful, darling! What do the doctors say?"

"They think that in time she will come home, but I need to talk with you about David. Can you meet me at the tea shop tomorrow morning?"

"Yes of course, I'll make a point of it." They arranged a time, at Candella, and Jeremy put the phone down, perplexed about what she wanted to discuss that had to be in person. Chiefly he was worried for her, knowing how she had depended on Gertrude all her life. Nan would be irreplaceable, yet with both his parents in the acting profession, young David at the age of eight still needed a nanny. Anna was dedicated to her career; she was not Tarn. And Jeremy at that time looked forward to the challenge of starring as Count Danilo in a forthcoming BBC production of the Franz Lehar operetta *The Merry Widow*.

Next morning at Candella they had a strong English tea, not a flavored one, with sugar and cream; and the warm scones were flaky—nearly as good as Cook used to make at the Grange.

"I left David at a friend's house, a neighbor boy," Anna explained. "From here I must go to the hospital to visit Nan."

"You know I will do whatever I can to help out, Anna," Jeremy volunteered. "Don't hesitate to call. But what is it you wanted to talk about?"

Anna thanked him for his kindness, slowly refilling his tea. How gorgeous he is, she was thinking: the grey-green luster in his eyes, the shadow of a beard under his cheek bones and over his strong jaw line, just square enough to suggest muscularity. She never stopped loving him, and perhaps stood somewhat in awe, as did many others as he matured.

"I have been thinking," she went on, "that with Nan so ill, the best course might be to enroll David in boarding school for the upcoming term. There is one in Sussex that still has an opening."

"Isn't he too young?" He could not help but think of his own experience being wrenched from home to attend Eton, and he was thirteen at the time.

"It's a very good place. They have many boys David's age. Fresh country air, room to play. What do you think?"

"Corporal punishment?" The conversation was uncomfortably reminiscent of those hushed quarrels between his parents that summer before he entered Eton.

"Heavens no, Jeremy, no one believes in that anymore!"

She was correct about this, except for Eton.[94] He lit a cigarette, and sat silently, his brow furrowed in thought, creases that already were there to stay. "I suppose then it would be best, under the circumstances," he agreed finally, just as his mother had.

Nanny Gertrude did come home for a while, but in March of the next year she succumbed. It was just as well that David was away at school, because his mother went to pieces, in a paroxysm of grief and anxiety over facing life alone.

* * *

Robert Stephens claimed in his memoir that only once in his life had he ever been jealous of another actor, and that was his good friend Jeremy Brett for his role in *The Merry Widow* in 1968. Brett's costar was the American opera singer Mary Costa, and in preparing for the part, he took three months to study and practice the operatic style. The performance was outstanding, the stars perfectly matched in those famous, beloved duets from the score.

He must have enjoyed this production immensely. We know that he loved opera, and the music of Lehar, the late Romantic Austrian composer, is universally appealing. Not since his voice had reverberated in College Chapel at Eton, singing Mendelssohn, had Jeremy felt so elated. But he also loved to dance, and this operetta not only has entrancing waltzes but spirited Hungarian folk dances as well, resonant of the gypsy strains he would have recalled from his childhood, when bands would encamp at the Grange. He was stunning as the dashing playboy Count Danilo, enlisted by the king to seduce a wealthy widow and falling for her in the end, as they waltz together singing "Love Unspoken." It was a two hour film, quite a special event for television, and no doubt received kudos. A recording of highlights came out also, though Brett was the only original cast member on that Columbia Records label.

But like water off a duck, praise rolled off Jeremy Brett without spoiling him. Indeed he would remain baffled by it, as he had been when he first sang in church as a child in Berkswell, telling his nanny, "Anyone can sing!" Neither did his physical attractiveness result in vanity. To the contrary, he would have preferred to perform disguised as a hunchback if he would thereby be recognized for his acting skill. In the National Company with the guidance of Olivier, he was perfectly positioned to develop his abilities. Sir Laurence had been trained at the same Central School, and as has been noted was a great proponent of the Stanislavsky method. With this influence, Brett often described himself as not merely an actor but a "becomer." He used the analogy of a sponge, explaining that he would squeeze out his own personality and absorb that of his character. His professional skill was enhanced by the ability to enter the mind of another, leaving his own, the weakness of which he could not have foreseen.

The kind of adoration that accompanied his growing celebrity was another side of his profession that puzzled and disturbed him. He was a mere mortal, and his mother's own son, descended of Quakers, a humble servant, using his particular gifts to bring joy. No pedestal for him! But of course we do not control the responses of others.

Along with *The Merry Widow* that year, Brett was on stage at the Old Vic in Bertolt Brecht's adaptation of Marlowe's sixteenth century tragedy *Edward II;* he was the King's brother Edmund, Earle of Kent. He was also in the Shakespeare comedy *Love's Labour's Lost* as Lord Berowne, one of three friends of the King of Navarre, all of whom along with the King challenge themselves to give up the company of women for three years. They are thwarted in this upon their encounter with the lovely French Princess of Aquitaine and her ladies in waiting.

The next BBC production that he appeared in was Oscar Wilde's *An Ideal Husband*, their Play of the Month in May 1969, a tale of blackmail and political corruption. Brett portrayed Viscount Goring, with the same comedic playfulness he brought to Count Danilo. The play opens as he is musing with his butler about the stylishness of a "button hole" or boutonniere, uttering one of Wilde's trademark epigrams: "Fashionable is what one wears oneself. What is unfashionable is what other people wear." Followed by: "To be in love with oneself is the beginning of a lifelong romance."

Margaret Leighton, at age 47, was perfectly cast as the blackmailer, a no longer young but still handsome Madam Cheveley. In a clever plot twist, so typical of Wilde, Lord Goring foils her scheme to blackmail his friend, Sir Robert Chiltern. Of course Wilde specialized in satire, never missing a chance to skewer conventional morality. Thus in the course of this play, Goring must also persuade Robert's wife Gertrude to bend her rigid principles and forgive her husband's long ago mistake, since in reality no one should be judged by impossible *ideals*. Happily he succeeds; the marriage is saved, and he himself marries the blithe Mabel, at last rewarding her coy pursuit.

Wilde was the flamboyant provocateur of Victorian London society, delighting to turn his razor sharp wit on its hypocrisy and pretension, but in the 1890s, he fell horribly afoul of the wrong man, that being the Marquess of Queensberry. We need hardly mention that the history of the case is infamous. Though married with two sons, Wilde became romantically involved with Lord Alfred Douglas, son of the Marquess, and was prosecuted under the sodomy laws, which covered homosexual activity. Convicted, he served two years in prison at hard labor. He moved to France after his release, never returning to England, and died in Paris in 1900 when he was just forty-six. A more enlightened view of the nature of sexual orientation awaited another six decades, and of course has yet to penetrate many parts of the world.

Still there was Noel Coward, gifted and versatile, playwright, composer, performer—and gay. Born the year before the death of Oscar Wilde, he was destined for the pinnacle of the London theatre world upon the success of his play *Private Lives* in 1930, a comedy of manners that featured Anna Massey's mother, Adrianne Allen, and Laurence Olivier. The play opened at the Phoenix Theatre on Charing Cross Road, and the British being so inclined toward nostalgia, it was there in 1969 that a grand musical tribute was staged on the occasion of Coward's seventieth birthday, 16 December.

The review was entitled "A Talent to Amuse" and included over two dozen of his songs with 120 performers. Billed as a "midnight matinee," it ran from midnight until four in the morning. And this show followed a party at the Savoy Hotel for three hundred people, surely every person involved in British theatre at that time. The guest of honor must have been hearty for his age to endure such a fete, but then he had only to eat, drink, and sit smiling next to his companion for the evening, the lovely Merle Oberon, just in from Acapulco.

It was at a rehearsal for this musical review that Jeremy Brett was waiting in the wings to go on stage with Anne Rogers to sing Coward's song "Time and Again,"[95] when dancers from the previous set came tumbling toward them. One young man lost his balance and hurtled into Jeremy, who reflexively grabbed both his arms to keep him from falling, noticing as he did so the palpable muscle, the musky scent of sweat and cologne. Embarrassed, the young man was profusely apologetic, then upon realizing that he had just collided with Jeremy Brett, excused himself, feeling even more awkward.

"What a fine looking chap," Brett commented to Anne. "Do you know who he is?"

"I'm afraid not. I really can't keep up with all the young people coming along."

A stage hand overheard this exchange and volunteered, "That's Gary Bond. He's on television quite a lot."

"Well, I'll have to start watching for him." Actually, Brett may well have jostled Bond before in the television studios of South London. Gary had had a good many such roles since coming out of the Central School in 1962. Jeremy was seven years his senior and was now well known and admired, especially by the younger actors.

Gary was normally a shy person, but he felt so foolish about the incident that afternoon that he waited outside the Phoenix to intercept Jeremy after the rehearsal.

"Mr. Brett, please allow me to apologize again. I really am not ordinarily so clumsy." It was then early evening, but at that time of year night was already falling. They stood under the theatre marquee as lights came on in gathering dusk.

"No harm done, Gary," and Brett lit up a cigarette, noting Bond's surprise that he knew his name. "It's early. Shall we go for a drink?"[96]

Gary was taken aback, but seized the moment. "The Salisbury?" he suggested, brashly naming the gay hangout.

"No, meet me in an hour at the Prince Albert, Notting Hill."

Though he was 29, Gary must have felt terribly young and green standing outside the pub waiting for Jeremy Brett, who had stopped at home to walk Mr. Binks, which he explained when he arrived. They went inside and took a table, ordering the fish and chips since neither of them had eaten dinner. At first they talked shop, then compared notes about the Central School. Bond attended after it had moved to the Embassy Theatre in the Swiss Cottage area of north London, and was intrigued by Brett's recounting of the days when it was at Royal Albert Hall.

They went on to swap their life stories. Gary was born in Hampshire during the war, 1940, and his father was military. The family had the usual expectations of a son, the eldest of two, which did not include an acting career. But the father died when Gary was just sixteen, removing any barrier to his chosen profession. A scholarship to the Central School soon followed, sealing the fulfillment of a dream.

While appearing to listen intently, Jeremy was not really taking in his companion's words. He had been very emotional for some weeks; the anniversary of his mother's death had just passed, and this musical review of Coward's songs heaped on nostalgia. Danny LaRue's[97] rendition of "I've Been to a Marvelous Party," for example, brought memories of that soiree in Highgate where Coward himself sang it, and where he had met the winsome waif he would marry. He was not so much listening to Gary as observing this interesting, handsome young fellow, who seemed somehow more mannerly and sensitive than his peers, with their loathsome tendency for aggressive vulgarity. Starting on the second round of Guinness, a wave of loneliness washed over him. He lit a cigarette and reaching across the table placed his free hand over Gary's, stopping him in midsentence.

Gary was stunned. He himself was tall and good looking, but Jeremy Brett was magnificent. How could this be happening? When he was able to breathe again, he said, "It was true then, what was said about you during your divorce."

"The man in Switzerland, yes. Well you must know Montreux is *very* romantic. He introduced me to opera, and skiing, but it didn't last. He was in Yorkshire and I was in London. Then I was off to Hollywood. I think when he saw me in *My Fair Lady* he was intimidated." He took a drag on the cigarette, studying Gary's reaction. "Are you intimidated, Gary?"

The question was at once plaintive and direct, but what was he to say? Was he being wooed by the most gorgeous man in the world? He was speechless. Then he got his answer.

"Come home with me, Gary." No more was said. They put on their coats and left the Prince Albert arm in arm, walked up past Ladbroke Garden, where the lampposts were decked with Christmas wreaths, their breath making snowy white clouds in the intermittent light, while the real electricity sparked between these two sudden lovers.

* * *

We may surmise that Jeremy took the initiative in the relationship with Gary Bond, who was younger and not as celebrated. Brett would have more likely been the first to make that tentative move suggestive of intimacy. He was very intuitive, and Gary, though reserved, would consciously or not have been signaling his attraction. Clearly the magnetism between them was mutually irresistible. They continued seeing each other, quickly discovering their remarkable compatibility of temperament and taste and values. They had all of Christmas together, reveling in new love, Jeremy once again in high spirits.

In the New Year though, 1970, came work for both of them. Bond was chosen for a leading role in a film titled *Wake in Fright*,[98] to be shot on location in Australia. In it, his character is trapped in the outback after gambling away all his money, and is brutalized by miscreants. With its graphic violence, nudity, and salacious content, the film exemplified a coarsening of the culture, particularly in the entertainment industry, with the British more often in the lead, defying stereotype.

Fortunately for the classic actors like Jeremy Brett there was the National Theatre. He was cast as Bassanio in *The Merchant of Venice*, the young suitor of the beautiful and wealthy Portia. Bassanio in his quest is aided by his friend Antonio, the merchant, who as a result becomes indebted to Shylock, signed to a contract giving the money lender a "pound of flesh" if he defaults. When he does, Portia, now married to Bassanio, disguises herself as a man in order to plead Antonio's case in court, cleverly freeing him of the ghastly forfeiture, and uttering in that proceeding one of the most famous and immortal soliloquies in Shakespeare, which begins, "The quality of mercy is not strained . . ."

But before Gary had returned from the filming in Australia, Jeremy's favorite cousin Daphne was widowed when her husband Alec Clunes died of lung cancer after a three-month illness. Alec had always been fond of his pipe. The family lived in a large Victorian house on Wimbledon Common, spending holidays on the island of Majorca, their hideaway from city life and from work. He was there alone when he took ill, and returned to London where he was diagnosed. Daphne confided in Jeremy that they had been separated at the time, and that she did not want the children to know. Clunes was sixteen years older than Daphne, but just 57 at his death. Their son Martin was eight and daughter Amanda ten.

The funeral was held in London; Alec was a native, born in Brixton. His mother was from Liverpool, his father from Cornwall, and both had been actors. Alec himself was prominent in the theatre world, so the service would have been well attended. As young as Martin was then, he recounts to his biographer that there was "a long line of people being horrid to me."

Jeremy had been very surprised to learn of the couple's marital problem. Of all the marriages, theirs seemed to him the least likely to break up. They were both solid citizens. Even Alec's pacifism in wartime had been redeemed by service as a noncombatant. Now with

Alec's death and the children so young, he was terribly concerned for Daphne, wanting somehow to protect her. She was close family. Before they parted the day of the funeral, they had arranged to meet for dinner at a restaurant she liked in Soho. She would hire a sitter for the children.

He was the first to arrive and waited outside for her. She soon came jostling through the throngs on the sidewalk in a long black cloth coat. It was a cold night in late March. "Sorry I'm late," she said breathlessly, and they hugged for quite a long while. He felt so good to her, like a brother.

"I'm reminded of how you would come pedaling fast up to the Cameo in Balsall," he commented, speaking of the cinema in the village near to Berkswell.

"Weren't those the days, Jeremy? Sir Laurence in *Henry V*, *Wuthering Heights*!" He put his arm around her shoulder, being a good bit taller, and pulled her close as they went in to dinner. They ordered, reminisced over cocktails, and he asked her how the children were adjusting.

"They don't really understand yet," she answered. "You know Alec was cremated, and Martin asked what became of the casket and its handles. He seemed perfectly satisfied when I told him that Dad always liked a bit of wood in the bonfire." They laughed.

"He's a delightful child, and you're a good mother, Daphne."

"I wanted to talk to you about him, Jeremy. Your David is in boarding school now, isn't he?" His mouth full of chicken curry, he nodded. "How is it working out?"

"It is a good place. He likes it well enough, though I'm not fond of the idea."

"I am thinking of sending Martin in the autumn."

"But why, darling? With us it seemed a necessity. Nanny was gone, and Anna's priority is her career. Even on school holidays, it is hard for her to supervise him. When I can, I take him places—Cornwall, the Lake Country, that sort of thing. But you . . ."

"I know, I'm home for my children, but now without Alec, Martin will not have a father figure. A boy needs a man's influence." Jeremy was increasingly uncomfortable with her implications.

"He could come with David and me, on trips."

"Just between us, Jeremy, my son is a bed-wetter."

"Oh, Daphne, don't you see? That could be a huge problem for him in a boarding school." The waiter came with coffee, and he lit a cigarette. "It's your decision, dear, but think it over carefully, please."

They ordered a dessert to split, and then changing the subject, she asked, "What is this I am hearing about you and young Gary Bond?"

That quick smile flashed at her and the sudden flush on his face was all the answer she needed. Daphne had been around theatre people long enough to be fairly sophisticated about such matters. She knew about Victor, being the only one in the family with whom Jeremy had shared the story. "Gary is a sweet guy," was all he said.

"But what about this film he is in?"

"I know, I've seen the promotions. Not our cup of tea, Daphne."

"I'm happy for you, dear heart," she went on. "You know I'm happy when you are happy. I just hope you will be careful, that's all." She smiled at him, and resisting an impulse to muss his hair, reached over the table with her hand and cupped his chin instead. She was so proud of him! But naturally she worried as well, and he understood, of course. However she had confirmed his inferences about this conversation, and his intuition told him that poor little Martin would soon be in boarding school because his mother feared that without a father he would become homosexual. As they parted ways with hugs and kisses and avowals of love and support, Jeremy was suddenly missing Gary extremely, excited that he would be returning next day.

The following afternoon late, Jeremy picked Gary up at Heathrow. They saved their greetings for the privacy of home in Notting Hill, but as soon as they were up the steps and in the house they embraced hungrily. Mr. Binks was excited too, jumping up and down on the both of them, causing Jeremy to say finally, "We've missed you awfully!"

Gary was eager to talk about his experience—Australia, movie making—and talk he did, while Jeremy warmed the lasagna he had waiting and tossed a salad. Within the hour, they sat down to eat with a bottle of Chianti, first toasting their happy reunion. Jeremy had been unduly quiet as Gary went on about the film, so Gary left off saying, "You should be able to see it soon."

"Do you seriously believe," Jeremy began, unsmiling, "that I would go to watch the brutal rape of a man I so love?"

Once again Gary felt young and green, a chastened boy; crestfallen, he realized that while Jeremy was not that much older, he was old-school. Yet at this time, there was nothing he would not do to keep this man's love. In the next moment, seeing the terrible frown he had caused, Jeremy smiled his broadest smile and poured more wine. "Don't look so glum, darling," he purred, in that sensuous baritone voice. Then the smile disappearing as quickly as it came, he reached his hand across and clasped Gary's forearm. Lifting his eyes from under his lowered brow, a characteristic gesture of his, he queried softly, "Move in with me?"

A tumult of emotion welled up in young Gary: love, joy, the surprised exultation that Jeremy Brett needed him. He took the hand from his arm, held it, kissed it, whispering, "Of course. Of course!"

As it turned out, Gary Bond never again appeared on the big screen.

* * *

Since Gary and Jeremy were already practically living together, the move presented no problem, which was fortunate with Brett about to take on a major part in Ibsen's *Hedda Gabler*. He was to play George Tesman, with his friend Robert Stephens as Loevborg, the rival colleague in academia, and Maggie Smith, Robert's wife at that time, as Hedda. The production was directed by Ingmar Bergman, and in his memoir Stephens tells the tale of how Olivier, rebuffed or ignored after several overtures, finally got Bergman's consent by banging on the door to his room at the Savoy Hotel. Then he quotes Ingmar as saying of Lord Laurence, "This man is a warlock!"

The work of Norwegian Henrik Ibsen, the nineteenth century playwright, often touches on the phenomenon of suicide, and his *Hedda Gabler* is typical. It has been found, sadly, from statistical observation that suicide is more common in the Nordic countries, quite plausibly as a result of the relative dearth of daylight so far north. Hedda is married to Tesman, whom she does not love, preferring Loevborg. In the course of a very intricate plot, also characteristic of Ibsen, she becomes involved in a love triangle with Loevborg and her friend Thea. She induces Loevborg to kill himself, supplying him a pistol, and when her role in the deed is later found out, she uses the same gun to commit suicide herself. These deeply psychological themes in Ibsen were Freudian before Freud's time.

John Osborne adapted the play for the National Company, and it was staged at the Cambridge Theatre which is near the Phoenix. Stephens writes that he influenced Olivier in casting him as Loevborg, an appropriate role since the character is alcoholic; and as Tesman, the suspicious husband, Brett was "wonderfully quiet and watchful." The two old friends surely must have enjoyed working together, as of old in Manchester.

Neither was Gary Bond idle. In fact his career had a major boost when he landed the starring role of Joseph in the Andrew Lloyd-Webber musical *Joseph and the Amazing Technicolor Dream Coat*, a pastiche of rock, calypso, and country music from the inventive twenty-two-year-old composer, who had already had a hit in *Jesus Christ Superstar*. The new musical opened at the Edinburgh Festival before coming to London and was so popular that it continued for two years.[99] From depravity in the Australian outback to a Bible story was quite a leap, but Bond was a very promising actor, acclaimed in both the movie and the musical. The film however was not received well by audiences, with Australians especially taking offense. Scenes of a drunken kangaroo hunt were hard to stomach, and the carnage had been filmed live during an actual hunt. We can be fairly certain that Gary's domestic partner was much happier with him as a flaxen haired Joseph.

The year had not ended before Brett reprised his portrayal of Bassanio in *The Merchant of Venice* for American television, with Sir Laurence in a masterful turn as Shylock. Olivier validated his stature by understanding the bitter unreason of antisemitism, and no less by finding this understanding in the sixteenth century play. His interpretation of the part evinces the fierce resentment of the wealthy

Jew, despised even as his help is entreated. Brett was likewise persuasive as the handsome suitor in his love scenes with Portia, played by Olivier's wife Joan Plowright. When he plants a passionate kiss on Portia's mouth, we can imagine Sir Larry urging him past incestuous misgivings: "Make it real, dear boy!" But truly just to be doing the Shakespeare he loved together with a man whom he had idolized since childhood surely never lost its thrill.

In 1971 Brett took on the role of the son in John Mortimer's play *A Voyage Round My Father*, adapted for the stage by the writer from a series he did for BBC radio in 1963. The story is autobiographical concerning Mortimer's own father, a barrister who becomes blind in middle age, but despite the handicap carries on, stubborn and cantankerous as ever. His devoted son follows him into the profession, all the while yearning to be a writer. Mortimer was the creator of the popular "Rumpole of the Bailey." Alec Guinness was the father in this production, staged at Theatre Royal in Haymarket.

Robert Stephens turned forty on 14 July of that year, and he planned a party for a number of his friends, including Jeremy Brett, on the patio of the Meridiana in the Fulham Road.[100] Unaccountably for July, the evening was very cold. Robert's wife Maggie was in a foul mood, perhaps because as he admits, he had been drinking all day. The group of ten or so sat around a long table shivering, and dinner took forever to arrive. The restaurant was just across the road from the house where Robert and Maggie were living, in Queen's Elm Square, so Jeremy walked over and brought back as many sweaters as he could find. That got them through dinner, and then they all retreated to the house, where of course still more drinking went on, and Maggie grew more cross. In order to salvage some vestige of celebration, Jeremy put on the record of highlights from *The Merry Widow* and sang along with himself. Nevertheless, Robert recalled the night as a catastrophe, exposing the serious erosion of his marriage.

While it was still summer, with son David on holiday from school, Jeremy planned a long weekend for them on the Isle of Wight,[101] stopping first in Chichester to take in a play at the festival. He even persuaded cousin Daphne to let her son Martin come with them. Once again this resort seemed a good summer getaway, especially with two young boys. David had just past his twelfth birthday, and Martin would be ten in the autumn. Jeremy reserved a suite at the Sandringham on the esplanade in Sandown, and Daphne furnished him with a rubber mat to put under Martin's sheet just in case.

The play in Chichester was the eighteenth century comedy of manners *The Rivals* by Robert Brinsley Sheridan, which introduced to the world the character of Mrs. Malaprop. The matinee performance was wonderfully funny, and Jeremy challenged the boys to remember as many *malapropisms* as they could, so the three continued laughing on the ferry to the island: "She's as headstrong as an allegory," quoted Martin; and David came up with, "Illiterate him from your memory!" It was past dinnertime when they got to the hotel, and as the boys were exhausted, they ordered from room service and ate on the balcony, which overlooked the water and a colorful sunset sky.

"How are you getting on at school, Martin?" Jeremy asked, eager to sound him out on his experience.

"It's all right, I guess. I come home on weekends you know, and I hate going back Sunday night. But it's okay." That was far from the truth, of course, as Jeremy knew immediately.

"Well Martin, I think you are a very brave young man. I know how hard it is to lose a parent, especially at your age."

"I'm almost ten!" Martin hastened to insist.

"Yes I know, lad, and mature for your years," which also was not true, but had young Martin beaming proudly. David sat quietly finishing his braised scallops. He was far more reticent than his second cousin. "The beach in the morning, boys," Jeremy announced, "and what shall we play when we tire of swimming? Badminton? Volleyball?"

"Volleyball!" the two exclaimed in unison.

"To bed early then, you will need your rest."

The hotel had its own private strip of beach with umbrellas and beach chairs. So after breakfast next day they staked out three of these near the volleyball court and went in for a swim. Martin had learned to swim in Majorca, and boasted loudly how he and his older sister could swim from there to the nearby island of Dragonera. Jeremy was duly impressed, while David was getting a little put off. They swam in after a time and decided to do some beach combing before lunch, gathering scallop shells and clam shells and sea snails, the occasional gull feather, as they enjoyed the views of water and beach and rocky bluffs. Martin continued going on about the wonderful shells that were to be found on the beaches of Majorca, superior to any he was finding here.

They had lunch from one of the food vendors, and then the boys wanted to play volleyball. Jeremy got them started by playing against the two of them, then let them play against each other while he stretched out in the sun.

"Go easy on Martin," he said to David. "He's younger than you." And being younger, Martin was not only getting tired, he was not yet as tall, though before many more years he would be over six feet. At this game however David, showing no mercy, was getting the better of him.

"You made me miss that on purpose!" cried Martin angrily.

"That's the point of the game," David rebutted, hitting the ball at his cousin even faster. Missing the volley again, Martin let loose a loud and furious stream of expletives, causing Jeremy to raise himself on his elbows and then sit up.

"Martin, watch your language!" he shouted. With that, the boy stormed off the court heading toward the water. "Wait here, David. Order yourself a cold drink," and Jeremy went after Martin, easily overtaking the youngster. They walked along the shore a while in silence; then Jeremy, putting a hand on the boy's shoulder, asked quietly, "Did you learn those words at school, Martin?"

That opened the floodgates. "They tease me about my ears," he cried. Those leprechaun ears of his were not so cute to the schoolyard bullies.[102] "They tease me because I don't have a father," then he mumbled, "and when I wet the bed."

They stopped walking and Martin hugged Jeremy tightly around the waist. "I'm so sorry, Martin," said Jeremy, holding him close and stroking his head, "so sorry. Here, let's sit," and they sat down in the warm sand near the water's edge, the waves lapping gently and a cool breeze coming off the Channel.

Then he told Matin how he was teased in school for the way he spoke. "They called me Peter Wabbit!" Mocking himself, he got Martin to laugh with him. "You see, lad? You have a sharp wit. Make them laugh. Let that be your best weapon, unless of course they're bigger than you," and they laughed again. The incoming tide was reaching their feet, so they started back to the hotel.

By the next day apologies had been exchanged and all was forgiven, but no more volleyball. Instead that afternoon, they bicycled along the Coastal Walk to Shanklin and to the cinema to see Peter O'Toole in *Murphy's War*, an action film set in World War II, not extraordinary but sufficiently macho to entertain two young boys.[103] Afterwards they returned to the hotel, where tea was being served on the veranda. Being summer it was not a high tea, but there was ice cream for the children. They took a table that had a most spectacular view of the Channel, and the boys chattered excitedly about the movie.

"What did you think of it, Dad?" David asked.

"Peter was excellent; he always is. But the production was sloppy."

Then Martin piped up. "I love Peter O'Toole. I want to be just like him when I grow up."

"You want to be an actor then! Well your father was a gifted actor," Jeremy observed. "What about you, David?"

"Not me, I would be too nervous," he replied. He took after his mother, except that he was independent enough not to follow his parents into the profession. "I would rather be a writer."

"A worthy ambition, son," his father asserted. Then the boys started comparing notes about their schools, and Martin told them of the animals kept on campus, which one of the teachers was allowing him to care for. Clearly the rabbits, chickens, and sheep were his favorite things at school.

Meanwhile, David was quiet; he had stopped listening and was studying his father's face. Both his parents were now living with someone. His mother had taken up with an actor twelve years younger than she, who had moved into the flat with them. George was his name, a nice enough fellow, and fun to play ball with in Hyde Park on school breaks. He had no say in such things, but at least, unlike poor Martin, he still had his father. He felt so blessed, so grateful.

Sensing his son's eyes on him, Jeremy beamed a smile his way and tousled his hair. The lad was getting too old for a father's kiss.

* * *

When they had gotten back to London, and Jeremy had seen each boy home and finally returned to Notting Hill, he climbed the stairs wearily, his bag suddenly heavy, even his head starting to ache with the weight of his thoughts: those two lovely boys subjected again to the rigors and torment of boarding school, Martin in particular. The school he attended in Surrey still practiced caning, or so Jeremy had heard. The outrageous barbarity, the perennial cruelty toward children and among them! He opened the door; the house was dark, quiet. Gary was at the theatre already. He would come home exhausted; Joseph was a very strenuous role.

Thank heavens for Mr. Binks! Despite his eleven years, at the sound of the door opening, he came tumbling downstairs from the bedroom and leapt into his master's arms, licking Jeremy's face exuberantly. On went his leash and off they went to the park together. They walked awhile, Mr. Binks visiting his favorite spots, but it was a hot summer night, so they soon found a bench and sat. In the companionship of his beloved dog, his spirits lifting quickly, Jeremy hatched a plan for a party.

"What do you say to a party, Binks? Day after tomorrow." The dog must have recognized the word *party* by now, because he barked in response, sealing the affirmation with more doggie kisses. Jeremy's love of parties was famous, and like his late mother he loved people. We may surmise that he kept no "B list" when it came to guests. Thus in a couple of days he had summoned a number of friends for a festive evening. The house had a veranda that was perfect for summer entertaining, lit with candles and lanterns, and Gary was very helpful, mixing drinks and seeing that all went smoothly.

Naturally Robert was invited, but Jeremy had not realized the extent to which his friend's condition was deteriorating. Stephens's marriage to Maggie Smith was in trouble; he was not getting along with his revered mentor, Olivier; he was depressed and drinking heavily. To make matters worse, true to his pattern, he was stringing along three other women on the side. When he arrived that evening in a taxi with one of these paramours, the poor girl's former lover was waiting for them and violence threatened. Noticing the kerfuffle from the window, Jeremy rushed out and managed to smooth it over. The other man was known to Robert, who seemed never to go far afield for his playmates.

Within days or weeks, nonetheless, it became clear that he would need a place to dry out, so his wife and their circle of friends found a private rehabilitation facility and made arrangements. Jeremy delivered him there and made sure he was checked in and was as comfortable as his condition would allow, having to stay sober.[104]

Maggie did not want him back at Queen's Elm Square upon his release; thus, it might have been then that he came to stay with Jeremy, whose house had that loft that he kept as a convenient guest suite. Yet as much as he cherished such a time-honored friendship, it must have been a strain at times. Robert was there for six months. Maggie eventually took him back, but he was incapable of fidelity, addicted to women as much as to alcohol. They finally divorced in 1975.

With such disquiet swirling around him, it is perhaps not surprising that Brett took on just one role in 1972. He was Gaston in *Traveller Without Luggage*, a play by Jean Anouilh. Ten years previous for the BBC, he had been in a farce by the same French playwright, but this more serious work was about an amnesiac, "luggage" being a metaphor for memories. Gaston is the protagonist, a veteran of the Great War, who discovers his true identity only to realize he had been a scoundrel. In his struggle to reconcile the dichotomous sides of himself, and his ultimate renunciation of his checkered past, are embedded the psychological and philosophical depths typical of Anouilh. This production was staged in Leatherhead at Thorndike Theatre.

By 1973, in contrast, Brett had gotten back to work in earnest. There was another Ibsen play, *Rosmersholm*, at Greenwich Theatre, London, in which he starred as John Rosmer, a former cleric and owner of the estate of the title. Again there is the morbid foreboding mood of the Scandinavian and the theme of suicide, but in a context of social and political change consequent to radical ideas, which Ibsen was wont to bring out in his dramas.

Rosmer's wife has died before the play begins, having thrown herself into the mill race. Her close friend Rebecca is in love with Rosmer and implicated in the suicide. Apparently, typical of Ibsen, his characters kill themselves at the prodding of friends or lovers. Rosmer goads Rebecca to jump into the mill race, promising to follow her, and the play ends as they jump in together. Ibsen wrote this in 1886, an era of high romanticism. Yet he was considered the father of realism and among the founders of modernism. He died in 1906.

In late March of 1973, Sir Noel Coward passed away at his Firefly Estate in Jamaica of heart failure.[105] A revival was planned in his memory of the comedy *Design for Living*, which he wrote in 1933 for his friends Alfred Lunt and Lynn Fontanne. The play, first produced on Broadway, is about the complicated relationships of three artistic people living together in Paris: Gilda, an interior designer; Leo, a writer; and Otto, a painter, played by Brett in this production, which took place at the Phoenix. The plot is not so much about a *ménage à trois* as a "three-sided erotic hotchpotch" as one character says at the end of the play. In fact, it was thought to be too risqué to be produced in London when it was first written due to the questionable sexuality of the two male characters, who love each other and also Gilda. Nevertheless, it would seem a great relief from Ibsen.

During the run of *Design for Living*, an American woman visiting London came to see it. Her name was Joan Wilson, and she had just been made an executive producer of Masterpiece Theatre, which had become a staple of public television in the States. She was already established in that arena as a producer at WGBH in Boston. Then in her early forties, she was a confessed workaholic, dedicated to her profession, independent, and determined. When she saw Jeremy

Brett on stage that night, she was overwhelmed, utterly captivated, and she later recalled it was then that she set her cap for him.

This was also the year that the National Theatre Company was able to leave the Old Vic and move into its far more commodious new building near Waterloo Bridge. Laurence Olivier stepped down from the leadership role of managing director, a position he had then held for ten years. Brett continued to appear on stage, but most of his performances after this point were on television.[106]

That year, for instance, he was in an episode of *Country Matters* for Granada Television, entitled "An Aspidistra in Babylon," the Aspidistra being a popular houseplant among the bourgeoisie in Victorian England. He played Captain Blaine, a soldier who seduces a village girl and then abandons her. It was adapted by screenwriter Jeremy Paul from a story by H. E. Bates; this was when the two Jeremy's first met. They became friends, and would work together again a decade later. Then Brett starred in the drama *One Deadly Owner* for ITC Entertainment, a murder mystery in which he was the villain, Peter Tower, a photographer whose ruthless ambition leads to homicide. The plot revolves around a white Rolls Royce that his girlfriend, played by Donna Mills, has purchased, unwittingly from the murder victim, whose spirit now haunts the car.

A third appearance in 1973 was as John Middleton Murry, the second husband of English writer Katherine Mansfield in a BBC series about her life. Vanessa Redgrave played Mansfield, who died of tuberculosis in 1923 at the age of thirty-five. Murry was a fellow writer, eminent and prolific, a friend of D. H. Laurence and T. S. Eliot. He lived until 1957. The series *A Picture of Katherine Mansfield*, included six episodes.

That November Jeremy turned forty. Considering recent debacles involving his friend Robert, he may have resisted his usual preference for a party, choosing to observe the day quietly, just he and Gary. It fell on a Saturday, and they decided to treat themselves to dinner at the Savoy and a ballet at the Royal Opera House, where Nureyev was dancing in Tschaikovsky's *Sleeping Beauty*.

"We'd have more fun at *The Rocky Horror Show*," Gary complained over dinner, thinking at the same time that he would be the sleeping beauty before the night was out.

"When you have your fortieth birthday, darling, we shall go to *The Rocky Horror Show*," Jeremy retorted, "if it's still around."

"I'll hold you to it, old man! It's an enormous hit. They had to move out of Royal Court Theatre to the King's Road to accommodate the crowds."

The move was made that very day in fact, and the musical, a camp satire of bad horror movies, became a long-lived cult classic. It was raucous and raunchy, featuring as its main character the mad transvestite scientist Dr. Frank N. Furter.

"Well then," Jeremy continued, "we'd be overdressed anyway." They were in formal wear for the occasion, and the red rose boutonnieres had become *de rigueur* ever since Montreux, in honor of his late mother, whose untimely death forever after impaired the happiness of his birthday.

Seeing the cloud draw suddenly over Jeremy's face, Gary remembered himself. "Of course, dear heart," he said, letting up, "of course. The ballet will be memorable, especially Rudolf!"

They did indeed enjoy themselves: a splendid dinner, beautiful music, Nureyev in his prime. It was quite late when they came home through the storied London fog of a cold autumn night. The house had a fireplace, which was not often used, but Gary had exercised the foresight of laying a wood fire and chilling a bottle of *Veuve Clicquot*, Napoleon's champagne. He set a match to the fire, fetched glasses, and popped the cork, while Jeremy slipped off his jacket and shoes and curled up on the sofa, a blissful Mr. Binks on the hearth rug at his feet.

Gary sat, poured the champagne, and toasted, "To you, dear Jeremy, health, happiness, long life!"

"Thank you, Gary, for shedding some brightness on this day. To reach this age is more a fright than a joy."

"Nonsense, old chap! In all honesty I must tell you, Jeremy Brett, you improve with age," and to that Jeremy flashed a quick smile.

The fire blazed awhile, and when the two of them had finished off the champagne, it was well past midnight. "Are you coming to bed?" Gary asked.

"In a bit." Jeremy stared into the embers of the fire, twinkling like the distant lights of a city. In the morning, Gary found him sound asleep, still on the sofa.

* * *

Gary was absolutely right; fully matured at age 40, Jeremy Brett truly was more attractive than he had ever been. He had matured professionally as well, and the power he was able to project as a result of this maturity greatly enhanced the pleasure he took in his work, though we are given to wonder whether he fully understood that power. Throughout his life, seemingly, he puzzled about being admired for his looks, a thing for which he could hardly take credit; but at this stage in his career his prowess had equally as much to do with the skill and intelligence he brought to each role. Ample confirmation came in the next two very busy years.

In 1974, a series of one hour dramas, *Affairs of the Heart*, was produced for ITV based on the work of American born author Henry James, whose life spanned the nineteenth to the twentieth centuries. He lived in England, and a common theme in his writing is the contrast between the Old World, feudal but alluring, and the New, a place of openness and freedom. Brett appeared in one of these, a Victorian comedy of manners, opposite Diana Rigg, known in Britain and beyond as Emma Peel in *The Avengers*. He played Captain Yule, heir to a family estate that is mortgaged beyond his means. The holder of the mortgage attempts to coerce him to marry his daughter, thereby to have the property free and clear. Meanwhile a friend of the daughter, a wealthy American woman played by Rigg, falls in love with the place, decrepit though it has become, and with the Captain.

This is considerable "dramedy" to squeeze into an hour broadcast, so it was fortunate that the costars were top notch. In the end, the wealthy American pays off the mortgage, and then some, taking over the estate and handing it to the rightful heir. Of course the Captain protests that he is undeserving this generosity, that he will pay her rent, but she will hear none of it. As she is headed for the door, having a train to catch, he stands across the room by the mantelpiece.

"Shall you like being called Mrs. Clem Yule?" he asks, and then, delivered with just the right whiff of male dominance, "You really can't come here, move mountains, clear my way, turn my head . . . and expect to be let go." This pronouncement is quickly punctuated with a robust kiss. Since the money lender's daughter was in love with another anyway, it is a fairytale ending. Yet as fast as the plot has moved along, Brett has been able to persuade us.

In another miniseries for ITV the same year, he again was the romantic lead in two of the seven episodes. The series was called *Jennie: Lady Randolph Churchill,* and it portrayed the life of Winston's mother, born in America in 1845. Jennie was played by American actress Lee Remick, and Brett was one of her several illustrious lovers, the Austrian Count Karl Kinsky, accent, mustache, and all.

For the BBC, he was in four episodes of the series *A Legacy,* based on the 1956 novel by the German-born English writer Sybille Bedford. The story was autobiographical, depicting the families of her parents in Germany prior to the First World War: the Catholic Feldens, on her mother's side; and the Merz family, who were Jewish. Brett played Eduard Merz, the eldest son, a rake and a gambler.

Then he accepted the starring role in an episode of *Haunted,* a series produced by Granada Television with studios in Manchester. Titled "The Ferryman," it dramatized a ghost story written by Kingsley Amis,[107] about an author, Sheridan Owen, played by Brett, who finds that the novel he has just published is not fiction. On holiday with his wife, they find themselves at an inn called The Ferryman, the title of his book, and they learn of the legend of a serial killer, a ferryman, whose ghost is said to haunt the place. Too eerie to be coincidence, he is living the plot of his book; and after nearly drowning in the very river used by the killer to dispose of his victims, Owen is possessed by the ghost. But only for one night. At the end, they have returned home and his wife has seen a doctor for a pregnancy test, lab results to come next day. Along with Owen, we are left with the ghostly, and ghastly presumption that the evil ferryman has used him to spawn an offspring.

For an actor to enter the mind of his character is one thing, but to enter a mind that has been possessed by a wraith would be no mean feat. There are aspects of this role which we might conjecture to have been unsettling to Jeremy: the Jekyll and Hyde notion of being taken over by a murderous spirit; and the blurring of a boundary presumed inviolable between fiction and reality.

After the show was "in the can" as they say of film, Jeremy decided to stop at the Abercrombie for a cask ale before taking the train home. It was autumn again, reminding him of those Manchester Library days two decades earlier. A fog was rolling in off the River Irwell as he walked, and he retained an uneasy feeling of demonic possession. He was glad to reach the pub, glad for the ale and a bite of supper.

As he sat alone at the bar, two young strangers were eyeing him and whispering. The boy approached, as though it was taking all his courage, and spoke. "Are you Jeremy Brett?"

Jeremy was nonplussed at being recognized, feeling both flattered and exposed. He might have lied, but not to two such innocents. He loved his fans, but working in television keeps the actor at some remove. That his acting was so meaningful to so many was a deep source of satisfaction, but added to the predictable tension for a private person in the spotlight of celebrity was Brett's modesty. It was not in his nature to be entirely comfortable with adulation.

"Yes I am, and you are?" The young man introduced himself and they shook hands.

"We watch you on television. We loved you in *Affairs of the Heart*!" His girlfriend reached into a large handbag and whipped out an autograph book, a thing Jeremy had not seen in years. He signed it, using their names, and they scampered off, thankful and excited. But he felt suddenly conspicuous, and on the train home the gloomy apprehension of "The Ferryman" descended on him.

Gary still had a good bit of work in television himself that year. He was in a Play of the Month for BBC, and did a drama for the ITV

Playhouse. But he was home when Jeremy came in, unusually quiet and withdrawn.

"May I fix you some tea?" Gary asked.

"No, nothing," was the brusque reply. "Would you mind taking Mr. Binks for a walk. I really don't want to go out again." Mr. Binks never walked far anymore, especially on a cold night, so he and Gary went out. When they got back, Jeremy had gone to bed in the guest quarters with the door closed. The lack of explanation was concerning, but Gary let him be.

When Jeremy was not up in the morning, Gary worried. He went to the loft to rouse him, and found him asleep face down, his head buried in the pillow. "Jeremy, are you all right?" he asked, shaking him.

"Oh, go away!" was the grumbled response. Then as poor Gary crept away, "Just leave me alone, darling, please."

What to do to get his partner out of this funk? Gary went down and started cooking breakfast—eggs and bacon—and put the kettle on for tea. Then he went out to the veranda, where they had a miniature red rose bush growing in a pot sheltered by the house, and cut some of the last blooms for the table. When he came in, Jeremy was standing in the kitchen in his long, woolen robe. The smell of breakfast had brought him down, and at the sight of the roses, a broad smile lit his face.

* * *

In some dark moods, Jeremy did not want to speak, seemed unable to speak, even unable to force himself. Gary blamed it on overwork; and as for dealing with autograph hounds, he offered the perfect solution: dark glasses and a high collar. Having danced around onstage as Joseph for two years, he also had occasion to be accosted by fans.

But Brett did not slack off; in fact 1975 was busier than the year prior. In a drama for ITV, *The Prodigal Daughter*, he played a priest, Father Michael Daley, living in the parsonage with two other priests, the senior one played by Alistair Sim. They are in dire need of a housekeeper, and so hire Christine, who works out splendidly, having had experience in catering. She is non-Catholic, and in her past has had an abortion. In the course of getting to know and to like her, Father Michael has a crisis of conscience, questioning the value of celibacy. How can a priest, he argues, minister to his flock, advising them about human relationships of which he himself has no experience? And then he questions the unforgiving doctrine that condemns Christine for a past sin. Can God truly be so unmerciful? In the end he leaves the priesthood. The screenplay by the prolific writer David Turner was a very thoughtful and sensitive commentary on organized religion as it relates, or fails to relate, to the inexorable conundrums of human life, with Brett's unparalleled subtlety making this one hour teleplay a dramatic jewel.

For the BBC, he repeated the role of Berowne in *Love's Labour's Lost*, which he had played on stage at the Old Vic in 1968; and he made an appearance with Twiggy, who had her own weekly variety show at that time. More challenging were two classic comedies by Robert Brinsley Sheridan, which he took on, also for BBC. He played Joseph Surface in *The School for Scandal*, that rollicking spoof of eighteenth century courtship involving the convoluted intrigues of Lady Sneerwell to spread gossip, and thereby match up the right people.

The second BBC production was Sheridan's *The Rivals*, another such satire, in which Brett took the role of Captain Jack Absolute, a "rival" for the hand of Lydia. This play, the same that was done at Chichester four years earlier, offers the added complications of mistaken identity and threats of a duel in an uproariously complex web of romantic entanglements. In his gleeful delivery of Sheridan's witty asides to the audience, Brett revealed the great delight he took in his work. At the beginning of the play, for example, he tells the audience wryly, "My father wants to force me to marry the very girl that I am plotting to run away with!" And later, even as he is embracing Lydia, he whispers behind her back, "She holds out now, the Devil's in it!" As Captain Jack, he gets the girl, unlike Joseph Surface.

In nothing he did that year would there be the slightest hint of any trouble in Jeremy's personal life. He was the consummate professional, able to leave behind any private concern to enter his role completely. But his beloved Mr. Binks, then sixteen, was showing his age. The vet said his heart was failing, and Jeremy could not but notice that the dog's symptoms were reminiscent of his late father's. Like the Colonel, Mr. Binks was sleeping most of the time, tired and short of breath. Jeremy would carry him to the park when the weather allowed; otherwise they stayed close, on the veranda or in the small yard of the house.

This little terrier had been Jeremy's bosom companion since his mother's death, seen him through the breakup of his marriage, his father's passing, and the sale of his childhood home. Mr. Binks was always there with innocent love and enthusiastic affection, typical of dogs, but surely exceptional in his case. Here was mutual devotion.

The two returned from the park one night, and Mr. Binks went straight to his cozy dog bed in the bedroom. When Jeremy turned in, the dog was sleeping peacefully, his breathing slow and regular. Usually toward daybreak he would jump up beside Jeremy in bed, and when next morning he was not there his master's heart sank. Sure enough Mr. Binks had died in his sleep. Gary awoke to find Jeremy sitting up on the edge of the bed, holding the dog's body closely to him and weeping softly. It was obvious what had happened.

"Oh, Jeremy," Gary tried to soothe him. When his loving arm was rebuffed, he was hurt. Deeply. Then he cried as well, as Jeremy put the dog down and retreated into the bathroom. We have the advantage of hindsight, knowing that Jeremy had a mood disorder, which by definition a person does not control. Yet Gary must have had the gift of intuition, because like Anna, Jeremy's first wife, he never stopped loving the man. Indeed at this particular moment, even smarting from his snub, he loved Jeremy more than ever.

Many people, perhaps most, have had the awful experience of losing a pet. They become entwined in our lives intimately, leaving a vacuum when they are gone in all the places they formerly inhabited: the places where they ate and slept, their master's lap, waiting by the door. This loss can bring a loneliness like no other, the fellow creature who would always listen, always love, gone.

Jeremy did not speak to anyone for many days. He did not answer the phone nor leave the house. He stayed in his robe all day, chain smoking, and pacing the floor, not sleeping. Gary had to explain the situation to concerned friends, all the while yearning to break through the wall of silence and somehow ease the sadness. It was too much for him.

He went to see *The Rocky Horror Show*, comic relief indeed. It was still running, of course, eventually joining the list of longest running musicals in London history. Robert Stephens had seen it, and had told Jeremy it was smashing good entertainment. He especially liked a young Irish actress named Patricia Quinn, whom he met backstage. Many years later, twenty in fact, he married her.

Might it have been Robert, his jolly ribaldry always at the ready, who finally brought Jeremy around, at least enough to go to the show with Gary?[108] In any case, off the two of them went one night, in their dark glasses and hooded jackets, to King's Road. Jeremy easily would have been more appalled by the audience of youthful followers than the show on stage, as loud and smutty as that was, a horror show indeed. Watching Gary laugh and sing along he began to worry for him. He was so young yet. They came out of the theatre, arms linked together, and as they walked toward the tube station, Jeremy spoke.

"Gary, darling, I am so very sorry for the way I have been, for shutting you out . . ."

"No, no, no," Gary interrupted. "Please don't apologize. I understand completely. You were so attached to Mr. Binks for so long, of course you are grieving."

"Thank you. You are too good!" and he held Gary closer. They walked on silently awhile and into the station.

Then Gary asked, "Did you like the show?"

"No."

"But it's camp, Jeremy."

"Unalloyed!" and they smiled at each other.

Jeremy continued to be restless, pursued by the memories of his dear dog, whom he now took to calling the Hound of Heaven. He needed to get away—from the house, from London, and dare he think it, from Gary. So when his agent presented him the opportunity to appear at the Stratford Shakespeare Festival in Canada, he jumped at it. They wanted him for two plays: *A Midsummer Night's Dream*, in the dual role of Theseus, Duke of Athens, and Oberon, King of the Fairies; and *The Way of the World*, the Restoration comedy written by William Congreve in 1700, in which he would play Mirabell, lover of Millamant, that latter role to be played by none other than Maggie Smith, Robert's ex.

The agent had received another request that Brett might wish to fulfill while overseas. An executive producer for Masterpiece Theatre, Joan Wilson, had seen *The Rivals* and acquired it for public broadcasting in America. She wanted him to introduce it. Her office was at WGBH in Boston, so the diversion would be simple enough. He would fly to Boston before the Festival, and she would pick him up at Logan Airport.

* * *

From all reports and descriptions of Joan Sullivan Wilson, she was a powerhouse. Born and raised in the Midwest, she studied drama at the University of Wisconsin before coming to Boston to work for the public television station. She dedicated her career to the idea that public broadcasting could bring classic English drama to the masses through quality television. An ardent anglophile, she found that quality in Britain, specifically the BBC, bringing many of their productions to America on such programs as Classic Theatre, Masterpiece Theatre, or Masterpiece Mystery.

She was older than Jeremy, the same age as his brother Patrick; and if we may assume that Sullivan was her maiden name, she may have had Irish antecedents. She had been married twice, but was single when she met Brett in 1976, with a son Caleb in college at her alma mater, Grinnell, and daughter Rebekah in high school.

Joan was of average height, with long, wavy brown hair and large expressive eyes. She had an outgoing personality, hardworking, disciplined, well organized. She was not a waif. Instead, we might observe, she had a good bit in common with Elizabeth Huggins. When Jeremy arrived at Logan airport early that spring, she was waiting at the gate. As we have noted, she already had eyes for him, and he stood out in a crowd. Shaking his hand and introducing herself, her heart skipped a beat. She led the way to her car, a black Ford Mustang with the license tag "WITCH."[109] He was intrigued. She confessed an interest in the occult, and after all they were in Massachusetts.

Their first stop was M. J. O'Connor's, one of many Irish pubs in Boston and not far from the airport. Most of the bars in Boston, it would seem, are Irish pubs. Over their mugs of stout ale, they discussed the work she had for him. She told him about what they called "wraparounds," the prologues and epilogues framing each weekly edition of Masterpiece Theatre, written and delivered by host Alistair Cooke. While Brett was not expected to write anything, she assured him that his suggestions would be welcome.

It was then supper time, and Joan would of course have planned the evening. They walked across the street and down a block to an excellent steak house, where she treated him to dinner. There the conversation turned to their personal lives, their Irish grandfathers, their children. Jeremy's son, who would turn seventeen that year, was about the same age as her daughter. They finished eating, raved about the steaks, and as they waited for the crème brûlée and coffee, he offered her a cigarette from his silver case. She took one, he lighted it, then his own, and they sat back, relaxed and content.

There was something about her; she was easy to be with, and years later he would reflect that it seemed they had always known each other. Lowering her head slightly, her eyes would look up at him from under her brow in a gesture strongly similar to a habit of his.

"I saw you in *Design for Living* in '73 at the Phoenix," she revealed.

"Ah, yes, just after Coward died." Then he lowered his head in like manner. "How was I?"

She puffed on the cigarette, pausing to search for an appropriate adjective. "Extraordinary!" Her tone, her expression suggested to him somewhat of a crush, which he found enormously flattering and charmingly youthful.

"I'm glad," he said, relieved that she had not chosen a word to describe him physically. Now she was embarrassed and moved to get up.

"I really must get you to your hotel, Jeremy. You must be exhausted." A veteran air traveler herself, she was sensitive to the effects of the time changes. "Sleep as long as you want tonight," she added, "just call me when you get up," and she wrote her number on a dry cocktail napkin.

They emerged into a cold fog, which she declared must have followed him all the way from London. A good head taller than she, his arm fell easily upon her shoulder with a spontaneous affection that was characteristic.

He did not sleep very late next day, having slept on the plane, so they met in the hotel cafe midmorning for tea. This being America, the waiter brought a tea chest which offered a variety of tea bags. She chose Earl Grey, and he took Darjeeling. He watched closely as she added cream and sugar. He had seldom seen an American drink tea, and never in the English style. She noticed him puzzling and understood at once. "English grandmother," she explained. He was liking Joan more and more. Then he had to tell her about the Cadbury family, his ancestors and their history, which he rarely discussed with anyone. They talked and talked, flitting among topics: English drama and literature, about which she was very knowledgeable; the London theatre world, where they knew many of the same people; the Boston origins of Edgar Allen Poe, near the old hotel where they sat, in the Bay Village area.

"Did you know that Poe was a favorite of Sir Arthur Conan Doyle?" she asked. "We must go visit Poe's birthplace if there is time. Both his parents were actors here in Boston." She glanced at her watch. "But first to the studio."

Apparently this filming of Brett's introduction to his performance in *The Rivals* was an emotionally charged experience for them both. By no means would we venture to say that she was starstruck, yet here was Jeremy Brett, *in her workplace!* In later interviews she would use the word "chemistry" to describe what they had felt between them on this occasion; and Jeremy had never had such instant rapport with anyone, the sense that he might absolutely drop the mask and be himself.

But he had to move on to Stratford, so next morning he hopped a small plane to London, Ontario, where the Festival would send a car to meet him. Before they parted, Joan told him she would be up to see him in *A Midsummer Night's Dream*, and he informed her that she would find him at the Queen's Inn, an old hotel near the center of town. Stratford, a delightful small city, has lakes on all sides: Huron to the west, Ontario to the east, and Erie to the south. In addition it has its own Lake Victoria, a small lake fed by the town's own Avon River. The Festival theatre and grounds in Upper Queen's Park are on this lake, and a Shakespearean Garden borders it as well.

The Canadian spring weather was glorious. Jeremy could walk to the theatre from the Inn, or in the opposite direction take the lakeside path to the Shakespearean Garden, where parrot tulips were blooming in all colors. He did not miss London at all, and the Congreve play, *The Way of the World*, was a therapeutic distraction from haunting thoughts of dear old Mr. Binks.

A Midsummer Night's Dream was to begin in early May, and on opening night, Joan showed up at his dressing room door with a dozen red roses. How did she know? They hugged like old friends, but with a wordless understanding that they would soon be more than friends. Could there be a more fantastical entertainment on a warm, clear night in May than this beloved play of the Bard? Brett was regal in robes of laminated gold and a tall feathered headdress as Theseus, Duke of Athens. The audience was most appreciative. After the show Joan was waiting outside the theatre for him.

"I'm so glad to see you, darling!" he exclaimed. "Where are you staying?"

"Well the summer crowds are not here yet, so I got a room at the same Inn where you are."

"Wonderful! Come, let's walk together," and they set out down the dark street, half expecting Puck to jump down from the occasional lamppost. Maybe he did.

They had not yet reached the intersection with Ontario Street before he stopped, turned her toward him, and took her in his arms, running his fingers through her long hair and kissing her. It was an impulse, but not an ill-considered one. For the benefit of later interviewers, he would always say that he and Joan were soul mates. They shared a birthday, so perhaps it was in the stars. Joan looked up at him, her eyes wide and serious. Having come to know Jeremy however briefly, she understood that here was so much more than a handsome man, more than one tends to expect of someone so attractive. He was a wonderful, warm, intelligent person. Before there could be any misapprehension, she reached up, kissing him right back—the first kiss of a romance, the blessed joy of mutuality affirmed! He held her tightly, feeling something he had not felt for a very long time: that he had a friend in this world.

Adjoining the Queen's Inn is the Boar's Head, a traditional English pub, and it was still open, so they went in for a nightcap. He had a gin and tonic, she ordered a sherry, and they took a booth. It was late and few other patrons remained. He had snipped one of the roses she brought him, and it was wilting in the buttonhole of his lapel.

"You must be a mind reader, Joan; the rose is my favorite flower. My mother kept a beautiful garden at home," he told her, "with lots of red rose bushes. All summer long, she would fill the house with them." Joan listened quietly as he went on describing his mother. "She was such a special person, fun loving, generous; the best mother, caring, nurturing, kind, strong."

In this loving portrait, his attachment was evident. Joan adored his voice, his accent; he was so, well, so *English*. "How old were you when your mother died?" she asked him.

"I had just turned 26. My son had just been born." He started to get emotional. "I was so angry!" and clearly he still was.

"I understand." Now Joan's eyes brimmed with tears. "How unbearable!"

Jeremy stopped then, touched by her empathy. "Dear me, look what I've done!" He reached over with a napkin and daubed the tears from her cheeks, feeling an irrepressible need to comfort her and thus himself. "Joanie darling," he said, downing the remainder of his drink and standing up, "I have a suite, and there is a skylight above the sitting room. Why don't we go up and see if the moon his risen?"

He didn't wait for an answer. He took her hand and pulled her up; then with his arm around her shoulders, led the way to the elevator.

* * *

Here we might reiterate, at the risk of belaboring the obvious, that what transpires between two people in a committed relationship can never be known for certain, and in this case no one involved even wrote a memoir. But more than one source indicates that Jeremy Brett broke up with Gary Bond in 1976, around the same time that he met Joan Wilson. Had Bond and Brett been drifting apart over time? Had they grown incompatible, restless, bored? We have no reason to believe that either of them stopped caring for the other, but based on what we do know of Jeremy Brett, we should be allowed to surmise that he was not the kind of man who would string someone along. He did not equivocate with respect to his affections, for example, with his first wife Anna, by whose own account he reported to her of the romance in Montreux. So when he fell in love in this precipitate, unforeseen manner with Joan Wilson he would have been honest with Gary.

It was awhile, however, before he returned to London. Joan had another project for him.[110] It was called *Piccadilly Circus*, a monthly anthology of British drama, comedy, and variety, and she wanted Brett as the host. So when he was done in Stratford, he returned to Boston. There were fourteen installments, but as the production was already in the works, they would have been able to film several of his introductions at once.

While he was back in Boston he was able to meet Joan's two children, Caleb, the eldest, home from his college out west, and Rebekah, off from Marblehead High School for the summer. The natural awkwardness of adolescents upon being introduced to the gentleman friend of their mother would have evaporated as fast as dew in the Boston heat; because Jeremy was exactly that, a gentleman and a friend, with a genuine, caring interest in whomever he met, but especially in these two young people. To Joan as to any mother this unequivocal embrace of her children vindicated all her earlier impressions of the man.

By the time she drove him to the airport to fly home, Jeremy had been away for some months. They parted with a kiss, a long hug, but having discovered such an uncanny connection between them, no sadness, just understanding. Both he and Joan thrived on work, and he had engagements awaiting in London.

On the long trans-Atlantic flight, he studied the part of Basil in *The Picture of Dorian Gray*, which he would be playing for the BBC Play of the Month. He had played Dorian for them in 1963, but was now a bit old for the role. A very young Peter Firth would have the lead, and John Gielgud would portray Lord Henry, the self-indulgent hedonist who corrupts Dorian and represents Oscar Wilde's clever embodiment of the Devil himself. The screenplay was written by John Osborne, adapted from Wilde's novel published in 1890; it was Wilde's only novel.

Basil is the artist who paints Dorian, falling in love with him at the same time. Osborne's script emphasizes this homosexual attraction more than the original. Dorian is not responsive to Basil's confession of love, but they remain friends, until Dorian murders him in front of the hideously altered portrait. Ironical that Brett should have had this role at that particular time.

Let us propose merely for the sake of this narrative that Gary Bond was still living at the house in Notting Hill when Jeremy returned from the States. He may have known about the new relationship with Joan Wilson in the same way she would know of him, through the grapevine at the various British television studios.

Jeremy took a cab home from Heathrow; Gary was working. The house was eerily still, haunted by the Hound of Heaven, a mustiness mingling the smells of damp dust, tanning lotion, and cigarette ash. His housemate must have enjoyed the summer was Jeremy's passing thought. He was too exhausted to prepare dinner, so he took the last beer from the refrigerator and sat in the armchair to wait for Gary. They would go to the Prince Albert.

"Jeremy, at last, my god, I've missed you!" cried Gary, bursting in exuberantly.

Jeremy stood up, grateful for the welcome, and they embraced. "It's good to be home," he could honestly say. Straight away they were off to the pub for supper, over which they engaged in the kind of small talk that belies the strong undercurrent of a serious issue.

"So Jeremy, how was Canada?"

"Absolutely delightful! Stratford is a lovely little town. But darling, what have you been up to all this time, besides neglecting the feather duster and tanning yourself on the veranda?"

Gary laughed, then defending himself, "Well between television parts, I did get over to Cornwall with some mates from the studio, hiking the cliffs, swimming in the ocean. That was fun." Awkward silence punctuated the conversation, and Jeremy intuited that his partner of the past many years already knew. "I heard that Joan Wilson got her claws into you," was Gary's opening salvo.

"Really. What's being said?"

"Some people believe it's just a career move on your part."

"That's ridiculous," Jeremy scowled, "and what do you believe, Gary?"

"Whatever you tell me, dear fellow."

"Come on, let's go home." The pub was no place to play this scene. It was a pleasant late summer night for the short walk, but once home they stayed inside in the living room. Jeremy poured them each a sherry and stood by the mantel of the fireplace while Gary sat on the sofa. "I know you will struggle to understand this," Jeremy began, "but when I met Joan there was such an immediate sense of familiarity. We both felt it, a natural, spontaneous connection, and when she came up to Stratford to see me play Oberon, well . . . I'm sorry, Gary, so sorry!"

Gary was no longer looking at him, but sat forward holding his head in his hands. "I can't believe you are attracted to a woman!" He was choking back tears.

"Oh Gary, that's unworthy of you." Jeremy refilled their glasses, sat by Gary on the sofa, and lit a cigarette. "I love her. I can't explain it."

Then the tears came, quietly. Not that Gary had not seen this coming, but with Jeremy there in the flesh, the ache of longing, the pain of this loss, surfaced. Jeremy, choking on the lump in his own throat, put his arm around Gary's shoulders, but it was his turn to be rebuffed. Gary stood up. "I'll look for a new place tomorrow," and he went upstairs to bed.

Jeremy took his sherry and his cigarette out to the veranda and sat in the dark, alone but for a terrible, heavy sadness. He thought of his Hound of Heaven, who had spent so much time there in his last days. The loneliness and now the weight of hurting a man he still and would always love felt crushing. But in a glimmer of reason, after chain smoking through a whole pack, he knew that being young and good looking, Gary would surely find someone else to love before long.[111]

* * *

Even when laws are changed relating to homosexuality, the discomfiting aspects of dealing with bias are hardly eliminated. With no clear way to discern who is or is not intolerant, the gay person must be circumspect with everyone, conceal his orientation for both personal and professional reasons. The kind of information that would be readily available about a heterosexual relationship may therefore not exist for gays. Someone knew these things, for example, whether Brett and Bond were still living together, or had broken up before Joan came along. We know from their own accounts that Jeremy Brett and Joan Wilson were drawn to one another from their first meeting. It is probable, all skepticism aside, that Brett was bisexual. He was then 43, and we should begin to suspect also that his mood disorder may have begun to affect his personal life. Was he having manic states, periods of deep depression? Often it is only in retrospect that episodes or traits regarded as eccentric are seen to be early signs, and only recalled because the condition has worsened noticeably and dangerously.

But in 1977, Jeremy was newly in love. He returned to Canada in the operetta *Robert and Elizabeth* as Robert Browning, a role he had just performed in Guildford, England, before coming to Ottawa. This musical setting of *The Barretts of Wimpole Street*, the 1931 play depicting the romance of the Brownings, was first produced in London in 1964. The music was written by contemporary Australian composer Ron Gainer with lyrics by Ronald Millar. The score, while not quite measuring up to Franz Lehar, has a memorable love duet, "I Know Now," with beautiful and novel harmonies at its climax.

For Brett at this time, there could have been no better role in which to pour out his heart in song every night. It may well be that Joan came up from Boston to see him, and that they were both swept up in the story and the music, because it was 1977 when they were married, in a civil ceremony. There was apparently no question about it. They meshed perfectly and reveled in one another. In Joan, with her strength and independence, Jeremy once again had an anchor in his life, a refuge; and for her, a believer in the occult, it was a stroke of fate to have found this bond. By no means would theirs be a settled life; neither wanted that. Joan was moored in Boston, but often traveled to London or wherever her job might take her; and Brett at this stage of his career found himself accepting work on both sides of the Atlantic. They loved each other in no small part it seems for this mutual dispensation to pursue a shared calling.

While he was still in the States, he took on a television role for CBS, playing the Captain in an episode of *The Young Dan'l Boone*.[112] Then it was back to England for the BBC anthology series *Supernatural*, in which he was Mr. Nightingale, heavily made-up as an old man. The connecting theme to the eight episodes was the "Club of the Damned" to which prospective members were inducted on the basis of how frightening a horror story they were able to tell, death being the price of failure.

Of course, the first person he wanted to see in London was his son, so it was a pleasant surprise when no sooner had he returned to the house in Notting Hill than he had a call from David who had just turned eighteen in August.

"David, how good to hear your voice, son!"

"Yours too, Dad, welcome back. I read that congratulations are in order." Jeremy had sent a card from Ottawa to say he had met up with that wonderful Bostonian again, but he had not had the chance to tell David of their marriage. David however loved reading about his father in the papers.

"News travels faster than I do. Thank you, son. We need to get together, don't we?"

"Definitely. You know we're living in Fulham now." Anna had taken a small house there the year before.

"Why don't we meet for lunch at the Meridiana tomorrow?" Jeremy suggested.

And so they did. Jeremy arrived first and sat waiting with a glass of wine, ruminating. The place reminded him of that disastrous party some years previous for Robert Stevens's fortieth birthday. But soon David came, amazingly grown up and resembling a young version of his grandfather, Colonel Huggins. Jeremy stood up and they embraced.

"My god, son, look at you, a man already!" Jeremy beamed, and David blushed. "Sit, sit! A glass of wine?" He caught the waiter's eye and signaled for another glass.

"So, Dad, tell me about Joan. This was so sudden."

"Indeed. It is most unusual to meet someone and to know at once you belong together."

"But how will it work being on opposite sides of the ocean?"

"She comes to London often, and I will be traveling more. I think maybe that's why we married, in order to feel we are together even when we cannot be. Of course what sealed the deal was the way she takes her tea."

"No! Really? Cream and sugar?"

"That and her black Mustang with the license plate WITCH," and they laughed. This would be hard for David to explain to any of his friends with whom he had shared the entertaining irony that his father was gay.

They ordered lunch, and as they ate David told his father about the move, and the new house.

"It sounds awfully small," Jeremy commented.

"Very," David said, and then with some hesitance, "I need to ask you something, Dad."

"Yes? Go on," said Jeremy, slicing into his London broil.

"May I come to live with you?"[113] It is not usual in adolescence for a boy to identify more strongly with his father, yet the request was unexpected. Anna of course thought their son was still too young for that much freedom.

"I would love that, David! You can have the loft; it is a flat unto itself. I will appreciate the company." Gary had moved out, and Robert Stephens, who seemed incapable of living alone without serious depression, was safely ensconced with a gay couple of their acquaintance. "But what about your mother?"

"She's too busy to miss me, doing a play, plus television and radio, and she sees her analyst three mornings a week, before work."

Jeremy sat back, holding his wine glass and pressing his index finger against his lips, a mannerism that was becoming a habit whenever he was listening intently and thinking. He reached into a pants pocket for his house key and handed it to his son. "Here, lad. I keep a spare by the back door, and I will have another key made. You can move in whenever it suits you."

"Thanks, Dad!" David exclaimed, his excitement evident.

Jeremy grasped David's shoulder and shook him affectionately. They ordered dessert and coffee. "So, you still like peppermint ice cream," Dad remarked, and they smiled. "Do you ever see your cousin Martin?"

"Rarely. He's become somewhat of a delinquent, smoking and loitering on Wimbledon Common, in trouble with the law.[114] I feel sorry for him, without his father."

"Yes, it is very sad." Jeremy thought to himself about poor Daphne, but she was warned. "And you, son, do you still want to be a writer?"

"It's a tossup now between that and art."

"Ah, taking after your Uncle Michael! Perhaps you will do both."[115]

"But what's next for you, Dad?" David was reluctant when it came to talking about himself.

"I have the opportunity to play Count Dracula on stage next year. I think I will do it."

"That's fantastic! You'll be the best Dracula ever, I know it."

"It means going to Los Angeles; not my cup of tea, but I need to spread my wings, professionally."

"Angel wings or bat wings?" David quipped, and they laughed at the irony of going to the City of Angels to play a vampire.

"Joanie will be here for Christmas, David. You'll have a chance to meet her." Jeremy lit the inevitable cigarette, offering one to his son, who declined. "I know, let's have a party! We'll invite a few friends, have champagne, maybe fix up a scavenger hunt. It will be fun!" David was dubious of that suggestion, but didn't let on.

Thus as the year waned, a time when he was often depressed, Jeremy was unusually lighthearted, his son at home with him, and the chance to be with Joan again. She offered to stay at the Dorchester to allay any awkwardness but Jeremy would not hear of it. This time it was he waiting excitedly at the airport to meet her. Just the sight of her brought him a sense of calm relief; and tired as she was from the flight, she fell gratefully into his arms, which lifted her easily off the floor. He kept his arm around her, and they walked in step out into the cold December fog to hail a cab.

The house was decorated for Christmas. He and David had put up a tree and hung a wreath on the door. A fire was warming the living room, where David sat studying an eggnog recipe, for the party of course.

"David darling, please meet my wife Joanie," his father said. We will not presume to imagine what young David's first impression was, unless perhaps that she really was *American*.

"I am so glad to know you, David. Your father speaks lovingly of you," Joan began. "You may call me Joan," she continued, sensitive that the manner of address would be a question.

"Welcome, Joan. I have heard high praise of you as well," and they shook hands. She joined him on the sofa as Jeremy took her bag up to the bedroom. David then began telling her about the party planned for the coming weekend. "I'm thinking of making eggnog. Do you like it?"

"Love it! I use lots of vanilla and nutmeg. If you want, I'll make it for you."

"Would you? That would be wonderful."

Jeremy returned and lay another log on the fire. "Are the tea things still out, David?" he asked.

"In fact, I just made a pot before you came. I'll fetch the tray," and he went to the kitchen.

"What a dear young man, Jeremy," Joan remarked.

"He is that, isn't he?" David came shortly carrying a very crowded and heavy tray, which he placed on a butler's table near the sofa, where they all three now sat together. It was not high tea at the Savoy, but there were biscuits and shortbreads, and warm slices of stollen, the smell of which mingled with the pungency of wood smoke. A genial mood settled on them, and Joan offered to pour, unaware how closely she was being observed. When they each had their cups, she added to hers a teaspoon of sugar, then cream from the pitcher. She did not notice Jeremy smile at his son over her head, nor see them wink at each other.

* * *

"Where shall I hide the toilet brush, Dad?" It was the day of the party, and David was helping to prepare for the scavenger hunt. Joan had gone to lunch with a colleague from the BBC. His father looked around.

"Put it in that potted plant by the front door."

"And the nail?"

"The crystal chandelier in the dining room," Jeremy instructed. "I hope you're keeping a list." After a dozen items had been hidden about the living area, he waxed nostalgic. "This reminds me of Parish Sunday at the Grange in Berkswell, hidden treasures in the shrubbery, a bonfire at the end of the day. Your grandmother was a genius at entertaining. Oh, the parties we had there!"

"Well, Granddad always used to say she lives on in you, Dad."

"I know, I remember," Jeremy mumbled hoarsely, tearing up all of a sudden.

"And I love to hear your stories about her," David continued, though now his father suspected he was being disingenuous.

"Come on, we still have to take out the stemware and the punch bowl, the silver one, for the eggnog."

The guests were friends in the theatre world. Robert Stephens would have been there, doubtless with his new flame, Patricia Quinn, the young Irish actress from *The Rocky Horror Show*. Perhaps Jeremy's bridge group was included. Penelope Keith, the comedic actress, had gotten him into the card game, and the other two in the foursome, according to Stephens's memoir, were actor Charles Kay, and the aging grande dame of character actresses, Patience Collier.[116] It was a late evening, after dinner party with desserts, plenty of champagne, Joan's eggnog, and Christmas music on the stereo, which was drowned out by laughter once the scavenger hunt got underway.[117] Jeremy leaned on the mantel, sipping his champagne, laughing, and giving clever clues, though no one ever found the toilet brush. Joan had a marvelous time, and those who did not already know her were impressed with her sense of humor, her savoire faire, and her eggnog. David especially, to his father's relief, found her to be an amazing woman, easy to be with, confident and likable.

That Christmas was the merriest for Jeremy in a long time, with Joan there and David. But when 1978 arrived, she returned to Boston and he made plans to go to Los Angeles. Before leaving home however, he accepted a small part in *The Medusa Touch*, a movie starring Richard Burton as John Millar, who uses psychokinetic abilities against people who have wronged him. It was based on a novel, a psychological thriller by Peter Van Greenaway. Brett played Edward Parrish, a playboy actor who runs off with Millar's estranged wife. Of course, he and the woman are then killed mysteriously.

Then Brett was off to America to take on Count Voivode Dracula[118] in a revival of the 1924 play adapted by Hamilton Deane from the 1897 Gothic horror novel by Bram Stoker. There had been a revival just the year before on Broadway at the Martin Beck Theatre, with Frank Langella, who then moved on to star in a film version. The Hollywood show was staged at the Ahmanson Theatre with sets by Edward Gorey, artist of the macabre. The Ahmanson had had ties with the National Theatre Company of Great Britain in the past, but we found no indication that this production came about through such a connection. In fact it toured from Los Angeles to Denver, San Diego, San Francisco, and finally Chicago in February of 1979.

The part was strenuous for Brett, who was no longer twenty-five. His thirty pound cape notoriously gave him tendonitis—"Dracula elbow"—as he flung it around night after night. He also complained of having to roar a good deal, which was hard on his throat. Then there was the love scene, where he lifts his 110-pound heroine and carries her to bed. The effect on the audience of this extremely sensuous scene amazed Brett, as he told Jeff Lyon, a reporter for the Chicago Tribune: "I think it affects women terribly. To be swept off their feet, to be possessed, is their wildest dream. Men got an enormous fizz from it too." In the same interview he explained his interpretation of the role. He decided to play it "as if Dracula were in love," basing this on the script where the Count says, "I'll set my Lucy above all else." Like his idol Olivier, he brought originality to a part by going directly to the creative source, avoiding any imitation of a prior portrayal.

As physically demanding as the role was, however, the more difficult aspect of playing a vampire would have been psychological for an actor with a mood disorder, and trained in the method.

Because he would be in the States for an indefinite period, Jeremy had taken a house in Hollywood Hills. His ex-wife Anna had come to California to see her father, who was still living in Los Angeles with Dorothy. Anna needed his signature to get a green card allowing her to work in America. Jeremy offered to put her up, and she accepted, since the prospect of driving in that sprawling town was daunting.

She obtained the required signature, but the visit was far from pleasant. Dorothy kept her from being alone with her ailing father, and it turned out to be the last time she was to see him. Yet even more disturbing was Jeremy's behavior, which she describes in her memoir. Obviously it is a retrospective report, but she implies that even at the time she knew that he was "extremely troubled." We might question certain details of her description, for example that he was "embarrassingly generous." Perhaps she was easily embarrassed. That he drove her to the airport wearing a Mickey Mouse hat? This was Hollywood; he was trying to fit in. But one sentence justifies her concern and demands our attention: "He hardly slept, and could not be still, and his restlessness was disturbing."

In a bestselling classic on the subject of bipolar disorder, Dr. Kay Jamison gives her firsthand account of the illness. Not only has she struggled with a serious case all her life, but she made the study of it her life's work. She has been fortunate that her illness is controlled with medication, and indeed when she wrote the memoir, *An Unquiet Mind*, in 1995, she was a professor of psychiatry at Johns Hopkins University. As of this writing, she continues to teach and practice there and remains a leading authority on mood disorders.

Where the average person thinks of mood swings as between happiness and sadness, the states Dr. Jamison describes are a misery at either extreme. She tells, for example, of "white manias" that bring "feelings of ease, intensity, power . . . euphoria," but also of "black manias, with their agitated, ferocious, and savage sides." Surprisingly, she writes that these manic states were to her far worse than her deepest depressions, bringing a loss of control over her thoughts and behaviors, the terrifying sense of going mad. Very successful people can be bipolar, often self-medicating with alcohol when depression comes, but firmly refusing to give up the euphoria, energy, creativity, charisma of the highs. We may know such individuals, those who will not acknowledge a problem, who seek a diagnosis only when the illness worsens, and even then will not take medication for it.

Imagine the kind of person who dominates a room full of people: outgoing, confident, convivial, seeming to radiate an invisible field of positive energy attracting others to him. Then imagine he is over six feel tall, possesses the most astonishing good looks, and is blessed with a deep, resonant voice whether speaking or singing. Depending on the keenness of one's imagination, that is a vivid picture of Jeremy Brett in the prime of his life and the height of his acting career. In hindsight, he was bipolar; and we must reluctantly submit that even while he remained well compensated to use the technical term, there would have been signs. But pertinent to our story at this point is that according to Dr. Jamison, "Decreased sleep is both a symptom of mania and a cause."

With all the traveling he was doing, crossing not just the ocean but then the continent and back again, Jeremy's diurnal patterns would have been frequently interrupted. The consequent lack of sleep, added to the strain of playing the diabolical Count Dracula for an extended period, may well have caused manic states, though Anna's is the only such report we found. He was of course electrifying as Dracula, which in itself may have been owed to a manic phase. When not too extreme, such a mood may give the individual a most magnetic charisma.

But Hollywood was not without its comic relief. While he was there, he was nabbed by casting for an episode of *The Incredible Hulk* and also of *Hart to Hart*, which starred Robert Wagner and Stefanie Powers as amateur detectives Jonathan and Jennifer Hart. The types of roles available in American television must have seemed silly to a classical actor like Brett, and this was of course the very condition his wife Joan was devoted to changing through public broadcasting.

When Dracula had its final run in Chicago at the Shubert Theatre, we would like to suppose that Joan took the opportunity to see it.[119] There can be no doubt that Jeremy Brett was thrilling as the Count; and with her love of the occult and of her husband, she would have to be the most thrilled member of the audience, attending every performance. Her son Caleb may have come from Grinnell College to see it, proud and excited to have his stepfather playing this popular character, and to such acclaim. Any possible jealousy in that relationship would have been nullified by Jeremy's kindness and openness.

The night Joan arrived, she came backstage with roses for the dressing room, and Jeremy embraced her with a big sigh, conveying better than words their mutual belonging. They held each other so long that the makeup and wardrobe girls were exchanging smiles and raising eyebrows.

"Meet me here after the performance, darling. I have a suite across the avenue." He was staying at the Palmer House, an opulent and historic hotel famous for the fresco, done by a French artist, on the ceiling of the lobby.[120]

"Yes I know, dear." Indeed she had already had roses delivered to the hotel room, ordered a bottle of champagne chilled, and a fire laid in the fireplace. To find that many red roses in Chicago in February was no small accomplishment; Joan was a resourceful woman.

It was late of course when the show was over and they were able to go to the hotel. They were tired but animated by the play and by being together. Jeremy opened the door to the suite, then picked Joan up in his arms and carried her in, pushing the door closed with his foot. He did not set her down, but began kissing her on the neck. Even as a chill shot through her whole body, Joan laughed.

"Oh Jeremy, if we are going to replay that love scene, I am going to need some champagne!" She was also disciplined.

"I'm sorry, Joanie. The Count is a terribly gripping fellow," he said, putting her down.

"Hard to let go?"

"Yes." They shed their wraps and their shoes, opened the champagne, lit the fire, and sat together on the settee. Joan cuddled close to him, her legs over his lap.

"You are the best Dracula, Jeremy," she began, "much better than that Italian," referring to Langella. "But I'm glad this is the last stop on the tour. It is too stressful for you I think. You must get back home to England." Her words of concern were sweet balm to him.

"You read my mind as always, Joanie. I am going back soon. The BBC has offered me Maxim deWinter in their miniseries of *Rebecca*."

"Good God, darling, that's the dream part! You were born for it, you know."

"But listen to this: my ex-wife wants to play Mrs. Danvers."

"Anna Massey? Well, why not, you're still friends."

"The producer thinks she's too young."

"No, no, makeup, costume, she would be very good." He filled their glasses, and they sat sipping as the night wore on. Feeling the combined effects of fatigue and alcohol, he began slipping into that love scene from the play; and this time, feeling the same effects, she succumbed.

Joan fell into a deep sleep, but just hours later—the middle of the night—she was awakened. The light was on, and Jeremy sat up in a chair smoking and intermittently getting up to pace. She got up and went to him as he stood by the window looking out at the lights of the city.

"Are you all right, darling?" She put her arm around him.

"Oh yes, I've been having trouble sleeping, that's all. I'm sorry I woke you."

"I know a bar up the street that's probably still open," she suggested.

"If this were London . . ."

"I know what you mean," and she did. "I'm afraid America doesn't really suit you, Jeremy." He took her in his arms; she always knew just what to say. "I could call the night clerk and have him bring up some tea." He smiled at the idea.

"No, darling, nothing, thank you."

"Come to bed then. Let me see if I can help you," and she took charge of him. He lay down and she gave him a back rub, starting at his neck. The muscles along his spine were like steel cables as she kneaded them. When finally she felt them soften and relax, heard his breathing to become slow and regular, she turned off the light. As Count Dracula, he made her deliciously afraid of him; lying beside him now, she was afraid *for* him.

* * *

We must digress here lest we leave the utterly false impression that Jeremy Brett was a dour fellow. To the contrary, the word he later used himself to describe his personality was "ebullient." Throughout his career, moreover, there were press reports of his off-stage antics, which may or may not have risen to the level of manic. For example, when he was at the Stratford Festival in Canada in 1976, one source[121] quotes a young actress recalling, "For much of that season, a group of us younger actors would sit in the pub of the Queen's Hotel while Jeremy, eyes twinkling, elegant fingers flying, Borsalino hat tilted rakishly atop his movie star head, held court." Did she forget the word "fedora," or was it really the famous fedora of the Borsalino hat company, made of felt from Belgian rabbit fur?

Then Jeff Lyon, who interviewed Brett for the Chicago Tribune when *Dracula* played there, apparently averred that "at a recent cocktail party a woman begged him to bite her neck and he consented, repeating the gesture several times over the evening." And there was of course that Mickey Mouse hat.

Still, Brett must have welcomed returning to England to film *Rebecca*, adapted by Hugh Whitemore from the classic novel written in 1938 by Daphne du Maurier when she was 31. Maxim de Winter, owner of the Manderly estate in Cornwall, was indeed the role he was born to play: gallant, aristocratic, genteel. The woman of the title, his deceased wife, was beautiful but malevolent; presumed to have been drowned in her small sailboat during a storm, she was murdered, we learn, by Maxim after considerable and brazen provocation. In a clever literary device, the name of the young woman telling the story is never mentioned. She is played by Joanna David, with just the right girlishness. The paid companion of a wealthy American woman, she is swept off her feet by Maxim in Monte Carlo, then back in Manderly, undermined by the sinister housekeeper Mrs. Danvers. Anna Massey did get that part, and was most convincingly malicious.

The location for the four-part BBC production was Caerhays Castle, a half mile from the tiny village of St. Michael Caerhays in Cornwall. The castellated mansion dates to the thirteenth century and overlooks Porthluney Cove on the English Channel. It has been privately owned by the Williams family since 1854, but is on occasion used by film makers; the gardens are extensive and renowned. What a pleasant place to spend the spring! And Anna does write that the filming took three months. The vintage 1930s cars and costumes were wonderfully congenial for Brett, who got to wear the fedora, the cashmere scarf, the driving gloves, though it was not just his appearance that outshone past actors in the role. He was simply the best Maxim ever, better even than Olivier, who was in the 1940 Hitchcock film with Joan Fontaine. In the proposal scene, for instance, where Maxim stuns the unnamed heroine with an offer of marriage so far above her social station, Brett's uniquely expressive face reflects the perfect nuance of the upper-class gentleman, first fearing rebuff, then joy of reciprocated affection. The BBC production was of course picked up for Masterpiece Mystery in America, a series created by Joan Wilson.

Anna Massey recounts just one complication due to their relationship. During rehearsals she was enraged to discover that Jeremy had given their son David a motorbike, knowing that she was against it. Their interactions became a bit chilly at that point, but very soon David had taken a spill, incurring a minor injury to his leg. The bike was soon given up.

Later that spring, Jeremy was contacted by his brother Patrick concerning a parcel of land that the brothers had retained when the Grange was sold. An adjacent neighbor had approached him about purchasing it, and Patrick felt the time was right if they all agreed. Jeremy was amenable to it as were John and Michael, so they arranged to meet again with the family solicitor in Birmingham, who would see to the details.

While they were together, it became clear that they all felt at least some of the money from the sale ought to go toward a memorial of some sort. There already was the plaque in the Lady Chapel of St. John the Baptist Church in Berkswell, which they had donated in honor of their parents. They could contribute to the parish charities, but Jeremy leaned toward something more permanent. John then suggested a lych-gate for the churchyard. The lych-gate is a roofed archway standing at the churchyard entrance. In Medieval times the first part of a funeral rite would be performed there, with the deceased resting on a bier under it. It is still used when a burial takes place to lead the funeral procession into the churchyard. John would consult with the rector, Reverend Dingle,[122] and Patrick and Michael would look into construction.

Arrangements were expedited and a date of Sunday, 24 June, was set for the dedication. Reverend Dingle, who had been the rector since the year after Colonel Huggins death, was able to enlist the Rev. John Gibbs, bishop of Coventry, to do the honors following morning service. There had been few opportunities to visit his hometown after the Grange was sold, so Jeremy was staying in Coventry. He drove down early and parked near the church, leaving his suit jacket and tie in the car and taking the two bouquets of red roses he had procured in Coventry to place on the graves of his parents. He was impressed with the lych-gate, already installed, with its memorial plaque which read: "This lych-gate is dedicated to the glory of God in memory of William and Elizabeth Huggins on June 24th 1979 by the Lord Bishop of Coventry." This was not the loose gate that long ago Nanny Ellen would close as she passed, but a substantial construction interrupting a stone wall, with two wide walls also of stone. The roof had four gabled sides meeting at the top. As he walked through it into the churchyard, the morning sun was sending long shafts of light through the trees, causing the dewy lawn to glisten. Together with the sweet scent of roses, the damp summer air suddenly made him light headed. Coming to his mother's headstone, he fell to his knees. He laid his head on the grass, as if he would hug the ground, and soon the tears came, surprising him with their intensity after twenty years. How he missed her strength, the deep well of her love from which he drew confidence, courage!

The beauty of tears is that to a degree they may assuage the grief they vent, so Jeremy had begun to compose himself just as John, the Reverend Huggins, approached in his clericals, alarmed at the sight of his brother prostrate on their mother's grave, reminding him of that terrible day at Jeremy's house in Chelsea when he had to break the news that their mother had been killed. He extended Jeremy his hand and helped him up.

"Are you all right, little brother?" Jeremy was by no means little, but his eldest sibling was the closest thing to a parent left to him. They embraced, unusual for two proper British gentlemen, but not for Elizabeth's sons.

"This place, John, the sweetness, the sadness . . ." Jeremy moaned.

"I know, I know. I had my moment yesterday, inside, Geoffrey found me—the rector, a lovely, kind man." John stopped, turning to face Jeremy and look him in the eye. "My god, it's good to have you back in England! We miss you here," John declared, "even as we are sinfully proud of your wonderful success."

"Thank you, John," Jeremy smiled, near fully restored by these gratifying sentiments.

"Come, we'd best go in before we are set upon by your fans," and they walked back through the lych-gate arm in arm. But before Jeremy could fetch his jacket and tie, one of his biggest fans drove up in a chauffeured Bentley. It was Mrs. Wheatley, who was then eighty-one and still living at the Hall. She stepped out of the car and greeted them warmly.

"Jeremy dear boy, how good to see you back where you belong!" She offered her hand, which he kissed, always gallant as expected. "But what a triumph as Dracula! I read that you were dazzling, putting that Hungarian to shame."

"Langella? Isn't he Italian?"

"Who? No, no, Bela Lugosi.[123] There I go dating myself. Come to think of it, John, he played the part the year you were born, the same year as my daughter Ann. Your parents were so excited! There was rejoicing at Holly Lodge." As we have noted, Christobel always had the right words. "I must tell you, gentlemen," she went on, "that the generosity of their sons is of itself a tribute to your parents, but to have Bishop Gibbs here this morning to dedicate this lych-gate to their memory brings us all such joy." Whereupon the six bells of St. John the Baptist Church of Berkswell rang out, seeming to underscore this avowal while calling the faithful to Sunday worship.

"Run get your coat and tie, Jeremy," his brother said.

Then Mrs. Wheatley called after him, "Come to tea this afternoon, dear, before you leave!"

"Yes, ma'am, thank you!" He was the last of the four she could still count on to accept such an invitation, and she was just the kind of gracious lady he adored.

The service was well attended. Uncle Richard and Aunt Anne were there from their mother's side, and Uncle Leslie, retired from the Stowe School, on their father's. The dedication took place in the churchyard afterwards in fair summer weather, Jeremy's red roses standing out against the headstones and framed by the lych-gate.

He did stop at the Hall for tea on his way home to London and reminisced with Mrs. Wheatley about such things as Parish Sunday, which had just passed. "It wasn't at all like the old days," she said, "not enough Scouts!" He told her about Joan and about filming *Rebecca*, which she promised to watch with great enthusiasm. She expressed concern about his traveling so much, and he assured her that he always slept on the plane, or at least tried. The widow was beginning to have health problems herself, but her daughter and son-in-law were a big help to her.[124] They parted as they always did, with another soft kiss of her hand as she easily wrested from him his promise not to forget his old hometown.

We like to think that Jeremy was able to stay in London at least until early August for his son's birthday. David turned twenty that year, and he had decided after all to study graphic design. While it was not fine arts, his Uncle Michael surely felt that at last he had an heir.

But then in 1980, it was back to Hollywood and the Ahmanson Theatre. Was it providential that Brett was slated to appear there in a Sherlockian pastiche? Not when we observe that so many actors, nearly all it seems, had been involved in productions of Sherlock Holmes stories since the first adaptation in 1899. Even his friend Robert had played the venerable sleuth in New York in 1975.

The play at the Ahmanson was titled *The Crucifer of Blood*, based loosely upon Conan Doyle's story *The Sign of Four*. Charlton Heston was Holmes and Brett had the role of Watson. The mystery, so familiar to Sherlock buffs, surrounds a killing over treasure purloined from the fort of Agra in colonial India. American Paul Giovanni, who was the same age as Brett, wrote the play.

Never lacking for work, Brett also took a part in the science fiction series *Battlestar Galactica* on the ABC network, no doubt while he was in Los Angeles for the play. The same year, for BBC Play of the Month, he appeared in the drawing room comedy *On Approval*, the 1926 play by Frederick Lonsdale, in which a vain, wealthy widow, Maria, invites her suitor Richard to her home in Scotland, promising to marry him if she still likes him after a month. Brett played George, Duke of Bristol, a mutual friend, with Penelope Keith, his bridge partner, as Maria. These two characters are spoiled aristocrats, who cannot tolerate each other, while Richard and a young woman named Helen, who loves George, are their more gentle and reasonable partners. In the end, a heavy snow begins to fall, and Richard and Helen decide to run off in the only car, leaving the Duke and Maria without transportation, snowed in at her Scottish manse. Dressed only in robe and slippers, the Duke runs out after the car, slipping and sliding in the snow. But he and Maria are stuck for at least a month, their forced togetherness perhaps instilling some maturity.

In a very different role, Brett played David Malcolm, the psychopathic killer in *The Secret of Seagull Island* for ITC Entertainment, a feature length film based on the series of the same name. This Jekyll and Hyde character preys on blind women, and the sister of one of his victims comes to the island pretending blindness in order to trap him.

The next two years, 1981 to 1982, were extremely busy for Jeremy Brett, frenetic if we dare say it. In the spring of 1981, he was back in America to appear in the musical revue *Noel*, a tribute to Noel Coward and his songs, which played at the Goodspeed Opera House in East Haddam, Connecticut. Surely here was a chance for he and Joan to be together for a while, because he also took on a role in an NBC film, *Madam X*, based on a French play written by Alexandre Bisson in 1908. Tuesday Weld starred as the tragic heroine, thrown into a life of depravity by a jealous husband. Twenty years later, accused of murdering her lover, she is defended in court by her grown daughter, an attorney who is ignorant that her defendant, "Madam X," is her mother.

Brett's role as Dr. Terrence Keith was limited. His character is the physician who treats Madam X in hospital following an overdose. He falls in love, and in several ensuing scenes attempts to romance her out of her depression, without success.

A much more significant undertaking the same year awaited Brett back in England, and that was *The Good Soldier*, which was being produced by Granada Television in Manchester. As Captain Edward Ashburnham, he had a chance to play his own father, except that this character is a serial philanderer, who leaves a trail of suicides ending in his own. It was adapted from the novel written in 1915 by the prolific British author Ford Madox Ford. As in the book, the story is told by an American, John Dowell, played by Robin Ellis, who along with his wife Florence has befriended the Captain and Mrs. Ashburnham at a health spa in Nauheim, Germany. The two couples meet there every summer.

The production was filmed at various lush locations in Germany and England, including Nauheim itself, a German town known for its healthful mineral waters and thermal springs. Opulent Croxteth Hall in Liverpool, the perfect setting for period drama, served as the interiors of the "Park Hotel" where patrons of the spa were accommodated. The Ashburnham estate in England was Stanway House in Gloucestershire, while the interiors of their manse, "Branshaw Teleragh," were filmed at Holker Hall, in Cartmel. Chetham's Library in Manchester stood in for Martin Luther's study in Marburg, Germany.

In the stylish dress of that prewar period, Brett portrayed the dashing, taciturn soldier to perfection. The Captain's wife, a punitive, self-righteous Irish Catholic, who goads and manipulates him, was played by Susan Fleetwood with a blend of emotional intensity and psychological subtlety. The story may have been somewhat autobiographical, motivated by Ford's own unhappy marriage; he separated from his wife and moved to France, where he took up with another woman.

The following year, 1982, Jeremy made a good many television appearances. He again played Robert Browning in a BBC film of the play *The Barretts of Wimpole Street* by Rudolf Besier, which premiered in 1930. We should recall that he was in a musical version of the same play in 1977. His costar in the film series was Jane Lapotaire, quite appropriately waifish for the sickly, oppressed Elizabeth Barrett, suffocated along with her eight siblings by a narcissistic father. Naturally Brett was at his most passionate in this role, as he woos and spirits her away to Italy.

Also for BBC, he was King Arthur in *Morte d'Arthur*, based on a fifteenth-century reworking of traditional Arthurian tales by Sir Thomas Morley. This film was part dance piece, staged reading, mime show, and drama, in which Arthur watches his kingdom collapse as his knights squabble over the guilt or innocence of Guinevere. Then Brett starred as Vincent Tumulty in a BBC drama called *The Last Visitor*, adapted from the 1953 novel *Sleeping Beauty* by British writer Elizabeth Taylor. It is set in a seaside town, and Tumulty is the last visitor remaining at season's end.

Yet another important role for Jeremy that year was in the series *Number 10*, produced by Yorkshire Television, which presented stories of Britain's more famous prime ministers. In the episode entitled "Bloodline," Brett appeared as William Pitt the Younger, whose father also served as prime minister in the late eighteenth century. The family had a history of hereditary mental illness, and the younger Pitt swears to his father on his deathbed that he will never have children. But then he falls deeply in love with a young woman who is equally passionate in her devotion to him. It is assumed that they will marry, but realizing that she would sacrifice her future motherhood because of his sworn promise, he turns her away, pretending cold indifference even as his own heart is breaking. It was a masterful portrayal of anguished renunciation.

But as Jeremy approached the age of fifty, looking back upon his acting success on stage and screen, he might have considered, like many another actor before him, that it was time to broaden his skills into directing and producing. Some actors have achieved this goal; the dynamic and masterful Laurence Olivier comes to mind, giving Brett all the more reason to believe he could do it. Other successful examples include Charlie Chaplin in the silent era, and Americans Clint Eastwood and Woody Allen. It is not difficult to assume that Joan would have encouraged this effort, being an executive producer herself. The idea was not unrealistic. Or was Brett having the delusions of grandeur that are symptomatic of manic depression?

Back in the States, Brett was Macbeth in what actors refer to superstitiously as "the Scottish play," for Century Home Video.[125] He had played Malcolm, a very different role, in London in 1960. This production, intended to be authentically Shakespearean, was filmed on a stage built to resemble that of the Globe, with costumes that also were appropriately primitive and an unusually hirsute Jeremy.

The director was Arthur Allan Seidelman, renowned for his extensive work in American television, but no Shakespeare. Jeremy was not credited as his assistant, yet at least one critic implied that he had a hand in directing the play. The interpretation was idiosyncratic, though still true to the text.

Brett portrayed Macbeth as a man driven mad by a guilty conscience, having been lured by the prophecies of the three witches, the "weird sisters," and lashed by his wife's ambition, fortifying his own, to commit evil deeds that exceed and corrupt his innate character. It was a most persuasive rendering of the part, completely consistent with Shakespeare's words. American actress Piper Laurie gave a very sensual version of Lady Macbeth, her body language alone giving fresh connotations to such lines as: "Come you spirits that tend on mortal thoughts, unsex me here. Stop up the access and passage to remorse." Macbeth then enters stage left, returning to Inverness from the battlefield and the strange prophetic encounter with the witches, and the scene of their greeting is ardent to the point of erotic.

By Act III he mocks and taunts her, but then embracing her from behind utters this poetry, clearly savoring every word: "Light thickens; and the crow makes wing to the rooky wood: good things of day begin to droop and drowse, whiles night's black agents to their preys do rouse." The speech exemplifies his relatively slower delivery, especially compared with the Americans in the cast, who seem to spew their lines as though they might otherwise forget them.

As the play progresses, Brett's Macbeth, tormented by terrifying hallucinations, is seen to slip into psychosis, signaled by the uncontrolled tics, the stiff paralytic gate, and before the last act a loud, screaming rage even at his wife, at whose bidding he has brought this guilty terror upon himself. In the famous soliloquy that begins, "Tomorrow and tomorrow and tomorrow," he delivers the ending with a loud snarl, "Life is but a walking shadow . . . a tale told by an idiot, *signifying nothing!*"

We are fortunate still to have access to so much of Jeremy Brett's work in film, though knowing of his later fate this *Macbeth* is quite unnerving. How much of his angry portrayal could be based on his personal experience of what Dr. Jamison called "black mania"? And we are moved to reflect on the many parts he had played dealing with mental derangement or demonic, occult themes, as in *Seagull Island*, *The Ferryman*, *Dracula*, even *Number 10*, and others. The combination of good looks and villainy in a character would seem to be a stock device for writers, although the sardonic effect of a good looking villain is lost over time as it becomes the stereotype.

While Brett may or may not have taken part in the direction of *Macbeth*, we know that he directed and produced *The Tempest* on stage in Toronto also in 1982, an ambitious undertaking for an actor without such experience. He played a rather young Prospero, the wizard who has learned to command the spirits while marooned with his daughter on an island for thirteen years. The play opens as Prospero's treacherous brother together with an entourage are shipwrecked on the island, and a complex drama ensues. The critics were not kind, but Brett continued to believe in his production and set about looking for the means to make a film of it.

* * *

At this point, readers may begin to wonder when our story will come to the role that made Jeremy Brett world famous, and we confess that the delay has not been unintentional. Just as we took care to provide the back story of Peter H. in the first two chapters, we have sought in this chapter to illuminate the many other attainments for which he might and should be remembered. Intelligent, insightful, gifted, original, as an actor he was more than a pretty face—because as a man he was more than an actor.

But now here we are, and we will propose that back in Manchester when he was working on *The Good Soldier*, he received a phone call at his suite in the Midland Hotel, an old Edwardian building opposite Manchester Library, where his career had begun decades past as a recent graduate of the Central School.

"Jeremy?" queried the man on the phone.

"Yes, who is this?"

"My name is Michael Cox. I'm a producer here at Granada Studios, and I'm working on a series that I thought might interest you. I would really rather tell you about it in person though. Perhaps we could meet for dinner tomorrow."

"Well, you have piqued my curiosity, Michael! How about the restaurant here at the hotel, seven o'clock?"

"Splendid!"

The next evening was rainy; it was late spring and Jeremy was glad he did not have to leave the hotel. Before seven, he went down to the bar for a drink and a smoke. Michael Cox, in a wet trench coat, found him there, and furling his dripping umbrella, introduced himself. He seemed to be brimming over with some exciting agenda, so they went straight in to dinner.

"I'm hearing wonderful reports of your performance in *The Good Soldier*," Michael began, not unmindful of the pleasantries, "and I must tell you that I feel blessed that we have not lost you to Hollywood."

"Why thank you, Michael, that is very kind of you to say." They ordered, both having the petite filet; and when Michael insisted upon a bottle of cabernet, Jeremy suspected a lengthy conversation.

"Now tell me about this new series you are doing."

The wine came and they settled back studying one another. "Let me first explain to you, Jeremy, that since I was a boy I have been a great fan of Sir Arthur Conan Doyle," Michael began, clearly having rehearsed this presentation in his head, "especially the Sherlock Holmes mysteries. I read every one, over and over. As you know, there have been many adaptations for stage and screen, but none to my knowledge that have hewn faithfully to the stories themselves. Even the first play in 1899, a collaboration between William Gillette and Sir Arthur, combined four of the plots. When I got into this business in 1956, right across the street here at the Manchester Library Theatre . . ."

"Really?" Jeremy interrupted with amazement. "I got my start there too, about the same time! What did you do?"

"I began as an assistant stage manager."

The waiter brought the steaks, and Jeremy poured more wine. "Sorry, Michael, please continue."

"Well, I have had this dream of producing the authentic Conan Doyle tales as unadulterated as possible, just as I read and enjoyed them as a child, and Granada is prepared to back me." The steak was excellent, the wine perfect, but by this time Jeremy must have been thinking, "Good God, the man wants me to play Sherlock Holmes!" Sure enough, "After a good deal of careful consideration," Michael went on, "I want you for the role of Holmes," and he sat back, a bit breathless.

Jeremy sipped his wine, trying not to register surprise. "But why me? My stock in trade has been romantic comedy, the occasional psychopath, nothing like Holmes. The closest I have come is Dr. Watson."

"No, no, the way I see it you are the perfect Holmes. You have the versatility, the physicality, the voice, the presence. I am convinced, Jeremy, that you are the best man for the part, and I hope you will accept. What's up next for you?"

"Robert Browning for the BBC." Brett was pensive, not wanting to disappoint the poor chap.

"There is no rush," Cox concluded, with enough experience to know this casting was a tad outré. "The project is not immanent. In fact, there may be a legal issue with another studio.[126] Take your time, but please," he paused, "please give the idea serious thought." Jeremy liked this fellow; he was plain-spoken, sincere, enthusiastic, not the stuffed shirt stereotype of a producer.

"Of course I will, Michael. I'm flattered that you think me so capable. You know my oldest brother John, the Reverend Huggins, is also a Sherlockian."

They went on discussing the Holmes mysteries, and Cox was excited to talk about his favorite stories, the ones he considered most appropriate to dramatize of the fifty-two composing the canon. They had dessert and coffee, and after a brandy and a cigarette Michael retrieved his coat and umbrella from the cloakroom. "You must learn to smoke a pipe, Jeremy," he joked on his way back out into the wet night.

"Quite right," Brett smiled, shaking Michael's hand warmly. "It was awfully good meeting you."

"And you, old chap. Thank you for hearing me out. I hope we will be in touch."

"I promise, Michael, I will get back to you." The bellman hailed a cab for Cox, and Jeremy retreated back into his hotel, bemused if unpersuaded by the thought of playing Sherlock Holmes.

* * *

Chapter 4

Though Scottish by birth, Sir Arthur Ignatius Conan Doyle was descended of Irish Catholics. His paternal grandfather, John Doyle, born in 1797, married Marianna Conan in 1820, and they moved from Dublin to London. John was an artist who won renown as a political cartoonist and caricaturist. In London he was acquainted with the great authors of the century, including Dickens, Coleridge, and Thackeray. Of the couple's seven children, their son Charles Altamont Doyle became the father of Arthur, born 1859 in Edinburgh. Charles had settled in Scotland after marrying Mary Foley, also from an Irish Catholic family. He attempted to follow his father's path as an artist, but from young adulthood suffered from depression, and the Irish curse, alcoholism. Life became so disrupted for the couple and their children that it was thought best to send Arthur away at the age of eight to a Jesuit boarding school at Stonyhurst. With Charles unable to provide for them, the family relied for support on his brothers.

More than 150 kilometers from Edinburgh, Stonyhurst is set in the fields and rolling hills of rural England near the Yorkshire Dales, overlooked by the Pennines. But in spite of this natural beauty, the boy Arthur, who was very close to his mother, was terribly homesick. Life under the priestly regime of a Catholic boarding school was harsh, and he felt the onus of his family's penury, their enforced dependency, especially as it weighed on his mother, even at that young age.

Mary Doyle was a masterful storyteller in the Irish tradition; and she would enthrall her promising young son with folk tales, lowering her voice to add suspense as she delivered the denouement. She also had a strong interest in the history of medieval England, the age of chivalry, with its jousting knights. Arthur's later career obviously drew on this maternal influence.

But before he became a successful writer, he was a doctor, following in the footsteps of his Uncle Michael Doyle. A close friend of his mother's also urged him in this direction, so he enrolled in Edinburgh University to study medicine. One of his professors there was Dr. Joseph Bell, noted for his amazing gift of deduction. Through just the careful observation of a patient, Dr. Bell was able to gather considerable detailed and accurate information about him, and even to make a diagnosis.

Arthur went into medical practice with a classmate, George Budd, in Plymouth. They had a falling out, however, upon which Arthur opened his own surgery in Portsmouth. It did not flourish. He continued to write stories, as he had done in fact since his youth, hoping to sell them to magazines to help his mother financially. Writing was his true vocation.

He married in 1885 to Louise Hawkins, and they had a daughter. With this added motivation to earn, he set about writing *A Study in Scarlet*, a mystery novel which introduced the characters Sherlock Holmes and Dr. John Watson. Sherlock's talent for observing and deducing was based on Dr. Bell of the medical school, but there were several other inventive aspects that led to the popularity of the many similar stories that followed. The very idea of having the same cast of characters feature in each mystery was new and allowed readers to enjoy an immediate sense of familiarity. Setting the stories in and around London added to that sense for London readers. The clever device of having Dr. Watson be the chronicler of these tales gave their author the means to create suspense, as we cannot know what Holmes is thinking until the end when we learn it from Watson and the mystery is solved. Since Doyle was himself grounded in science, his character's methods were forensic, even becoming influential in promoting forensic science in crime solving.

By 1891, Arthur and Louise had another child, a son, and had moved to the Norwood suburb of London. Arthur had been to Europe to study ophthalmology and had set up a London office as an ophthalmic surgeon. Before this practice got off the ground, however, he realized that his writing was earning him a living, to the extent that he would be better off devoting his full energies to it. This support came not only from the Holmes stories, published each week in the Strand Magazine, but also from what he considered his more important works, his historical novels, such as *The White Company*, a grand saga of crusading knights and their ladies. Mystery stories were popular, and Arthur wrote for money, but as the years went by he began to find Holmes an annoying distraction.

Then Louise was diagnosed with tuberculosis. They began to travel back and forth to Switzerland in hope that the clear mountain air would slow her decline. With this complication Doyle decided to stop the mystery writing, so in 1893 he wrote "The Final Problem," sending Holmes to his death over the Reichenbach Falls—in Switzerland—with his archenemy Professor Moriarty. It was a famously black day in London when that story appeared. Sherlock Holmes already had developed an avid, fanatical readership. Yet it was not until 1903 that Doyle agreed to resume the mystery stories, when the American magazine Collier's offered him such a princely sum he could not refuse.

In the tale called "The Empty House," Holmes reappears and explains to Watson that he did not go over the falls with Moriarty but had overcome the professor and escaped, wandering Europe and the Orient for the next three years to elude the revenge of Moriarty's henchman, Colonel Sebastian Moran, with his ingenious air gun. By way of apology, he declares, "I have taken up my pen to write you, Watson, but feared lest your affectionate regard for me tempt you to some indiscretion that would betray my secret."

It seems odd indeed that this return of the great detective has ever since presented Sherlockians such a perennial conundrum, to wit: how could Holmes have been so cruel as to let his friend Watson believe for so long that he had died? Here we are compelled to observe that what has been lost on these devotees is the perspective of the writer. Feeling the need for some continuity, Doyle simply devised an explanation for Sherlock's long absence, cleverly weaving it into the murder mystery that bags the old *shikari*[127] Colonel Moran.

We would submit, furthermore, that Doyle did not recognize any requirement to elaborate the personal qualities of his hero. A mystery from the writer's viewpoint is about plot, not character. Thus apart from allowing Watson allusions to Holmes's coldly rational albeit superior mind, there are no real discussions of his personality or his background that would flesh out the character in a different genre.

But Sir Arthur was a talented writer. He wanted to earn a living certainly, but over and above that he wanted to do so engaged in what he loved. He enjoyed writing. His portrait of Sherlock Holmes may seem as sketchy as the Sydney Paget drawings that accompanied the stories in the Strand Magazine; but Doyle could not resist giving us clues to Holmes's nature, however indirectly, dialogue being perhaps the most revealing. Ironically any paucity of characterization allowed readers the free rein of imagination, which may have enhanced Holmes's lasting popularity.

To have any understanding of Sir Arthur's own image of his creation, though, a person must read the stories in the Holmes canon. Unfortunately, the iconic version that became accepted derived from numerous adaptations for stage and later film. The actor most closely associated with the role of Holmes was Basil Rathbone, who made fourteen movies as Sherlock, with Nigel Bruce as Watson, starting in 1939, nine years after Doyle's death. These films were simple detective stories, divorced from the author's work apart from expected conventions such as the deerstalker hat, the Baker Street rooms run by Mrs. Hudson, the violin, and curiously the calabash pipe, which Holmes never smoked.

It was Basil Rathbone, the Hollywood Sherlock, who made famous the phrase, "Elementary, my dear Watson," which Sir Arthur Conan Doyle never wrote. In contrast, did the actor ever utter these words from *The Adventure of the Abbey Grange*? In that story Holmes says to Lady Brackenstall, whose cruel, alcoholic husband is murdered by her champion, Captain Crocker, "My whole desire is to make things easy for you," the sentiment of a chivalrous gentleman, a compassionate person.

MORE THAN AN ACTOR

Doyle's wife Louise succumbed to tuberculosis in 1906, and he remarried in 1907 to Jean Leckie. He had another three children with her, and his youngest, Dame Jean Conan Doyle, lived until 1997. Sir Arthur died in 1930, having spent his last years advocating for spiritualism, a strong conviction held by many after the devastation of the Great War that the soul lives on after death, and through a medium can communicate with the living.

As for the phenomenal popularity of Sherlock Holmes, it only grew keener after a play by the charismatic American actor William Gillette opened in 1899 on Broadway and in London. Gillette had gotten Doyle's approval of the script, and took the role of Holmes himself. Thus in spite of his own personal inclination, Sir Arthur Conan Doyle is best remembered for his clever detective, the chronicle of whose adventures eclipsed all of his creator's many other literary works.

* * *

Afternoon tea was served on the porch of the Sweetfield Manor Inn, where hibiscus bloomed by the white wooden railing and tables covered in white linen were each adorned with a red or a purple flower of the bougainvillea. The ocean view from Britton's Hill, upon which the Inn stands, was framed by palm trees that swayed gently in the sea breeze. On the velvet green lawn in front of the porch a peacock strutted.

Sitting alone enjoying a pot of a most delicious Taylor's Earl Grey tea, with a lovely fresh tea bread, was Jeremy Brett, in white slacks and a black polo.[128] He had come to Barbados chastened by the bad reviews of *The Tempest*, but nevertheless searching out a potential location for filming it, in the hope that financial backing might still be found. This tiny coral island, easternmost of the Lesser Antilles, with its silky white sand edging the shimmering aquamarine of the sea, was indeed the perfect spot for Prospero to be beached, but also the perfect refuge for Jeremy to find solace in the warm, caressing sun and the bright tropical flowers.

Yet he sat on the porch of the Inn reading a book, his feet propped on the rung of another chair so as to balance it on his lap. It was heavy: *The Complete Sherlock Holmes, Volume I*. Here he was in this languorous paradise immersing himself in the pea soup fogs of London, captivated.

The Tempest had played for just over two weeks in Toronto, and Joan had come up toward the end. Naturally she adored him as Prospero; and when the critics panned it, she was there with moral support. When the run was over they were able to fly back to England together. First class on British Airways was a comfortable journey even in those days: steak dinners with champagne, wide reclining seats. They sat back with their wine, and Jeremy lit two cigarettes, giving one to his wife.

"I don't know, Joanie, I really felt the lack of a director in that play."

"You missed Seidelman," the director beloved by actors, who collaborated in *Macbeth*.

"Maybe. Something was missing."

"Affirmation."

"You read me like a book, darling."

"You know very well how hidebound critics can be when it comes to Shakespeare, Jeremy. I loved the play. I've never seen a more exciting Prospero."

"But you're biased," he remarked sweetly, squeezing her arm. "I really want to make a film of it nonetheless. What do you think?"

"It would be even better as a film. Of course you could do it! When we get to London, you'll make the rounds of the studios, talk it up, get some backing. And I will call my connections also." Joan had contacts with corporate donors to public broadcasting, such as Mobil Oil.

Jeremy cupped her chin and kissed her softly, those limpid eyes of his brim full. "You are so good for me, Joanie."

She took his hand in both of hers and kissed it as if to quiet him. "I hope so," was all she could say, her eyes brimming too. Soon the stewardess, in her wonderfully decorous dark pinstripe suit, white shirt, and the uniform silk scarf, came with pillows and blankets.

"Now, Jeremy darling," Joan commanded, "you promised me you would sleep."

"You and Mrs. Wheatley!"

Arriving back at Notting Hill, Jeremy was full of energy, no jet lagged fatigue, and he went straight to work at the BBC on *The Barretts of Wimpole Street*. He was delighted with his costar, Jane Lapotaire, so lovely and demur, and a talented actress into the bargain. He was able to throw himself whole heartedly into the part of Robert Browning, falling for her and wresting her from a despotic father. At the same time he arranged to see various producers of his acquaintance regarding *The Tempest*.

Unfortunately he soon learned that the time was not right; a modern version of it was about to be released by Columbia Pictures starring John Cassavetes.[129] His discouragement grew, feeding on itself; the cloud of depression seeped in around doors and windows like a fog, and everything became a terrible effort, energy gone. He began to feel hopeless, inadequate, and strangely ashamed of his dreary despair. In this mood, he was very nearly struck mute, which must have alarmed Joan, being herself such a positive person.

"Listen, darling," she said to him one night at bedtime, "this movie coming out isn't even Shakespeare, and if it succeeds, it doesn't necessarily preclude your version. On the contrary it can benefit yours by creating interest." He was unresponsive in a way she had never seen, so she kept talking. "I know just the place too. Why don't you check out Barbados as a location? You could use the sunshine and sea air right now anyway."

So he arrived on this enchanting, if not enchanted, isle, which did indeed lift his spirits. The manager of the Inn arranged for an employee to give his guest a tour, with an eye out for filming locations; and Jeremy found the natural beauty very suitable for his vision. In his mind's eye he could see footage of a tropical storm opening Act I, high winds whipping up the waves and lashing the palm trees. Moreover, Barbados as a former British territory, had the necessary infrastructure: tea, tobacco, hotels. Then there was the delightful, exotic flora and fauna: the perfume of oleander in the air, goats wandering the dusty back roads. As he sat at tea, in fact, a cheeky, dove grey Barbados bullfinch hopped from the porch rail onto his table after the tea cake, and was of course rewarded. He made a mental note to tell Joanie about it. She had been unable to come; and while he missed her, this retreat from the world came as a relief.

He interrupted his reading just long enough to have a quick supper, then took his book to the patio where there was an outdoor bar. The lengthening rays of the sun were coloring the cumulus clouds a deepening pink over the sea, and the cool breeze of evening rustled through the palms. Tree frogs started up their quiet peeping, joined by the lazy, sleepy rhythm of crickets. When it was dark enough, those essential pollinators of tropical fruit, the bats, flitted across the sky, reminding Jeremy of Dracula's cape. Two gaslights lit the patio, and under one of them he was able to continue reading, as he slowly sipped a Paradise Punch.

Before leaving for Barbados, he had borrowed the two volumes of Sherlock Holmes mysteries from his brother John, who was happy to loan them, but confounded. "You can't be Holmes, Jeremy, you don't smoke a pipe!" he had exclaimed, "and you are nothing like him." But then he went on to offer his advice on how to play the part; so Jeremy came away with some reassurance, and along with the two books, the card of John's favorite tobacconist in London.

Now he was devouring the Conan Doyle stories with fascination. He took them to the beach, where he sat in one of the striped canvas chairs with a shade cover, digging his bare feet into the warm sand, taking a dip when he got hot, then back to his book again.

One night he decided to treat himself to dinner at Champers, a seaside restaurant, formal enough that he wore his white dinner jacket. As the maître d' led him out to the open balcony overlooking the water, where naturally everyone wanted to sit to watch the sunset, Jeremy was spotted.

"Jeremy Brett! What a delightful surprise to see you here!" It was none other than Claudette Colbert, the French-born film star. For some years she had had a cottage on the island, and now at age 79 divided her time between Barbados and Manhattan. "Come join me, please." Though she often came with neighbors, she was alone that night, a widow since 1968.

"How kind of you to recognize me, darling," Jeremy greeted her and took a seat, glad for the company, "especially considering the guests you had most recently." In April of that year, 1982, President and Mrs. Reagan, old friends of Colbert's from their Hollywood days, vacationed in Barbados at her invitation.[130]

"Oh indeed, that was quite a to-do. But what brings you here? Is your wife with you?"

"Joan is dedicated to her work with PBS. She sent me to get some sun and sea air."

"Well, you came to the right place! I've been here for years." Colbert was amazingly youthful for her age.

"I know. I thought I might run into you." They ordered mai tai's and studied the menu, which offered enticingly fresh seafood. "Truthfully though, I'm also working, scouting locations to make a film of *The Tempest*, which I recently played in Toronto."

"Dear me, darling boy, I don't mean to be discouraging, but you should know that John Gielgud has had that very dream all his life, and it hasn't come to pass. Instead we have this travesty with Cassavetes. Is nothing sacred?" They went on discussing the merits of various beaches, then over a leisurely dinner, a variety of topics: the regrettable lack of support for the arts, including theatre; the dreadful coarsening of the culture so evident in the entertainment industry. She blamed it on the Americans, until he reminded her of that "angry young man," John Osborne.

The sky had darkened and the stars twinkled, a near full moon showing itself overhead, when they got up, deciding to venture down nearer the water's edge. A path of pebbles marked the way to a gazebo, where other patrons were dining, but as they approached it, Jeremy stepped off and began to walk over the sand toward the surf. Claudette was taken aback briefly, but soon enough he turned facing her, and taking on his stage voice declaimed, "I have done nothing but in care of thee, of thee my dear one, thee my daughter, who art ignorant of what thou art, naught knowing of whence I am . . ."

Earlier that day, with his driver, a swarthy young fellow, as his reluctant Caliban, Jeremy had been rehearsing his Prospero on the beaches. After this speech to Miranda from Act I, a round of applause erupted from the gazebo, and from Claudette. She was a petite woman, five foot four. He towered over her.

"Jeremy darling, you can be my Prospero any day!" she said affectionately, taking his arm as they made their way to the street to fetch a cab. He saw her home and insisted upon paying the fare, recalling some gossip that due to her extravagant tastes she had a struggle to live within her means.

On the ride back to the Inn, his thoughts returned to Conan Doyle. His son David was opposed to the idea of this taking on Holmes. "It's been done to death, Dad," he had said, "and it's not your kind of role." But Joan, beloved Joanie, supportive always, told him sincerely, "In my view, Jeremy, you have transformed every character you have ever portrayed, and you would do the same for poor old Sherlock Holmes if you chose."

He sat up for a while that night with his book, the white sheer curtains at his open window moved by a gentle breeze, awakening his very oldest memories of childhood at the Grange. Framed by the window, the moon was getting ready to set on the distant horizon over a pearlescent sea. He was reading "The Naval Treaty," where Holmes is interviewing Watson's friend Percy Phelps concerning the disastrous loss of an important document entrusted to him. There is a famous passage in which Sherlock offers his philosophical reflections on the goodness of Providence as evidenced by the flowers. "What a lovely flower a rose is," he says as he holds up "the drooping stalk of a moss-rose, looking down at the dainty blend of crimson and green." In an odd digression, he goes on, "This rose is an extra. Its smell and its color are an embellishment of life, not a condition of it. It is only goodness which gives extras, and so I say again that we have much to hope from the flowers."

This offer to play Sherlock Holmes was beginning to seem to him much more than just a backup plan.

* * *

Jeremy Brett not only took on the starring role in the Granada series, giving up the idea of filming *The Tempest*, but he succeeded so spectacularly that he became and remains the definitive Sherlock Holmes. Much has been written about how this occurred, the most reliable source being the book *Bending the Willow* by Sherlock scholar David Stuart Davies, who consulted on the series.[131] Brett used to say that as faithful as they might be to the short stories, the demands of dramatization forced them to at least "bend the willow" in adapting them for film.

But in our view, Brett's enormous success as Holmes derived from the simple fact that unlike previous pretenders to the role, he had read the stories. Those glorious nights and days in Barbados immersed in Doyle were key. He gleaned a strong affinity for the author, identifying not with Sherlock, but with Sir Arthur. That was the source of his insight. The Abbey Grange might have been Berkswell Grange; Baskerville Hall could have been Berkswell Hall; the Hurlstone manse in "The Musgrave Ritual" had a moat like the estate of Sir Charles Hyde in Brett's hometown. Then there were the racing stories: "Shoscombe Old Place," and "Silver Blaze." Had he not dreamed of becoming a jockey all those years ago? And of course "The Priory School" was Stonyhurst, the boarding school where young Arthur was sent. Echoes of Eton.

As for Holmes, Brett must have been truly amazed to find that the stereotype, which had calcified in the public perception since Sir Arthur's death, was far from accurate. Yes, he was brilliantly analytical and unemotional, with the cold heart of a scientist; yet he was also eager to help those who came to him, especially to defend them from injustice. He was not inhuman, but laughed, enjoyed music, food, tobacco. Brett was astute enough to recognize that while Doyle had created two fictional characters in Holmes and Watson each was in some way expressive of the author himself.

The language, the writing, must also have appealed to Jeremy: the eloquent formality of Victorian English; the long, carefully constructed sentences. The stories are told in large part through dialogue, which he would see could be lifted in many cases to become the script, particularly since it was Cox's intention to be as authentic as possible. He must also have noted with delight the many opportunities there would be to use disguises, a frequent device used by the author.

Nonetheless, as Brett approached the actual portrayal of Holmes, he could not help but to be intimidated by the past: the long accretion of expectations; the history of other actors in the part. He knew he could not be Basil Rathbone; and who was he to believe his unorthodox interpretation might be superior? This insecurity came across in the several interviews he gave on the subject. He was uniformly self-deprecating, perhaps the lasting effect of a self-image as the youngest child. As though to forestall criticism or disappointment, he continually repeated that he was "miscast," that his personality was too animated. But these avowals contradicted his own statements concerning what he had discovered in the actual stories, i.e. the human aspects of Holmes heretofore overlooked, and which moreover were in keeping with his own nature. Recall John Gielgud's reflection that an actor can conceal only 10 percent of his personality in playing a role. It was Jeremy Brett's own nature that leavened the character of Sherlock Holmes and brought it back to life fully as his creator intended. Fortunately in his acting, Brett showed ample self-confidence, his supremely expressive face registering subtle emotion, like mist on glass. As we have observed, the only picture of him in which he is devoid of expression was significantly his Eton photograph.

By the time Jeremy got back to London from Barbados, things were coming together for this Granada project. The rival studio, Mapleton, had lost the legal battle over the American copyrights, even though they had gone ahead and made two films starring Ian Richardson. These were versions of *The Sign of Four* and *The Hound of the Baskervilles*, quite divergent from the original stories. At the end of *The Sign of Four*, for example, when the one-legged man Jonathan Small is pursued down the Thames by a police launch, he does not throw the treasure into the river but conceals the jewels in his wooden leg, which Holmes cleverly deduces, though it makes for an awkward ending. Neither production met with excitement at Cannes that year, so both were shelved, clearing the way for Granada.

The courage and confidence it must have taken for producer Michael Cox to go forward with this series can hardly be exaggerated. Setting the stories in the original Victorian era meant creating Baker Street on a lot at the Manchester studio as authentically as possible. Cox would brook no anachronism, and his commitment to his choice of a star was in a word, gutsy. What clinched it for him, as he told Davies for his book, was the reaction of his wife Sandra, who was initially against yet another rehashing of the genre. But when Michael suggested Jeremy Brett, she said, "Ah, well that's different!"

There in a nutshell we have another secret to the success of Granada's Sherlock Holmes. The appeal of Conan Doyle's detective has always been masculine. The innumerable clubs and societies, for example, that sprang up worldwide among his myriad fans were men only. A woman wanting to attend would need to go in drag. Sherlock's relationship with his friend and colleague Dr. Watson may have raised an eyebrow of some few unfamiliar with the sentimentality of Victorian friendship; but with a careful reading, it seems more kin to the camaraderie of schoolboys. Jeremy Brett was attractive to both genders in the sensuality he exuded as a bisexual man, and for women this attraction was intensified because the emotionally repressed Holmes is unattainable. In this role, unlike any other before, Brett does not get to kiss the girl, but instead is left brooding by the fire across from Watson, nursing a brandy, sweet torture for his female fans.

When Jeremy accepted, Michael Cox was thrilled, having perfect confidence in his choice for Holmes. Joan, we can only imagine, was over the moon, because knowing Jeremy as she did, his intelligence, his perfectionism, she foresaw that he would not only succeed, he would be the best Sherlock Holmes there could ever be; and the series would be readymade for her own Masterpiece Mystery on American screens.

Thus despite lingering misgivings, to Manchester he went. He worried about carrying a lengthy series; thirteen one hour episodes had been authorized. Brett had guest starred in various series, and he had starred in miniseries, but this long commitment was uncharted territory. He knew Manchester of course and liked the Midland Hotel well enough. He would take a suite and settle in.

The Baker Street set, large as it was, went up with amazing alacrity, all sixty yards of length, authentic Victorian facades hung from steel girders. John Hawkesworth, the gifted and experienced writer and producer, had worked with Cox to have the stories adapted for the screen. Their independent selection of the most suitable adventures was virtually identical, and the order would adhere to the original chronology in the Strand Magazine. The first to be broadcast would be "A Scandal in Bohemia." But cleverly, Cox did not want the initial broadcast to be their maiden effort, so he began filming with "The Solitary Cyclist."

Looking back at this episode, we can see in the first moments of Brett's being Holmes that he retained some confusion. He is trying to be Basil Rathbone, but for no more than two minutes. By the time he has gotten up from his beakers and Bunsen burner, where he is doing an experiment concerning "the persecution of tobacco millionaire John Vincent Harden," and gone over to Miss Violet Smith, examining her hand and deducing that the spatulate fingertips show she plays the piano, he has taken possession of the character, the true Conan Doyle version. He goes on to explain that he could tell she was not a typist, because of a "spirituality about the face." Then cupping her chin, he says, "This lady is a musician!"

Brett was confident of his portrayal when the British audience first saw him in "A Scandal in Bohemia," which aired in April of 1984. It begins with Dr. Watson, played by David Burke, lecturing Holmes about the damage of using cocaine. Sherlock, who is facing the fireplace, turns slowly to face the camera and replies, "I can highly recommend a 7 percent solution. Would you care to try it?"[132] He then goes on to justify his habit: how it "clarifies the mind"; how he "abhors the dull routine of existence"; how he has had to create his own particular profession as the only "unofficial consulting detective."

In this speech with its nuanced delivery is the first evidence that Brett has created a psychological profile of his character as a highly intelligent man who does not fit in with human society and beneath a veneer of arrogance, is insecure in regard to his position in it. Holmes has been given a human dimension more explicit perhaps than the author ever provided yet nonetheless implicit in Doyle's words.

But before that first episode aired, Jeremy turned fifty, and as they shared a birthday, we imagine Joan would want to share the celebration. She may have come to Manchester during the filming of "The Blue Carbuncle." Since this story takes place at Christmastime, appropriate weather was required. Joan was enormously impressed with the set, as she told Michael Cox, whom she knew and respected. He directed her to the interior Baker Street rooms where Jeremy was preparing for one of the opening scenes. He was sprawled on the settee in a long grey woolen dressing gown over a white shirt, open at the neck, his hair combed straight back. "Here," she thought to herself, "is the most sensuous Sherlock Holmes the world is ever likely to see." She could scarcely contain her excitement, but she did not interrupt the filming.

It was Thursday, the third of November, the very day of their birthday, and the cast and crew had planned a party in the canteen following the day's shoot. Upon the director's last call of "Cut!" Jeremy spotted his wife, went directly to her, and throwing his arms around her, lifted her off the floor.

"Happy birthday, darling!" he bubbled with exuberance. She blushed, a bit embarrassed by this spontaneous demonstration.

"And to you! Yours is a milestone."

"Don't remind me. Let me change, and I'll meet you in the canteen. It seems everyone wants to celebrate."

Though the series was just getting off the ground, its star had already charmed every person involved, with his humor, his warmth and kindness, his modesty. He was his mother's son. He became renown for taking candid photos of people during filming and pinning them to his dressing room door. He made everyone feel important, knitted the group together through his magnanimity, and so the champagne flowed.

Michael Cox offered a toast, "To our friend and our star, the ever youthful Jeremy, a splendid birthday!" With which the room broke into singing, "For he's a jolly good fellow . . ."

Jeremy thanked them all, adding, "And since it is also Joanie's birthday, we must all drink twice as much!"

Was there cake? But of course! Jeremy loved cake, and the celebrating didn't stop there. Next day he and Joan returned to London on the train, and that evening had a party for their friends in Notting Hill.[133] The place had never felt so cramped, what with their expanding guest list.

When the last person had left, and they were cleaning up, Jeremy said, "I think we are going to need larger quarters."

Joan agreed, but wondered, "What would David do, though?"

"His mother now has a house in Holland Park with a flat above it. I'll ask him. Shall I start looking?"

"Why not!"

That weekend Jeremy's brothers, with their wives, took him and Joan to dinner at the Savoy on the occasion of the big birthday. They loved Joan; she was so funny, so *American*, even in light of her charming and flattering anglophilia. It was Saturday night, and she wore a black cocktail dress, looking unusually slim. Jeremy was in a dinner jacket and tie. They had a tableful, with John at the head, paternal as ever.

"Well, baby brother," he said after they had been seated, "may I still call you that now that you are fifty?"

"Please do, John. It's good to know that you remain older," Jeremy replied with a good natured smile.

"How is it going in Manchester?" John continued eagerly, "and when will we see you as Holmes?"

"It is a gargantuan effort on the part of the studio and the producer, meticulously authentic period drama; and you in particular will be pleased to know that I have *The Complete Sherlock Holmes* on the set to keep them honest."

"And the star of the show?" Patrick chimed in, always worried about the youngest.

"Oh, a lot of hard work, Patrick, dialogue to memorize, and you know in film you stay in costume most of the day. That black Victorian suit with the turned under tie . . ." All three older brothers broke into laughter.

"Say no more! Shades of Eton!" Patrick went on, and more gales went round.

"How awful for you, Jeremy!" Michael was sympathetic. "But when?" he begged, "When does the series start?"

"I believe they are aiming for next April." Sitting next to him, Joan could read his face, could see the fleeting cloud pass over it, the pressure of expectations. She put her hand on his arm, and he put his hand over hers. Their eyes met in that glance of understanding that is silent reassurance. More than anyone, she "understood the hell actors go through," as he later said of her.[134] She also knew how gifted he was, and more even than he himself, how intelligent.

It was a wonderful evening, much laughing and reminiscing, sharing news of their families. When Jeremy and Joan got home to Notting Hill, they lit a fire and collapsed onto the sofa, each with a glass of port. She planned to stay for their anniversary, the sixth, on 22 November, returning afterward to Boston and to work. Not that she did not also have work in England. She would certainly be arranging terms with Granada, for example, to bring *The Adventures of Sherlock Holmes* to Masterpiece Mystery. Neither was Jeremy to have a break from Manchester. As they sipped their wine, he explained to her that even when they completed the first seven episodes, the first season in other words, Cox wanted to push on to the remaining six before critics could weigh in, possibly dampening prospects.

"Oh, I can't see any risk of that, darling," Joan remarked, kicking off her black satin heels and curling up beside him.

"But Joanie, wait till I tell you what he has planned for the grand finale, 'The Final Problem.'"

"Is that when Holmes goes over the falls with Moriarty?"

"Precisely. Well just between us, Michael wants to film it on location in Switzerland and have them go over the actual Reichenbach Falls."

"Good heavens, Jeremy! He will need to find two stunt men as brave as he is."

"Or as reckless!"

And so their anniversary came and went, and Joan left for the States. Jeremy would look for a larger house when he had a chance, and by spring would grab at least some few days to come to Boston. They both loved their work, with the dedication of professionals.

* * *

On 24 April, 1984, "A Scandal in Bohemia" aired on British television, beginning the series of seven weekly mysteries. Any worries Michael Cox may have harbored that the fulfillment of his boyhood dream might be disparaged by critics were quickly allayed. The Guardian called it "a very posh job indeed . . . luxurious, even luscious," and Philip French in the Times wrote, "Jeremy Brett and David Burke are the best Holmes and Watson I've ever seen." But most treasured of all was a note that Brett received from Douglas Fairbanks Jr. "Could this really be our darling Freddy Eynsford Hill?" he wrote, referring to *My Fair Lady*. From such a renowned film star, Jeremy took this affirmation as high praise.

By the end of May he finally had a chance to break away for a trip to Boston. He had also found a penthouse for sale overlooking Clapham Common that he was considering, and had sounded out his son about the possibility of moving to Holland Park. In the event, David was understanding, realizing it was time for a change.

Jeremy arrived at Logan in the late afternoon, and Joan was waiting to pick him up. She seemed to him thinner than ever, her complexion sallow, or maybe it was just the waning light. If absence makes the heart grow fonder as they say, that is certainly how this couple kept romance alive. He loved holding her in his arms, the very place she loved to be.

"Joanie, my darling, you look like you need something to eat. Why don't we stop at that steak house downtown on the way home?" He was thinking of the place where she took him to dinner when they first met.

"Good idea! Come, let's get your bag."

They came to the restaurant, ordered drinks, and sat back awaiting steaks. She had heard about the rave reviews he was getting as Holmes, and was terribly excited about it.

"I knew you would be superb, Jeremy. I hadn't the slightest doubt!" He started to speak, and she stopped him. "I know, I know, I'm biased, but the critics aren't. Cox must be enormously relieved." Dinner came, sizzling and perfectly cooked. "What about the Switzerland shoot?"

"We go in September. They are planning the stunt and have two of the best men lined up. Obviously there is no margin for error."

"Of course. Michael will see to it; he is painstaking. I'm so anxious to bring these adventures here to public broadcasting!"[135]

"Patience, Joanie darling! We are working as hard as we can." He went on to tell her about the penthouse on Clapham Common in south London, and she begged him to send pictures, which he promised to do. Joan ate little of her dinner and wanted no dessert. When she got up to leave she winced, clutching her left side. "Joanie, what is it? Are you all right?" He took her arm to steady her.

"I see my doctor next week. I've been having this pain."

"You must have an ulcer, the curse of the executive. Let me drive home; you rest."

Uncharacteristically, she handed over the keys to the black Mustang, and they set out for home in Marblehead, about fifteen miles north of Boston, a small suburb on a peninsula between Salem Harbor and Marblehead Harbor. Night came on as they drove, and a full moon was rising, its light glinting off the water as they approached the coast.

"Such a beautiful night, darling! Shall we stop by the lighthouse for a while?" Jeremy suggested. "If you are feeling better that is." The Chandler-Hovey lighthouse has a park around it and beautiful views of the ocean.

"A lovely idea; I feel fine now."

All along the harbor sailboats and yachts of different sizes were anchored for the night, their bows facing into the current. Jeremy and Joan walked a bit, encountering not another soul. Then they stopped and she leaned her back against him as they looked out over the waters, the boats appearing spectral in the pearly light, their rigging softly clanking as they bobbed.

"This reminds me," Joan began, "of that night in Stratford at the Festival."

"Ah, Canada! The night I swept you off your feet," and he turned her around, kissing her exactly as he had then, eight years before.

"Like that" she whispered, "except it was only a first quarter moon that night." They laughed and held each other. How she loved having him here, and for him being with her was blessed peace.

Within the week she had seen her doctor in Boston, and as expected he sent her for tests at Mass General, a barium swallow and an abdominal ultrasound. She was surprised how quickly these were scheduled, but she went. It was not a fun day. Naturally, she and Jeremy were anxious for the test results, and very soon her doctor's office called: he had the results, but wanted to discuss them with her; when could she come in?

"You are starting to worry me, Joanie. Why does the doctor want to talk to you? I'm coming with you," Jeremy insisted.

The doctor came out to the waiting room to greet them and led them back to his office. They all sat, and after a few minutes of small talk, he got to the matter at hand. "The barium swallow showed no abnormality, so Joan, you do not have an ulcer." He smiled, but Jeremy, as a student of facial expressions, particularly those of concealment, was growing more and more uneasy. "However," the doctor went on, "it appears from the ultrasound that there is a mass on your pancreas." This is the kind of dreaded news that doctors shudder at delivering. There was a loud hiss as his patient and her husband simultaneously gasped for air. "It will need to be biopsied. I want you to go to Dana-Farber; they are tops in the field, affiliated with Mass General and Harvard Med School. My receptionist will get you set up."

He had referred to the Dana-Farber Cancer Institute[136] without using the word any patient fears. "You think it could be cancer then," Joan stated calmly, but her heart was racing.

"Let's not get ahead of things, Joan, but do get that biopsy without delay; and I'm giving you two prescriptions for your symptoms." He took his pad and scribbled. "This one is for any pain, and another for nausea. Take them as needed, and please try not to worry."

Physicians are notoriously disingenuous when it comes to this kind of terrifying report. Who are they, comes the rationalization, to dash anyone's hopes? Fear and gloom, after all, might even affect a patient's outcome. So while in an agony of anxiety, Joan and Jeremy tried to remain confident.

He accompanied her to the appointment at Dana-Farber, paced the floor of the waiting room and smoked. After the procedure she came out, and they waited together for the verdict. Finally they were brought back to the oncologist, a very trim, tall, younger man with thick horn-rimmed glasses. He introduced himself, and they shook hands.

"I'm so sorry for the need to tell you," he said, "but it is not good news." Joan looked at Jeremy. She had half expected this since she began feeling ill, a premonition; Jeremy was her worry. "The pathology clearly shows the mass to be adenocarcinoma of the pancreas," the doctor continued. "It is the most common form of pancreatic cancer."

From a disorienting sense of unreality, Jeremy began to feel a tidal wave of rage rising within him. Joan could see it, and so did the young oncologist. "But we have treatments," the doctor went on, throwing up a dyke against it. "Our facilities at Dana-Farber are state of the art, our staff the very best. We will start you on a course of radiation right away, Joan. We will take care of you."

Jeremy jumped out of his chair, barely able to restrain himself. "Is it curable?" he asked.

Given his specialization and position, the oncologist had experience with this question, enough to have practiced evasion. "There is always hope, sir," he replied. "We must never lose hope."

The truth is that pancreatic cancer is among the worst forms in its treachery. There is no screening test and no early sign; symptoms arise only after it is far advanced, and surgery often is not an option. Radiation and chemotherapy therefore simply postpone the inevitable course, which is generally rapid. Joan would learn this from her family physician in time; there was no need to accost her with such information immediately. Of course she signed on for radiation and she and Jeremy left, both in a tremulous state, headed for the closest Irish pub.

Jeremy was speechless as they sat at the bar, so Joan said, "He didn't tell me not to drink, did he?" thinking a little gallows humor was in order. She did get a smile out of him and an arm around her shoulder.

"How will we tell the children, darling?" Jeremy was hoarse from the double gin and tonic.

"Honestly, just what the doctor said, there is always hope."

"By God, I cling to those words, and you must too, Joanie."

Of course he accompanied her to the first radiation appointment, and he was allowed into the treatment room. Anyone who has seen a loved one sucked into the maw of modern medical science can appreciate the experience, the horror. There was his beloved wife and soulmate lying flat on the steel table in a hospital gown, and looming over her this mammoth machine, moving slowly down as if to crush her. Jeremy fainted dead away, caught by an orderly, who luckily was standing near him and led him from the room.[137]

The summer dragged on, and he was able to go to these appointments without passing out, though he did not go to every one. Joan became very weak from the radiation, a brutal, scattershot treatment; but the tumor was shrinking, and the next step was chemotherapy. September was approaching.

"I want to stay with you, Joanie. Switzerland will have to wait," he said as he helped her out of the car, coming home from the clinic. He got her into the house and into the easy chair to recover herself.

"No, no, Jeremy, you must go. They will not be able to reschedule, and you are the lynchpin."

"I don't care, darling. I need to be here, to see you through all this," he insisted.

"These protocols will take some time," she reasoned, "and anyway, my mother is coming from Wisconsin. The children are here with me. I will have lots of support."

"What about your work?"

"My assistant will carry on as he has been doing. You go, Jeremy. Come back to me as soon as 'The Final Problem' is in the can."

September came, and with extreme reluctance, he returned to England. From there the whole troupe set off for Meiringen, an alpine village one mile north of the Reichenbach Falls, where cast and crew put up at the aptly named Sherlock Holmes Hotel. It is a stunning place; the falls are breathtaking. Brett and Eric Porter, who played Professor Moriarty, were petrified even to approach the abyss on those wet rocks. But the stunt men, Alf Joint and Marc Boyle, made the descent heroically, suspended by cables and lowered at thirty miles an hour. When they were hoisted back up, Jeremy was waiting with champagne!

This episode was the last of the thirteen initially planned, of which seven had been broadcast between April and June 1984, to critical acclaim and wide popularity. The remaining six did not air until late summer of 1985, concluding with "The Final Problem" at the end of September, a year after the filming. But before then, Granada Studios knew they had a hit series.

Brett's unorthodox Holmes was a breath of fresh air, because along with Cox he became a champion of the author. His wonderfully sensitive intuition resurrected Conan Doyle's conception of the character, with a portrayal praised by none other than Dame Jean Conan Doyle, the author's youngest daughter then still living. And naturally, Jeremy brought something of himself to the part: his supple energy, his unerringly emotive face, the flash of a quick smile, the index finger pressed to his lips like an exclamation point, and not least among his idiosyncrasies, the long dark green muffler around his neck. The cigarettes of course need no mention.

It was nearly November when they were done shooting in Switzerland. Snow storms were swirling over the mountain peaks, and cold autumn winds swept through the pine forest and down the village lanes. A party was planned to celebrate what they may well have believed was the end of the series. It would be held in the hotel for the whole troupe.

Jeremy, in a distracted frame of mind, was helping Michael Cox blow up balloons, listening to the wind whine in the chimney. Logs blazed in the large fireplace. "Cheer up, old man," Michael bade him, "our work is done and a good job of it I'd say."

"Indeed so. I'm sorry, Michael, I was thinking about Joan."

"Missing your wife?"

"You haven't heard then. She was diagnosed with cancer not long before I returned to England. Now she is undergoing chemotherapy."

"That's dreadful, Jeremy. No, I didn't know. What do the doctor's say?"

"Not to give up hope."

"Excellent advice!"

* * *

Before he left for Switzerland, Jeremy had made an offer on the penthouse on Clapham Common, which parenthetically was the neighborhood where Noel Coward grew up. When he returned, he closed the deal and prepared to move. David had already taken his things to the flat above his mother's house in Holland Park. He of course knew about Joan's dire condition and was ready to help his father however he could. He was then twenty-five and just beginning a career in graphic design. They spent many days together at the start of 1985 hauling boxes across the Thames to the new place, no small task since even after ascending in the lift there were stairs to climb to the apartment.

"Please tell me you have hired movers, Dad," David complained, getting out of the elevator with an oil painting in each hand. One was a work of his own and the other by Uncle Michael.

"Oh, yes, in fact they are coming tomorrow, dear boy. But I wanted to get the place reasonably presentable, because I promised Joan I would take pictures."

"Would you like me to hang the art for you?"

"That would be an enormous help, son. Thank you!"

The apartment sat atop four lower floors of an old Edwardian style building. An L-shaped living room had high ceilings and perfect views across the Thames. To the right of the living room was a dining area, with a small kitchen off of that, and a winding staircase to two bedroom suites. There was also access to a rooftop balcony.[138]

Once the movers had taken over, David grouped his father's paintings and prints in a tasteful arrangement on the wall of the living room. In addition to the oils, there was a hunt scene, and then miscellany related to theatre—posters, drawings, and so on. Jeremy saw to the furniture, and set up his small desk with a statue of Buddha, a crystal, a pipe rack, an incense burner, and a photo of Mr. Binks, the hound he never forgot. He was then ready for David to bring his camera. To this day there are pictures available on the internet of Jeremy Brett in this penthouse apartment, which we surmise to have been taken for Joan's benefit. His unsmiling expression of concern is a wordless message of "get well." The Buddha and the incense tell us also that he continued his practice of meditation.

When the move was complete he would of course return to be with her. He took a morning flight and chasing the sun in its westward course arrived in Boston where it was still morning. He was encouraged that Joan was at the airport to meet him, and overjoyed to see her looking like her old self, her complexion better, her weight up, her hair long and wavy, though in fact it was a custom wig. She had been through chemo and was waiting to see if another round would be needed, recouping herself in the meanwhile. Embracing her, he longed to protect her from these trials, though truly the sight of him was enough. On the way home they stopped for tea at a little shop on Boston Common. We like to imagine it was called the Boston Tea Party, in hopes that there was a Bostonian sufficiently fanciful to think of it.

As they sat in this warm refuge from the drizzle of a Boston winter with their pot of Twining's English Breakfast and a basket of assorted muffins, Jeremy took out the photos of the penthouse, eager to share them. Joan studied them pensively, then smiling, remarked, "What a long face, darling! You look so sad here."

"Well, I wanted so badly for you to be there with me, Joanie. What do you think of it?"

"Oh, it's fabulous, and these views!" David had also taken pictures from the roof. "Maybe soon, I can go . . . maybe?"

"Let's hope." They went on to talk about Switzerland and the stunning finale over Reichenbach Falls.

"So the series is complete. Will that be the end then? I mean, it has been so popular," Joan wondered.

"I have heard rumors at Granada, though I don't know that Michael Cox is keen. It's been awfully hard work."

"He can hand it off to another producer, Jeremy, but you would be indispensable. Your Holmes has been perfectly unique. It has those stuffy Sherlockians running to their canon to see what they missed!"

He laughed at that. "I'm afraid you're right, darling, but if so maybe I should quit while I am ahead! It's truly the hardest role I have ever taken on. I don't think I want to continue: all those scripts to memorize, living at the Midland Hotel for weeks on end to portray a character for whom I am miscast."

"I quite understand, my dear," Joan said with much sincerity, "and of course you must do what is right for you, but I don't believe for a moment that you are miscast. I think what you bring of yourself to the role is what has brought Holmes to life."

"You mean Sir Arthur's Sherlock is more like me than was thought?"

"And perhaps you are more like Sherlock than you admit." She instantly regretted saying that, and so went on, "But please, darling, I would not have you sacrifice yourself for any part."

"Then let's hope Holmes does not return!"

Of course, they had far more pressing concerns at that time. Further chemotherapy was advised for Joan, though they were encouraged that treatment was having some effect on the tumor. Jeremy often went with her to the clinic, consoling her through the harrowing side effects, the weakness, the nausea, and at home cajoling her to eat. Strong willed and ill though she was, she tried her best to respond to his entreaties. She really felt he needed to work, and when two opportunities arose, she was glad for it.

The first offer was quite unusual: to narrate a ballet called "Song" based on the "Song of Solomon" from the Bible, and one of several ballets choreographed by Martha Graham that were being presented at the Lincoln Center in early April 1985. The recitation of the biblical love poems came from offstage, and Brett's reverberant voice was perfectly suited: "For lo the winter is past, the rain is over and gone, the flowers appear on the earth; the time of the singing of birds is come, and the voice of the turtle is heard in our land!"

Conveniently, a recording could be used when he was unavailable, because the second part he took on was a revival of the 1920s play *Aren't We All?* by Frederick Lonsdale, which was to open 29 April at the Brooks Atkinson. Brett was adept at this sort of drawing room comedy and had appeared in a television adaptation of Lonsdale's *On Approval* five years before, so needless to say his portrayal of Willie Tatham was superb. Willie's wife, played by Lynn Redgrave, catches him kissing another woman, and refuses to believe his protests that it was not serious. He then tries to balance the scales by surprising her in some indiscretion. Rex Harrison played Willie's father, Lord Grenham, and Claudette Colbert was Lady Frinton, a society grande dame out to extract a proposal from the aging yet randy Lord, who is especially fond of the shop girls at the British Museum.

This was just the type of light fare to distract Jeremy from the dreadful anxiety of Joan's illness, and she was improving. The chemotherapy ended, and she began to regain strength, just in time for an opening night party at the Rainbow Room, overlooking the New York skyline from the sixty-fifth floor of the Rockefeller Center. While Boston is just a hop and a skip from Manhattan, Jeremy would no doubt have taken a hotel room for the occasion, perhaps at the Belvedere Hotel, dating from the twenties, with its splendid marble lobby and just a block from the theatre.

Jeremy came up to the suite after the performance, and Joan was getting into her evening gown, a gorgeous confection of scarlet and silver.[139] Before she saw him, he stood in the doorway, struck by a sudden vivid memory of his mother dressed for the Coronation Ball that long ago night at the Dorchester Hotel in London.

"Oh, darling, would you zip me?" Joan had glimpsed him in the mirror, and as he obliged her, she asked, "Well how did it go?" She had seen a preview performance of the play, as had all the major critics, who wrote rave reviews and were especially enthusiastic about Brett.

"Splendidly! I lost count of the curtain calls," he replied, "and you'll never guess who came to my dressing room afterwards."

"I never guess, Watson," she jested. "Who?"

"Martha Graham.[140] I was flabbergasted! I adore the woman."

"Good heavens, there are stairs to your dressing room, and she is 91!"

"I know, amazing," though more amazing to Jeremy at that moment was the sight of his Joanie. Her hair had started growing in, but she still was relying on the wig. "You are positively ravishing tonight, my darling. I can't believe how good you look, but how do you feel?"

"Like dancing! Now into your tux. There's a boutonniere in the fridge." It was a red rose.

With no stretch of our imagination, we may easily believe that Joan and Jeremy were that night the most graceful and handsome couple on the dance floor, which in the Rainbow Room famously revolves slowly to take advantage of the panoramic views; and after what they had been through lately, what a joy it must have been to be together, *dancing!* It was a fairytale evening; they ate and drank and laughed. Jeremy loved the cast he was working with, Harrison, Colbert, Redgrave. Perhaps Lynn's sister Vanessa was there with her husband, director Tony Richardson, and their grown daughter Natasha, whose film debut in "The Copper Beeches" on the Holmes series would be broadcast in August that year. But that night *the play was the thing*, and everyone was exuberant over its success.

* * *

Jeremy was in a visitor's lounge at Mass General, chain smoking. It was not allowed, but the staff was being indulgent. Joan's son Caleb was with him, and the doctor had just left to finish his rounds. It was the end of June, and Joan was not doing well.

"What do doctors know?" Jeremy protested. "Miracles happen. We can't give up hope, son." They looked at each other in unspoken desperation.

"I can't believe this is happening," is all Caleb could say. He was about the same age as Jeremy had been when his own mother died, only adding to a crushing sense of unreality.

"Come, let's go see her, lad," and Jeremy laid his hand on Caleb's shoulder.

Joan had tried to go back to work in May, but her stamina was gone. By June symptoms were returning. These were controlled for a while with medication, but in the all too familiar course of malignancy, the tumor was overtaking her. Cancer is diabolical; it does not kill outright, with quick mercy, like heart attack or stroke, but gradually, agonizingly, leaves the body unable to sustain life.

Jeremy was still doing the play on Broadway, so when Joan was hospitalized, life became ever more complicated. He fully expected, though, that she would go home in time, like Caleb refusing to believe what the doctors were predicting.

The first of July fell on a Monday when the theatre was dark, and Jeremy came up to Boston, going straight to the hospital. He was intercepted by the oncologist, who was leaving Joan's room.

"Jeremy, I'm glad you're here. I need to talk with you." He took Jeremy's elbow and led him into the visitor's lounge, then he continued, "Joan is on a morphine drip now," he explained, "but her pain is worsening. We will need to increase the dose."

"Of course, by all means," Jeremy said, still not acknowledging the doctor's implication.

"I am sorry to say it, Jeremy, but truthfully she is not going to make it, and the end may be soon." Jeremy listened, his head in his hands as if to close his ears. "I would advise you, if you can possibly have your understudy take over this week, to stay here in Boston with Joan and the family." Struck dumb, Jeremy simply nodded, clasping the doctor's hand.

He did manage to stay in Boston, and came every morning to the hospital. Joan slept most of the time. She was pale and gaunt, but the nurses would put her wig on so that she would look more herself. When she would wake, she and Jeremy would daydream together about going back to London and settling down in Clapham, the parties they would throw, or romantic dinners on the rooftop watching city lights come on. By Wednesday she was in intensive care.

Morphine was believed by the ancient Greeks to be a gift of the gods, and anyone bearing witness to a cancer death would have cause to agree. Some portion of those witnesses have come to know that, in addition to relieving pain, it also suppresses respiration. Physicians dissemble on this matter: is it used for comfort or euthanasia? But then as to death itself, their profession equates it with failure. In the ICU, Joan would have been given as much morphine as needed to control her pain.[141]

When Jeremy came on Thursday, 4 July, she was sleeping, the heart monitor beeping reassurance. He sat close to the bed listening to it, holding her hand, unmindful of passing time. Eventually she opened her eyes and smiled at him. He kissed her hand, her forehead, her lips. She said, "Are you going to be all right?"

"Don't trouble yourself, please darling," he whispered, and she slipped back into oblivion. The heart monitor beeped more slowly, then fitfully, and he thought his own heart would stop. Soon came the straight line; she was gone. The nurses were alerted, but of course this was the expected outcome. They would notify the doctor to make it official, but they left the bereaved husband alone lying over his beloved wife, sobbing.

* * *

In the hours and days ahead, Peter Jeremy William Huggins felt a renewed and redoubled respect and appreciation for his father and older brothers as he bore the grim, onerous duty they once had: breaking the news of a mother's death. Jeremy knew he had to hold up for the sake of his stepchildren, Caleb and Rebekah, then in their twenties. Joan's mother had come again, and in spite of the terrible distress of losing her daughter, was able to be of great help. She and Joan, facing the situation with some realism, had planned for her passing, perhaps even choosing the funeral hymns. Joan's colleagues, devastated though they were, would have spoken among themselves of who would carry on in her place, who might give a eulogy or write an obituary. One source quotes Alistair Cooke, host of Masterpiece Theatre, remembering her as a "marvelous boss," though fearing that her dedication to her work may have led to her early end.[142]

Aren't We All? continued on Broadway until 23 July, its ninety performances representing quite a good run for a revival. Somehow, Brett was able to get through it, in the time honored manner of a good showman. By the end of August he was back in England, where Granada Television was indeed going ahead with more of their wildly popular Sherlock Holmes dramas. As Joan may have predicted, Michael Cox would step back, becoming executive producer, handing the producer's role to June Wyndham Davies.[143] What was not foreseen was that the role of Dr. Watson, which had been filled by the amiable, avuncular David Burke, would be taken over by the more sedate Edward Hardwicke. Burke left to join the Royal Shakespeare Company, along with his wife, the actress Anna Calder-Marshall.

What an irony that like Conan Doyle, Brett was to be dogged by the popularity of Sherlock Holmes. For the actor though, the ongoing demands of carrying this television series in the starring role hit him at a time of great personal loss and at an age when he no longer had the resilience of youth. He would turn fifty-two that November. Joan had just died, the person whose love had given him confidence, security, solace. Now once again would come the sense of abandonment that combines loneliness and fear. We must surmise that a natural anger that is part of grief, the more so for a person with a mood disorder, was intensified by resentment at having to carry on in spite of it. Yet Jeremy kept his aplomb, for the most part.

It appears that as his fame grew in the role of Sherlock Holmes, Brett gave more interviews, and at this point we need to digress briefly with regard to them. In all those we have come upon, he is charming, witty, seeming familiar and without reserve. Nevertheless, the expected questions are met with stock answers, as for instance the similarities in two interviews he gave in 1985. One was on the Baker Street set at the end of the year with author Peter Haining, who was writing a book, *The Television Sherlock Holmes*. Asked about the beginning of the series, Jeremy tells of a screen test of his makeup, saying, "I looked like a gargoyle." To the question of how the part has affected him, he replies, "It has turned me into something of a recluse." These and other answers are the same that he gave Rosemary

Herbert in New York when he was there in April. That interview appeared in the magazine Armchair Detective, the fall edition.

Indeed even later personal appearances on television talk shows follow the same script, so that viewing a number of these one senses he is not really being open. When asked about his childhood, he tells of his father, a decorated war hero, and his wonderful mother, who had "open doors and open windows in her soul." He will go on to refer to his sense of responsibility toward his parents, though he was the youngest of four, with a favorite metaphor about the tail of the crocodile being heaviest. Particularly sad for someone knowing Brett's history is the impression that he is attempting to offset the upper-class background clearly evident in the very pronunciation of his words. He is self-deprecating, parodies the aristocratic smirk. Like his Quaker ancestors, including his mother, he was modest, humble; he had the common touch, never putting himself above others. But that really is class, in the truest sense, which needs no apology.

Any actor who has enjoyed, or should we say endured, celebrity will create a public facade, giving just enough personal information to endear himself. Jeremy Brett always wore that actor's mask, removing it only for Joan, perhaps his son David, and briefly for a young photographer by the name of Marcus Tylor. But more on that later, lest we get ahead of our story.

That day in December when Haining was granted access for the sake of his book, Brett's wife had been dead just six months, and he would spend two months of the year to come in a mental hospital. Despite appearances, he was emotionally fragile, which comes across reading between the lines in Haining's account; there is a certain edginess. Having to adjust to a new costar put added strain, but Jeremy was unfailingly generous, to fellow actors most especially. Thus before filming began, he invited Edward Hardwicke to meet him at a restaurant in Soho. They had both been at the National Theatre Company in the late sixties, but in different troupes, and so had never acted together. It was late August, a hot summer night, when they converged on Soho, bustling with hungry tourists.

"I must tell you, Jeremy," Edward began, when they had been seated and awaited cocktails, "I am so pleased to be able to work with you, and honored to have a part in such a fine production."

"Thank you, Ted, you are so kind. What do you think of the script?" They would begin filming with "The Abbey Grange," though the first episode of *The Return of Sherlock Holmes* to air would be "The Empty House," in keeping with the canonical order.

"It's absolutely splendid!" Hardwicke exclaimed, "and I don't have much to memorize."

"I think June wants to ease you into the part," said Jeremy, referring to producer June Davies, "but David Burke will attest to how often I have prevailed upon the writers to give Watson more lines."

"He did tell me that." Hardwicke and Burke were close friends. David had strongly recommended Edward as his best replacement. "I love the way David rescued poor doctor Watson from the old caricature, and the fact that the series is so authentically Doyle."

"That's what persuaded me to do it," Jeremy concurred. Over dinner Edward went on to say that as a child in Hollywood with his famous father, he came to know and love Nigel Bruce, who played Watson in the Rathbone films, and was a frequent guest.

"Your father was quite a figure to live up to," Jeremy observed. "Do you feel his shadow?"

"I confess to a bit of a complex on that score," Edward replied frankly. His father was Sir Cedric Hardwicke.

"Well, now it's your turn, old fellow." Edward was genuinely touched by this remark, reassured that they would get on well and make a good team.[144]

Jeremy did not eat or drink very much and seemed eager to leave. After dinner, he said suddenly, "Come on, let's go to a jazz club." And off they went in a cab to Tottenham Court Road. It may have been the 100 Club, which had been there since 1942, when it opened as the London Jazz Club. They were stopped at the door, as the club was private.

"Charles," Jeremy addressed the doorman, observing his name tag. "Charles darling, I was not intending to come to the Club tonight; but my friend is a visitor to London, and we decided on the spur of the moment. I don't have my card on me, Charles, but surely you will be kind to us." Of course, looking eminently respectable, they gained entry to the smoke-filled premises.

They sat listening to the featured combo playing classic jazz, ordered drinks, and Jeremy contributed to the cloud of cigarette smoke in the room. But he seemed restless. He fidgeted in his seat, and to Edward the silence between sets was feeling awkward. Finally he looked at his watch and excused himself.

"I had better get home if I want to catch the early train to Manchester in the morning."

"See you tomorrow then," Jeremy said. "Awfully glad we could meet this evening."

They shook hands warmly, and Edward left, impressed with Jeremy's kindness and support, though puzzled by his distracted behavior.

"The Abbey Grange" was a standout production among the next seven one hour episodes in the series. Edward Hardwicke slipped into the part of Watson so ably that viewers scarcely noticed the change. The story begins with Holmes standing over a sleeping Watson with a candle. He wakes him, quoting Shakespeare, "Come Watson, 'the game is afoot.'"[145] They have been summoned to the Abbey Grange by Inspector Stanley Hopkins upon the murder of Sir Eustace Brackenstall, who turns out to have been a drunken, cruel, and abusive husband to Lady Mary Brackenstall, the former Miss Mary Fraser of Adelaide. The murder was committed by Captain Jack Crocker, a mate on the ship that brought Mary from Australia. They are in love.

Upon suspecting where justice lies in this case, Holmes utters the famous line, "Once or twice in my career I feel I have done more real harm by my discovery of the criminal than ever he had done by his crime. I have learned caution now, and I had rather play tricks with the law . . . then with my own conscience."

Brett is athletic as ever: swarming up the great stone mantel to examine a bell rope, standing up to the burly Captain Crocker, played by Oliver Tobias. "Play tricks with me and I'll crush you,"

Sherlock brags, poking the Captain with his pipe stem. In the end he lets Captain Crocker go free.

But the closing scene is most relevant to our story. It is not in the Conan Doyle original, but makes a smooth conclusion added by the script writer, Trevor Bowen. Holmes and Watson are relaxing by the fire savoring their port, and the good doctor seems critical of Sherlock's rash indifference to legality.

"You are too bound by forms, Watson," says Holmes.

"Forms are society, Holmes," Watson counters, and Holmes snorts. "It's just as well you are unique," and Watson smiles broadly. Then Holmes flashes that quick smile that was a Jeremy Brett, *nee* Huggins, trademark. In this instance the smile falls so quickly that even viewed in slow motion it seems fast. And it falls very low indeed: his whole face droops, the corners of his mouth, his brow; his eyes go dark, the light gone out. On a face that was supremely expressive, it is an expression of profound, unfathomable melancholy. Knowing his story as we tell it, and as we hope readers may know it, the scene is chilling, foreboding.

Brett was beginning to crack. As told by Hardwicke in the Stuart Davies book, the first signs came during the filming of "The Priory School," when a crew member felt it necessary to explain that "Jeremy is not himself today." Always professional on the set, he became at other times snappy, snarling, icy, which was of course far from his normal behavior. Was the filming location for the school too reminiscent of Eton? It was Haddon Hall in Derbyshire.

Jeremy held up through the completion of the series of seven episodes, ending with "The Six Napoleons." It was terribly hard work through the dark winter months, when the Midland Hotel in Manchester became his home away from home. Luxurious though it was, it must have come to seem a prison. He was nearing a dangerous threshold. As Dr. Jameson describes her personal experience in her memoir, "Slowly the darkness began to weave its way into my mind, and before long I has hopelessly out of control."

* * *

"Penelope, dear, are we still playing cards tonight at Jeremy's? I have been trying to reach him since yesterday." It was Patience Collier on the phone wanting to confirm a bridge date.

"As far as I know we're on, darling, but I'll call Charles to be sure and get back to you." Charles Kay was the fourth partner as we mentioned in Chapter Three. But Penelope Keith was alerted, having heard rumors that Jeremy was behaving erratically. One mutual friend had been at dinner with Brett a week earlier when he insisted on buying a bottle of champagne for every table in the restaurant.

Unable to reach Jeremy by phone, Penelope called Charles. "Have you spoken to Jeremy lately, Charles?" she inquired. "He's not answering his telephone."

Charles had heard nothing.

"Do you think we should drop in on him, to see if he is all right?" However reluctant to intrude on his friend, Charles agreed.

"Meet me at Clapham then, half an hour."

They converged on the apartment building and ascended to the penthouse. Receiving no response to their pounding on the door, they entered. It was open. They called his name. Again nothing. They looked through all the rooms without finding him.

"Surely he has just stepped out for cigarettes, Penelope!" Charles was feeling awkward.

"No, I'm worried," Penelope insisted. "Wait! Let's check the roof."

It was lucky they did. Jeremy was sitting in a patio chair in the cold drizzle with night coming on, only his robe and slippers to protect him. He looked at them as though they were strangers and resisted their efforts to get him inside, struggling with them physically.

"We're going to need help, Penelope," Charles decided. "Go call an ambulance."

We know that Jeremy Brett had a breakdown in 1986; we do not have details of just how he came to be admitted to Maudesley, the psychiatric hospital in South London. From his own account in the Davies book, had his situation not come out in the newspapers, he would have kept it even from his family. So we surmise it was not a relative who discovered him.¹⁴⁶ He also spoke of the crisis in an interview for the London Times, describing it from his perspective: the world went pink, then white, and the next thing he knew, he was in hospital, unable to relate to anyone, lying face down, his fists clenched.¹⁴⁷ He remained there for two months.

Anyone who has had the misfortune to experience a locked psychiatric ward firsthand, even as a visitor, will know how grim and fearsome a place it is by its very mission. Lost souls wander the halls; muffled cries waft through the corridors; new patients arrive in restraints. The atmosphere is cold, clinical, sterile.

Jeremy's son David went immediately to Maudesley as soon as he read in the paper what had happened. By then his father would have been medicated, though the drugs used have their own terrible effects. David came often during that hospitalization, bringing flowers—red roses of course—and anything he could think of to lend a modicum of cheer. His mother Anna would drive him, and wait in the car.

Edward Hardwicke was also a visitor, as he reported to Davies. He related that what Brett feared most was the loss of his skill as an actor, that the drugs to subdue him would take away his edge, compromise him. He was discharged from Maudesley to a convalescent home, and then stayed with Edward and his wife for a short time. He now had a diagnosis of manic depression and no doubt a referral to a psychiatrist.

In Manchester meanwhile, executives at Granada waited anxiously for their star to get back on his feet. The plan was to produce *The Sign of Four* as a two hour television special, and sometime that year work began. The result was one of the finest dramas made. Brett was back at his best, interrogating Miss Morstan, played by the lovely Jenny Seagrove, recruiting the Baker Street Irregulars, a gang of London urchins, and running after Toby, a borrowed border collie on the scent of Jonathan Small and his aboriginal companion, who attempt to flee in a steam launch after murdering Bartholomew Sholto for the treasure chest. The chase down the River Thames, so picture perfect that every thirty-five-millimeter frame might be a Pre-Raphaelite painting, was actually filmed on the River Yare in Norfolk.[148]

A gruff and hirsute John Thaw played the peg-legged Small, and Ronald Lacey was Bartholomew's twin, Thaddeus, a character whom Conan Doyle is said to have based on his friend Oscar Wilde. The mystery was published in 1890, ten years before Wilde's death. The Granada adaptation, staying true to the original, aired late in 1987, to much approbation.

In retrospect, a person familiar with the Granada series from beginning to end, all forty-two productions of Sherlock Holmes mysteries, would likely appreciate the view that Jeremy Brett should have quit the role after *The Sign of Four*, in which he was still magnificent, lithe, strong, in good voice. Not that he ever ceased to be exemplary, always adding interest to the character he portrayed so truthfully. But in subsequent episodes his failing health was increasingly evident.

Nevertheless, no sooner was *The Sign of Four* completed than work began on four more one hour shows, and Brett was slipping back into mania. At some point in 1987, in a state perhaps mixing depression and extreme frustration, he took a scissors to his hair, lopping it off, leaving nothing but a bristly shag. He attempted a weak rationalization of this action, but Hardwicke confirmed the truth of the matter to Davies. The Sherlock of this period, moreover, is not only shorthaired, but emanates a distinct aura of dissolution. We might point, for example, to the first Baker Street scene of "Silver Blaze," where through a thick haze of tobacco smoke, he saunters wearily from the bedroom in his dressing gown and announces to Watson, "I'll have to go," meaning to Dartmoor to look for the missing race horse, Silver Blaze. Then there is the final shot of Holmes in "Wisteria Lodge," in a small, worn mirror, his face, his demeanor, heavy with *Weltschmerz*.

Why then if Jeremy had become unhappy playing Holmes did he not back out? There would have been a contract certainly, and had he begged off for health reasons his future in acting would be compromised. In any case, he was by then typecast as the super sleuth. But most of all he could never disappoint the legions of fans worldwide who loved him as Holmes, regardless of the cost to himself personally. He soldiered on.

* * *

The location shoot of "The Devil's Foot" was in Cornwall, a welcome break for cast and crew, we imagine, from the Manchester studios. The plot has an ailing Holmes, upon the advice of the Harley Street specialist, Dr. Moore Agar, on holiday with Watson. A full-bearded Denis Quilley played Dr. Leon Sterndale, famed African explorer, whose sample of a West African poison, *radix pedis diaboli*, "devil's foot root," is purloined by Mortimer Tregennis and used against his siblings. The sister Brenda, who was Sterndale's secret lover, dies.

In this tale, Conan Doyle rails against British divorce laws through the character of Sterndale, whose predicament reflects the author's. Sir Arthur was still a young man when his first wife contracted tuberculosis, and before she died after years of illness, he had fallen for Jean Leckie. But he could not divorce, so they waited; likewise in the story, Leon could not divorce to marry Brenda. When she is killed, Sterndale uses the "devil's foot" to take revenge on the murderous brother. Once again, Holmes takes the side of justice and refrains from telling the police of Sterndale's guilt.

The drama plays out on the southernmost point of Cornwall in the environs of Caerleon and the rocky peninsula known as the Lizard. We see Brett wrapped in his long knitted muffler and an afghan, which he flings over his shoulder in a very Shakespearean gesture. Without knowing the details, we might assume that cast and crew were put up at a Caerleon cottage or inn, or perhaps they took over the local pub.

"Quilley old chap, come join us!" Jeremy beckoned. He and Edward were having dinner, and everyone in the pub, for that matter, was associated with the production company. "Loved your Sterndale this afternoon."

"Thank you, Jeremy. I think we're ready to shoot, don't you?" They had finished rehearsing that day.

"Filming tomorrow!" Away together on location, the team felt even more like a family, and they were all in good spirits. Jeremy was finishing a glass of wine and lit a cigarette. "Do you like Rodgers and Hart, Denis?"

Quilley took a swig of ale and started to sing, "I'm wild again, beguiled again . . ." and Brett joined in, "a simpering, whimpering child again. Bewitched, bothered, and bewildered am I."

Denis Quilley was five years older but had also been with the National Theatre Company in the seventies. He had an excellent singing voice and had done musicals, including the very successful *La Cage aux Folles*. Jeremy was tickled to find someone who knew the score of *Pal Joey*. They were off, serenading the room to delighted applause. Hardwicke was embarrassed and excused himself.[149]

"Poor Ted, he tends to be a bit staid," Jeremy explained, smiling as Hardwicke left the pub.

Then Quilley sang on, "There's a small hotel," handing off the next phrase to Brett, "with a wishing well," then Quilley, "I wish that we were there," and in harmony, "together!"

Oh, it was a jolly good time, laughing and singing! Another evening they crooned "Joey, Joey, Joey" from *The Most Happy Fella*, the 1956 American musical by Frank Loesser. To Edward's consternation this after dinner cabaret was repeated every night. The only song that stumped Quilley was Noel Coward's "I've Been to a Marvelous Party." Who else but Jeremy Brett would remember those hilarious, limerick verses?

That year, 1987, was the centenary of *A Study in Scarlet*, the work that introduced Holmes and Watson to the reading public. Screenwriter Jeremy Paul, who had already scripted several episodes for the Granada series, was reminded of this by his good friend Jeremy Brett, and the two decided there should be some sort of commemoration. They had known one another since 1973 when they worked together on an episode of *Country Matters*, also a Granada series.

Setting his fertile mind to it, Jeremy Paul came up with the idea of a play, not a typical Holmes mystery, but one that delved into Sherlock's relationship with Watson, having just the two of them on stage. The result was a short work entitled *The Secret of Sherlock*

Holmes. It was a clever pastiche of familiar speeches woven together in dialogue between Holmes and Watson: "What a lovely thing a rose is!"; "My mind rebels at stagnation! Give me problems, give me work . . ."

The secret, arising in the second act, was that Professor Moriarty was really Sherlock himself, his alter ego, a strange notion that had come up once or twice in the past, though strenuously refuted by Doyle's youngest son Adrian in a filmed interview from the 1960s. In the play, Sherlock tries to convince Watson of this idea, challenging him to refute his proofs if he can.

The plan was for one Sunday evening performance of the work before an invited audience, to include Conan Doyle's last surviving child, Dame Jean Conan Doyle, who was then 72. The event, at the Mayfair Theatre, went well, and Jeremy was thrilled to meet Dame Jean; it was here that she blessed him with her assurance that his was the Sherlock Holmes of her childhood memories, surely no higher praise.

The play was then put on the back burner as production began on the next two hour special. By March of 1988, the company was on location in Liverpool filming *The Hound of the Baskervilles*, which aired in August. It was not as impressive as *The Sign of Four*, in spite of Neil Duncan as Dr. Mortimer and Kristoffer Tabori as the American Baskerville, Sir Henry, who inherits the family estate, including the title and historic curse. A great dane, conscripted as the hound, was unfortunately docile, but the scene of the villainous Stapleton sinking in the Great Grimpen Mire never fails to horrify.

In the meantime, Jeremy Paul had modified his play somewhat, and impresario Duncan Weldon took a chance on it. After previews in Guildford and Richmond, *The Secret of Sherlock Holmes*, came to the Wyndham's Theatre in the West End on 22 September, 1988. While reviews were mixed, critics concurred on the excellence of the acting, and people flocked to see the television stars in the flesh.

Jeremy enjoyed being in front of a live audience again, and as he had become so widely known and loved through the medium of television, fans lined up at the stage door for his autograph. Indeed, his dressing room apparently was a hub of activity, and filled with red roses always, even if he had to buy them himself.

Let it be said here that whatever skepticism may have been harbored about the intercontinental marriage of Jeremy Brett and Joan Wilson should be dispelled by his fate after she died, robbing him of the sole pillar of stability in his life, a cruel and untimely loss inflicted upon him *for a second time*. After losing his soulmate in Joan and suffering a psychotic break associated with manic depression, there was cause to wonder whether he ever again would know the sweet freedom of dropping the actor's mask, the comfort to be himself. Thanks to his accessibility backstage at Wyndham's we have photographic evidence of just one incredible instance.

A young, struggling photographer by the name of Marcus Tylor was exhibiting his work at the Palace Theatre nearby. His portraits of actors backstage were black and white mood studies, aiming to be deeper and more insightful than the common, smiling, celebrity shots. He left a note for Brett at the stage door explaining this intent and asking whether he might come with his camera. To his surprise, Jeremy responded, calling him on Monday, 10 October, and arranging for them to meet that Thursday evening at 6:45, before the performance, giving Tylor all of fifteen minutes to shoot a roll of film before Brett would need to prepare for the 8:00 curtain.[150]

Perhaps it was inadvertent, or it may have been the stipulation that he should not try to pose, but there in that dim light in just those few short minutes the mask came off. In the first four frames especially, we are given a glimpse of the real Peter Jeremy William Huggins that so few had ever seen and no one would ever again see, the depth of his character and intelligence, the genuine beauty of his nature. If ever a soul was captured on film, Jeremy's was that night in these remarkable photographs.

But young Marcus was hardly alone in that bustling backstage dressing room at Wyndham's. In November, Anna Massey remarried to a professor of metallurgy, Uri Andres, an Israeli. Jeremy was of course very happy for them, marking the occasion with a wedding gift and in addition box seats to the play, which Anna describes in her memoir as "brilliant."

Then in March 1989, Brett was visited backstage by three representatives of the Berkswell Historical Society, more specifically three among several members calling themselves the Offshoot Group, who wrote and published a yearly periodical titled *Berkswell Miscellany*. Given the fame of their native son, they wanted Volume 5 of the publication to include articles about him and his family. The interview was prearranged, and Jeremy was gratified to be remembered in his hometown. He even shared family photos, which appeared along with the articles, including legends naming those pictured. In the group picture from the farewell party, for example, after Colonel Huggins died, we have the faces and names of many of the house staff among whom Jeremy grew up.

The resulting articles that appeared under the title "The Huggins Family of Berkswell" give a sense of how thrilled Jeremy was to talk about those halcyon days. The separate pieces included "Colonel Huggins," "The Colonel's Regiment," and "Life at the Grange." Before leaving they informed Jeremy of the upcoming fiftieth reunion of the 120th Field Regiment, which his father the Colonel had mustered and trained in 1939 when war broke out. The reunion would be held at the Reading Room in Berkswell on 4 June, and Jeremy assured them he and his brothers would be honored to participate.

Also backstage in March, Brett was handed a letter from a young woman named Linda Pritchard. She was a short, rather prosaic looking individual, but muscular, being a marathon runner. She lived with her parents, had work involving computers, and though two decades younger had a huge crush on Jeremy. Commonplace as she appeared, however, she was a person of uncommon empathy. As she explained in her letter, her plan was to make a solo run around the whole of the United Kingdom to raise money for cancer research, sensing acutely the suffering inflicted by the disease, even the anxiety of a routine screening test, and the terror of a positive diagnosis. She needed support and publicity for such an ambitious undertaking and had found none.

Jeremy had a keen intuition about people; he was impressed with this woman's courage and initiative and naturally sympathetic to the cause, considering how Joan had died. So he called Linda and offered whatever service he could provide toward the run.

It is easy to imagine the shock and excitement the young woman felt actually speaking to the man she idolized.[151] But she controlled herself, and together they planned for a press release to announce her plan. She began the run on 12 April from Greenwich to much publicity. Jeremy was there, of course, family and friends, and newsmen. Over the next six months she ran five thousand miles, raising fifty thousand pounds for the Imperial Cancer Research Fund. Jeremy, who had been named Pipe Smoker of the Year, donated the three thousand pounds attendant upon that distinction.

* * *

"Pipe Smoker of the Year? You? Is there no justice?" Reverend Huggins was kidding his baby brother, who puffed on a cigarette over after dinner coffee at Coombe Abbey, their favorite inn in Coventry.[152] It was 3 June, the day before the regimental reunion in Berkswell, when they would converge along with Patrick upon the Reading Room. Michael was away. "Do you hear from Daphne?" John went on.

"Not recently," his brother replied. "I'm not complaining, John, you know I love my work, but I miss the opportunities to be with family," he paused, "like when Joanie was so ill."

Just what John was thinking. "But you were there, Jeremy, and she understood. Your son is close though, right?"

"Oh, indeed, he is a mainstay."

"Well, I heard that Daphne's son Martin is to marry next year, an actress named Lucy."

"That's wonderful news! He's finally settling down. I was glad too when he decided on acting."[153]

"Yes, he should do well if he takes after his father."

"But I think his success will come in comedy, John, mark my words."

"Really? You may be prescient, brother. You know Mrs. Wheatley died."

"Patrick told me. What a great old dame she was! A sad day," he paused, lit another cigarette and smiled to himself, recalling his last tea with her at the Hall, the day the lych-gate was dedicated in 1979. Then continuing, "And a sad day when the Hall was converted to apartments. The passing of an era."

"What is the world coming to"—and John grinned—"when Pipe Smoker of the Year goes to Jeremy Huggins rather than his eldest brother!"

They laughed. He no longer felt free to tousle Jeremy's hair; at fifty-five and sixty-four, the age difference seemed much smaller. Then he grew serious.

"I worry about you, Jeremy, you're working too hard. You know I'm a fan, and by God you are the finest Sherlock Holmes there will ever be—Sir Arthur is rejoicing in heaven—but please don't let this role be the death of you. Think of your health. Remember that rheumatic fever. Take care of yourself."

"I will, John, I will." Jeremy was touched by this speech and his brother's genuine concern. "You need not worry though," he added, "look who I have praying for me."

"That I do, believe me, that I do." John had the last word.

What a joy it was to be back in Berkswell the next morning, despite the inevitable poignance: the emerald pastures, where horses still grazed; the hedge roses in full bloom; the Village Green sparkling with dew; the smell of damp stone from the ancient Bercul's well outside the church, from which Berkswell takes its name. It was Sunday, the Fourth of June, the day when at Eton the wet bobs in their flower-bedecked straw boaters would be sculling on the Thames. But here in Berkswell the clangor of the old church bells soon filled the air.

Following morning service, the Huggins brothers were invited to the rectory for lunch with Reverend Gooderick and his wife. He had been appointed the new rector the previous year, taking over from Reverend Dingle. Then it was on to the Reading Room, where surviving members of the regiment and their wives were convening. Their chaplain, Joe Partridge, was regrettably too ill to attend, but his prepared sermon was read. A silver commemorative tray, presented to Colonel Huggins by the regiment when he retired, was returned to them on this occasion by his sons.[154]

Later in the day a wreath-laying was held at the Colonel's grave in the churchyard with villagers joining in, including friends and former staff of the family. There was Lily Knight, the cook, Joyce Jakeman, the housekeeper, Bob Creber, the gardener who succeeded Tom Houghton. These were the cast of Jeremy's childhood, the best years of his life.

The day ended with a service of Evensong, at which Jeremy read the lesson and added his still resonant voice to the hymns he loved. His eyes filled with tears of nostalgia as he sang "Now the Day is Over," recalling as it did the Parish Sunday when he sat on his father's shoulders singing with all the village children around the bonfire behind the Grange.

It must have been hard for Jeremy to leave his brothers that night, to acknowledge that time moves in only one direction, the only vector, curiously, that is thus restricted, and to realize that John was quite right. He was working too hard. Sustaining a nightly performance on stage for so many months—with no understudy—was physically exhausting and mentally numbing. But there it was: the public did not tire of the play. Tickets were still selling.

Jeremy took a late train back to London that night, and his brothers saw him to the station, waving as he boarded. They stood silently together as the train pulled away from the platform.

"Can you keep an eye on him, Patrick?" John asked, something of pleading in the question.

"I try, John, but you know how he is: 'I'm fine, don't worry about me!' We're always the last to know when he is in trouble."

"Yes, of course. I guess we'll just have to keep watching the newspapers," John sighed, putting a hand on Patrick's shoulder. They walked away from the empty station, under the stark lights that make such places seem like otherworldly outposts.

There is no significant information about Jeremy's brothers: where they lived; whether the two eldest married or had children. Obviously they had no interest in the limelight. They were private people; they wrote no memoirs. We might have cause to wonder what role they did play in the serious problems of their youngest sibling. However, anyone having the experience of a close relative with a mental disorder will appreciate how the illness drives a wedge. Adding to the social stigma of such a condition, to lose control over one's behavior is fundamentally embarrassing. No one wants to believe it is even a possibility; and posing an exasperating perplexity, the individual often turns away from those who most want to understand and help him.

By this time, Jeremy would have been taking lithium, the only drug found to be effective in managing manic depression. Dr. Jameson writes at length in her book about the struggle patients have accepting the need for medication. There is at first a reluctance to give up the euphoria, energy, and creativity of the positive moods; but when the illness worsens, when mania brings chaos and depression the risk of suicide, a person has no better option.

Tragically for Jeremy Brett, lithium has terrible cardiac side effects, which he began to experience as *The Secret of Sherlock Holmes* kept on. A fateful circle of affliction, a legacy of Eton—the diving event, the ear infection, rheumatic fever—was closing on him. While his heart struggled, his body was retaining fluid, until breathing and even moving were difficult. He was forced finally to see a doctor, who put him in hospital immediately. The play went dark for two weeks as he recuperated.

But then it resumed, running at Wyndham's for a year, then touring Britain for another three months. In the Davies book, Jeremy Paul recounts that he and Brett both looked upon the nightly performance as a kind of therapy for the actor. We would humbly submit that this view was misguided, underscoring the ignorance which prevails regarding mental disorders in general and bipolar in particular. In its later stages, manic depression may bring about schizoid and paranoid symptoms. The Jekyll and Hyde theme of Jeremy Paul's play, having Holmes revealed as Moriarty, was probably the last thing Brett needed at that time.

Hardwicke, a compassionate fellow and a good friend, saw that Jeremy's portrayal was deteriorating as the daily grind continued, and he attempted gently to suggest as much. Brett's reaction illustrates the lamentable manner by which the mood disorder ultimately isolates, through unreasoning, uncontrolled anger, vented most often at the closest targets.

He and Edward reached the point that they were no longer speaking. Then one evening Jeremy called him on the telephone, unleashing a loud, venomous tirade. Knowing how unlike the normally gracious, generous Jeremy this behavior was, Edward could not sleep all night, but stayed up, as he tells it in the Davies book, writing a lengthy letter, which he handed to Jeremy the next day. Jeremy looked at it, apologized, and carried on as usual. The mood had swung.

The final performance of the play took place at Theatre Royal in Bath on 16 December, 1989, doubtless to the huge relief of the exhausted actors. At last they would have a break from their roles until the spring, when Granada planned to start work on *The Casebook of Sherlock Holmes*, another series of six dramas. Jeremy took the opportunity to contact Linda Pritchard again. The charity run had ended in October, and he wanted to keep in touch with the plucky young woman. She received the call, as she recounts in her memoir of the period, with considerable excitement, but feigned sufficient calm to ask if they might meet for coffee. To her extreme delight he suggested Tea Time, a cafe near his home on Clapham Common.

Thus began a true friendship. Linda was young enough to be Jeremy's daughter, and her account of the relationship suggests that he may have regarded her in that light. They enjoyed one another and became regulars at Tea Time, talking for hours over pots of tea and whatever else they fancied, scones, muffins, tea bread. She found him to be open and friendly, unspoiled either by his fame or his extraordinary good looks. He liked her good humor and sense of adventure. She had been to Tibet, developed an interest in Eastern thought, and unlike most people did not shy away from serious discussions.

The principle question with which she struggled was a very common one: if God is omnipotent, why does he let good people suffer? Jeremy found himself in the ironic position of holding the brief for God, trying to help her and perhaps himself come to terms with adversity by realizing how it may instill wisdom, compassion and strength. At one point he took her to his apartment to demonstrate the practice of clearing the mind in meditation. The inference we draw from her account, however, is that his acquaintance with Eastern religion may not have been extensive.

Pritchard quotes him as saying that we are "not separate from God but a part of God," which expresses a certain remove from traditional theism. But the deeper wisdom of the East, the precept of Buddhism, for example, that the root of human suffering is a stubborn clinging to an individual, temporal selfhood, is a much farther reach, difficult even for many people raised in the culture. In any case, a probing into the transcendent oneness of ultimate reality is not something we find in Linda's story, which is not to denigrate either of them. He on his part was battling demons after all.

In the spring of 1990 it would be back to Manchester to resume production of the enormously popular Granada series, but there was still time for Brett to take a trip, perhaps a sentimental journey to Boston to visit his stepchildren.[155]

* * *

It was sometime after the New Year that he had the idea, and he called his son. "David, I'm thinking of going to the States, just to get away. Why don't you come with me? We could meet Caleb and Rebekah in New York and take in some Broadway shows."

"But, Dad, it's winter," David responded, initially disinclined.

"Are we not hardy Brits? Anyway it's the only time I am likely to have for a while."

Of course David agreed, knowing his father was far from hardy, and in fact needing the security of companionship. The fact of his dad's worsening health, a man who had always been so strong, so athletic, was surely an unhappy adjustment.

They took a suite at the Belvedere in Manhattan and had arranged for Caleb and Rebekah to come down and join them for a few days. Awaiting their arrival, David and Jeremy sat in the cocktail lounge of the hotel, drinking martinis.

"Are you going to Martin's wedding, Dad?" David asked. "It's going to be in Kent, near Canterbury."

"I'm awfully happy for him, son," Jeremy began, lighting a cigarette, "but I hesitate. I seem to have become so well known, you know?"

"You mean the paparazzi?"

"Quite so. My presence might cause a stir."

"So what? I really don't think Martin would mind," David cajoled. At that moment they spotted Joan's two offspring, and Jeremy stood up to wave them over. There were exuberant hugs and handshakes all around.

"Look at you!" Jeremy beamed, "No longer children! Please tell us all about yourselves." So they did, but Jeremy was not taking in the details. He was drinking in the sight of these fine young adults, conjuring in his mind their dear mother.

"When will we see more of Sherlock, Dad?" Rebekah enquired, interrupting his reverie. "You know the show is very popular here."

"Dear me! Should I expect to be accosted on the street?" They laughed.

"I will be back at work shortly, darling. Six more dramas are on the way, starting with 'The Disappearance of Lady Frances Carfax'." No doubt the youngsters had become enthusiasts.

"Mom would be so thrilled and proud if she were here," Caleb interjected, ever conscious of preserving her memory.

Sitting next to him, Jeremy clasped his arm, saying nothing. Only David might have been skeptical of the assertion, considering that Joan would more likely have been worried about his father's health, just as he was.

A substantial February snow had fallen on the city, making for that dirty urban slush, but Central Park just a few blocks away was pristine, a fairyland. Bundled in coats and scarves, hats and boots, the four walked to the park next morning and took a carriage ride, enjoying the crisp air, the sun glinting off the snow and making the bare trees sparkle. Then they rented skates and went ice skating on Wollman Rink. Only one man was bold enough to ask Jeremy whether he was indeed Jeremy Brett.

Rebekah jumped in saying, "My dad gets that all the time! Amazing resemblance, isn't it?" then skating away on Dad's arm before his accent could give him away.

So much like her mother! Jeremy could not help thinking.

That night they had tickets to a revival of *Gypsy* at the St. James Theatre, with Tyne Daly as Rose, the ambitious stage mother of stripper Gypsy Rose Lee. Jeremy emerged from the performance singing, "Everything's coming up roses!" from the score by Jule Stein and Stephen Sondheim, and Rebekah joined in with "Let me entertain you!" She may not have been the best singer, but at least she was not inhibited. Jeremy loved that about Americans.

The following night they took in *The Merchant of Venice*, with Dustin Hoffman in the role of Shylock. Hoffman was already a prominent film star, and Jeremy was favorably impressed by his Shakespeare, but no one would surpass Olivier as Shylock in his mind. Seeing this play was all the more poignant as Sir Laurence—idol, mentor, friend—had died the previous year at the age of 82.

The plan had been for David and Jeremy to visit Boston before returning home, but Jeremy was tiring, his legs and feet swelling from fluid retention. The cold of New York, the concrete canyons, made matters worse. He needed to see his doctors. Reluctantly they decided to go straight home, cutting the trip short.

In *The Casebook of Sherlock Holmes,* it is apparent that executives at Granada, typically when it comes to a highly successful television program, were resting on their laurels. Rather than go to the expense of sending a production crew to Switzerland, the original setting for "The Disappearance of Lady Frances Carfax," they filmed it in the Lake District. Extravagant spectacles like the one at Reichenbach Falls would not be repeated.

The first scene of this initial episode shows Holmes reading a letter from Watson, who is vacationing at the Lake Hotel and has met the intriguing eccentric, Lady Frances. Brett, in the long grey dressing gown, appears drawn, haggard, as though he has undergone diuresis, which might have been necessitated by a strenuous trip abroad. He found himself at this time walking a razor's edge, needing to control the extremes of a mood disorder while avoiding further heart damage from the medication.

Suffice it to say that it was a much different Jeremy Brett the public saw in *The Casebook*, which began airing in February of 1991, three years after *The Hound of the Baskervilles*. He was older and heavier. The relationship between Holmes and Watson in the dramas was also changing, forcing us to wonder whether off-screen conflicts were affecting the two actors, professional though they both were.

In "The Creeping Man," for example, Holmes summons Watson with a famously laconic note: "Come at once if convenient. If inconvenient, come all the same." When Watson arrives at Baker Street, Holmes is contemplating a mysterious case, looking for a loose end in the tangled skein. He says, "One such may reside in the question: does Professor Presbury's daughter wake or sleep?" Watson then proceeds to scold him for the peremptory summons on such flimsy grounds. If Watson is out of character in his petulance, Holmes is equally so in his timid response. Or is it Hardwicke and Brett we are watching?

This interchange is not in the original story, lavishly though effectively embellished by screenwriter Robin Chapman. As Davies points out in his book, Granada had already used the more adaptable of the Holmes mysteries, so that writers now needed to stretch the remaining tales extravagantly. But the bare bones of "The Creeping Man" are still there. Edith Presbury did not dream; a creature did look in at her second floor bedroom window, and that creature turns out to be her father, who in a misguided attempt to restore his virility has been injecting himself with a serum derived from the gonads of male primates, with the bizarre result of making him ape-like.

While this was the last episode in *The Casebook* series, it seemed there was always more Sherlock in the pipeline. Granada executives were eager to do more two hour dramas, even though it meant that writers, left only with the shortest and weakest stories in the canon, would be still more pressed to pad the material.

Again, Brett had put on water weight, the edema evident in his hands on close-up. Yet he was masterful in *The Master Blackmailer*, the first of the two hour productions, based rather loosely on "The

Adventure of Charles Augustus Milverton." Doyle was thought to have modeled Charles Augustus on a real person, a prominent Londoner rumored to be an extortionist. The script, another by Jeremy Paul, has an infamous kissing scene between Milverton's housemaid Aggie, played endearingly by Sophie Thompson, and Holmes, disguised as a plumber to obtain information about the household. The scene was a hit in the press, but even Brett could not convincingly force Sherlock into such a contortion. He did not like it.

Then came *The Last Vampyre*, also scripted by Jeremy Paul, based on another modest short story, "The Sussex Vampyre." The other Jeremy must have been relieved that at least he was not to replay the Count, though at the start of the episode, he startles Watson with a set of false fangs. The character of John Stockton, descendent of a family suspected in centuries past of vampirism, is not in the original. But the part, played by Roy Marsden, brings enough complication to the plot to fill two hours. Keith Barron, who appeared with Brett in 1982 in the series *Number 10*, took the part here of Bob Ferguson, the character whose family is visited with misfortune coincident with the arrival of Stockton. As in the original, Ferguson's crippled son Jack is the would-be vampire, who tries to poison his infant stepbrother with curare. But in Doyle's story the baby does not die, and in the end Holmes advises, "A year at sea would be my prescription for Master Jacky." The very thing Sir Arthur might suggest, considering his time before the mast.

The last of these feature length productions was *The Eligible Bachelor*, a wildly swollen version of the original story, "The Noble Bachelor." Stretching this simple tale to a two hour film was screenwriter Trevor Bowen. With all this going on in Manchester and numerous locations—several in Cheshire for *The Master Blackmailer* and *The Last Vampyre*, Croxteth Hall in Liverpool and Eastnor Castle in Herefordshire for *The Eligible Bachelor*—it would seem unlikely that Jeremy would have had time to go to his young cousin Martin's June wedding in Chilham. But his son quite possibly represented him, bearing his best wishes and a generous present.

* * *

A rare day of June perfection brought a good number of tourists to explore the quaint village of Chilham and snap pictures in the village square. Martin and Lucy would be married there in her home church, St. Mary's, she in a gown of white over green; and they would spend a brief honeymoon at a stately nearby hotel, which had been a seventeenth century manor house, surrounded by the rolling countryside of Kent.

What a glorious occasion it must have been for Daphne! David sought her out in the church when he arrived, and they sat together on the groom's side of the aisle.[156]

"You must be awfully excited for Martin, Daphne, starting his career, and now marriage."

"That I am, David. He is getting work in television, though at the moment he is doing Shakespeare in Regent's Park, which is why he needs to be back in London so quickly."

"What are they doing?"

"*Julius Caesar.* Can you believe it? Our Martin is Mark Antony!" Daphne exclaimed.

"Fabulous!" David was truly amazed. "You know my dad feels badly not being here today. He sends his love to you and the newlyweds."

"We understand, David, please tell him. This Granada business is consuming him, I'm afraid," Daphne remarked, openly concerned. "How is his health?"

"Truthfully? Worrisome." At that moment, the organ signaled the bridal procession, and everyone turned to watch Lucy enter on her father's arm.

There followed a rousing reception with champagne and dancing, all planned by Lucy's mother. We cannot imagine that it could have been held in the parish hall of a village church, so perhaps it was at a club or hotel. Whatever the case, it would be great fun. Martin is known to be a very gregarious, comical fellow. Making the rounds of the wedding guests, he was glad to see David.

"Wonderful of you to come, dear chap!" Martin beamed, shaking David's hand and slapping his back. "Where's Dad?"

"Busy filming *The Casebook* series. He hated to miss your wedding. Please know that," David answered, a bit awkwardly.

"Tell him we missed him too. We were all looking forward to ducking the paparazzi!" Martin jested. "No, no, your father is the best in my book. Now, cousin, meet my new wife." He motioned to Lucy.

"Are you going to let me dance with her?" David asked, as they watched her approach, gliding gracefully as her long gown swayed.

"If you promise not to steal her!"

The festivities wound down after a London black cab, specially enlisted for the event, whisked the wedding couple away to the manor house and their honeymoon suite, but David had not stayed in any case, driving back home before the champagne went to his head. It was late and few cars were on the road. He smiled as he drove, remembering how his father predicted Martin would be a comic; then he laughed aloud imagining Martin's Mark Antony declaiming to friends, Romans, and countrymen, "Lend me your ears!" He would call his father next day, and they would laugh together.

Brett was hard at work on the six mysteries in *The Casebook* series: "Boscombe Valley," with Peter Vaughn as the old Aussie John Turner; "Shoscombe Old Place," reuniting Brett with Robin Ellis, who starred with him in *The Good Soldier*; "The Creeping Man," in which Professor Presbury is played by Brett's bridge partner Charles Kay; "The Problem of Thor Bridge," with Senator Neil Gibson played by Brett's former brother-in-law Daniel Massey; "The Illustrious Client," who turns out to be the king; and the aforementioned "Disappearance of Lady Frances Carfax," with Cheryl Campbell in the title role.

Brett pulled them off ably in spite of his added weight, and the series was well received. His portrayal, however, is noticeably harsher. Holmes has taken to barking at Watson, and Watson scowls, seeming chronically annoyed. This dynamic becomes still more evident when they move on to the two hour films. For example, in *The Master Blackmailer*, when Holmes determines that the only way to foil Milverton and save his young client is to burglarize Milverton's house and crack his safe, Watson objects strenuously, and they get into a shouting match. Such anger, seen but rarely in the earlier films, became a signature of the later Sherlock.

Yet for Jeremy, surrounded by old friends, including Michael Cox, who returned to the producer's chair for *The Casebook*, this must have been a happy time. Acting was his passion, and while he surely may have wished at times to move on to other roles, the public loved him as Holmes. Moreover there were things he would love about these episodes: Shoscombe Prince, the beautiful white stallion who wins the Champion Stakes, redeeming Sir Robert's debts, and the Shoscombe spaniels, especially Jasper, the pet of Lady Beatrice; stunning location shoots, like Gawsworth Old Hall that served as an elegant Boscombe Arms Hotel; and of course the Lake Country, where Lady Frances sails off to her undoing. It requires no great leap of faith to imagine Jeremy, in defiance of his health problems, entertaining friends at the Midland Hotel.

Back at home in London, he and Linda Pritchard continued to meet at Tea Time, enjoying long, deep discussions of weighty spiritual matters; or they would walk on Clapham Common, and he would twirl her about in the old Victorian bandstand, humming a waltz. She came to know him not merely as an accomplished actor, charming and charismatic, but as a man who was kind and compassionate, generous, and grateful as well for any small thing that was done for him. He had a way of making others feel good about themselves and special to him. He found in her a friend for whom no sacrifice would seem too great.

The last of the two hour dramas was *The Eligible Bachelor*, with a script bloated out of all proportion by writer Trevor Bowen. The original story is quite short and simple: Lord Robert St. Simon marries an American gold heiress, and immediately following the wedding ceremony she disappears. As it turns out, upon leaving the church she has seen the man she had married years before, who had been presumed dead in the gold fields of California. Holmes is called in to find the bride and has no great difficulty locating her with her real husband at a hotel. He invites them for supper at Baker Street, along with Lord Robert, and all are reconciled. End of story.

Of the monstrous conceit made of this by Bowen it must be said first that it can scarcely be called an adaptation. But we are driven to add, albeit sardonically, that in terms of casting it is the ideal vehicle for an actor in the advanced stages of serious mental illness. On grounds of humanity, therefore, it is ugly and worse, cruel. Brett's own enthusiasm for the script excuses neither the writer, the producer, who was again June Wyndham Davies, nor the studio for letting it go forward, knowing his history.

The film begins with Holmes and Watson in a carriage on a foggy night driving past an insane asylum, the screams of a mad woman heard from within. The face of Holmes is seen staring through the darkness; and for the portly old man he has become, Brett is still magnificent. In the scenes following in Baker Street, Holmes, in a long white nightgown, is plagued by a terrifying nightmare that recurs whenever he sleeps. He draws pictures of the images in the dream, and wanders about the streets of London in the dark and the fog, his distracted mind pricked by the shrieks and bizarre behavior of crones, reminding him of the witch-like creature in his dream. When Watson comes to help, Holmes pounces on him at every turn in irrational anger.

As Bowen's eerie plot unfolds, it turns out that Lord St. Simon is not a bachelor, but has been married twice before. In order to save his neglected and crumbling family estate, he has commissioned the murder of his first wife for her money. He dispatches the second by having her declared insane, then imprisoning her on the estate in a deep pit, like an animal, for seven years. Sherlock eventually finds and liberates her, discovering in that place the strange visions that have haunted his sleep.

David Stuart Davies visited the set of *The Eligible Bachelor* in October of 1992, and by his account Brett was excited about the script. In an odd reversal of his commitment to authenticity, he was eager to explore Holmes alter ego, as the consummate logician is forced to confront this mystical dream that turns out to be prophetic. But Davies also reports "wild and whirling words," which caused him to fear that Jeremy was perilously close to another breakdown. What Davies describes is Dr. Jameson's "black mania." Unfortunately, we must consider then that what we see on screen in this episode is the very sad exposure of the actor's own mental illness; and if this is the case, the unreason and the wrathful outbursts were likely clouding his personal life. So typical of this disorder in its late stage, the angry moods alienate and ultimately isolate.

Should the reader have the opportunity to view the Granada series from its beginnings, we would draw his attention to a wall on the set of the Baker Street flat. It is to the left as one would face the door to Sherlock's bedroom. In the early days, hung upon this wall was a black and white drawing of bare trees. It had been changed for *The Casebook* episodes to a portrait, a three-quarter bust of some prominent man, perhaps a scientist. Most suggestive, and far removed from Holmes or even Conan Doyle, in *The Eligible Bachelor* this picture is replaced by one of the head of Christ wearing the crown of thorns.

* * *

After the filming of *The Eligible Bachelor* was complete, Linda Pritchard found a troubling message from Jeremy on her answering machine, asking why she had not met him at Tea Time as planned. There had been no arrangement to meet. It was worrisome, but when she was unable to reach him even the next day she became alarmed. Finally she heard back from his brother Patrick that Jeremy was hospitalized at Charter Nightingale, a psychiatric hospital. This was when she first became aware of the seriousness of his mental illness.

She went every day to visit him, horrified by the security of a locked ward, so like a prison. He was there for three weeks, and when he was released she wanted to stay with him while he regained his strength. But not wanting to burden her, he decided to check in at Grayshott Hall, a health spa in Surrey, fifty miles southwest of London.

It was December, that especially gloomy time after his birthday, and the graceful Tudor style Grayshott Hall was blanketed with snow, its towering chimneys smoking, the bowed window of the lounge jutting boldly into the expansive lawn, now all white. In the early dusk, light streamed from all the windows, and inside, fireplaces were blazing. With Christmas approaching, fragrant evergreen wreaths had been hung and vases of holly set about the common rooms. His driver brought Jeremy down, and he settled into a comfortable suite with a sitting room, where the large mullioned window overlooked a formal garden.

Staff brought up his tea right away. He did not want dinner, but sat despondently, thinking perhaps this would be a fine place to die. As in the typical case, the intensity of a manic state would likely be equaled by the depth of depression that would follow. Dr. Jameson in her memoir vividly writes of this morbid mood, its "despair, hopelessness, and shame," the terrible sense of inadequacy, and the incapacity for any joy or enthusiasm.

So after wrapping himself in a spa robe, he sat down to his tea, a sweet little china pot on the tray, with small sandwiches and even fresh flowers from the greenhouse. He knew this should make him happy, warm and contented. But he was not, and could not even respond to the kind friendliness of the girl who brought it.

Attendants and staff at the spa, or health farm as it is called, would see to his medications and make sure he availed himself of the whirlpool baths and massage. As he was nudged out of depression, he would enjoy the healthful meals and the company of other patients. But of course there were also symptoms of his heart condition, shortness of breath, low exercise tolerance, and possibly a deep cough if fluid gathered in his lungs.

He stayed until after Christmas, though he was still not well when he returned to Clapham Common. Linda persuaded him to go to his general doctor, who upon seeing Jeremy sent him to the psychiatrist. Initially the psychiatrist proposed increasing the dose of lithium, but took a blood test to be sure. This showed an already high level of lithium in his blood, and when the general doctor got the report the drug was stopped. Both physicians wanted Jeremy to return to Charter Nightingale; but when he refused, they accepted that he could stay at home provided there was someone there to care for him.

So it was that Linda moved into the penthouse at Clapham Common. She writes in some detail of this period in her book, and it is her information that causes us to consider a disturbing possibility: if the psychiatrist's first impulse was to increase the lithium, when a subsequent test revealed high levels of it in Jeremy's blood, the drug may not have been working. It is not effective in all cases. Dr. Jameson confesses that one of her worst fears about going on lithium was that it might not work, closing off the only means of managing a terrible illness.

It was now 1993, and on 3 February, *The Eligible Bachelor* was broadcast on British television. We shudder to think how Jeremy's family must have reacted to this public display of what they knew to be his own suffering. The next day David called his Uncle Patrick.[157]

"David, how good to hear from you! What's up?"

"Did you watch television last night, Uncle Patrick?"

"Sherlock! Good God, yes."

"I was horrified," David said, earnestly. "What are we going to do?"

"Listen, David, I'm coming down to London tomorrow. Can we meet for lunch?" Glad at this prospect, David suggested the Scottish Newcastle, a little pub on the Gloucester Road near Holland Park. He arrived early and was waiting when Patrick came in with his face red from the cold. He had walked from the train station. Before they had time to study the menu, David launched into the subject he was clearly anxious to talk about.

"I have to tell you, Uncle Patrick, I am furious after that broadcast the other night. Now we know, don't we, what put my father in hospital. All those people up in Manchester are well aware of his history. How could they saddle him with such a macabre story? They are just exploiting him!" David was unusually agitated.

"What's good for lunch here, lad?" Patrick asked calmly, bringing his nephew back to earth.

"The burgers are very good," and so they ordered.

"I agree with you, David," Patrick offered, taking up the burning topic. "I had the same reaction, but you know how much your dad loves acting. He lives for it."

"Of course, but he'll die for it."

"My point is that now, because of his health, the only role left to him may be this one. He will be uninsurable."

"I hate this, Uncle Patrick, acting I mean. It isn't right for my father."

"Funny you should say that, David," Patrick remarked as the burgers arrived with pints of Guinness. "Your grandfather felt the same way, until he saw what an exceptional actor your father became."

"But what can we do? Ever since Joan died, his health has gotten worse, and now this bizarre script. It is not even Holmes!"

"You are so right, far removed from Doyle, and it does seem that Joan's death was the crowning blow, so reminiscent."

"Grandmother, yes, two beloved women taken too soon." As David spoke, the shadow of a smile crossed Patrick's face, reflecting the memory of his late mother, which David, only just born when she died, was too young to share. But the smile faded instantly at the thought of his ill-fated brother.

"You know, son, you would have the best chance of influencing your father," Patrick suggested. "Tell him just what you've said to me."

"No, no," David objected, "he flares up so easily. There is no reasoning with him."

"That is part of the illness, the angry moods. The doctors warned me." Patrick was sensing David's desperation. "Calm yourself, dear boy. We must all be patient, and tolerant, and keep a close watch. I have to say his heart worries me more now than the mental illness."

"My god!" David heaved a loud sigh. He was close to tears. They looked at each other in a mixture of sympathy and fear. "Well, thank heaven for Linda Pritchard." The tension subsided, and they smiled.

"Indeed. She's a trouper."

David did arrange to speak with his father, who put on his best game face to convince his son not to worry. Yes, *The Eligible Bachelor* had been a strain on him, but he recovered, and his health was now under control. Linda was taking care of him at home, and he promised to stay out of the hospital. After a pint or two at the Alexandra, a very old pub in Clapham, they were laughing and joking. David left with some reassurance, which nonetheless could not shake a deeper unease. Jeremy went home knowing he had persuaded his son of many things he himself struggled to believe.

* * *

It must have been in the spring of 1993 when Granada went into production of the last series of the Conan Doyle stories, *The Memoirs of Sherlock Holmes*, which thankfully returned to the one hour format. Brett had been starring as Holmes for a decade; of course he would not give it up. To do so would be the end of his career. Naturally he feared that, as Hardwicke related to Davies. But his declining health was painfully visible in these last films.

One of the saddest effects of his heart condition was on his voice, that wonderful, deep, sonorous voice, which had always been among his richest gifts. Because of the breathlessness, his lines were often delivered in a weak, singsong cadence. Fluid retention affected his lungs and added to weight gain, setting up a vicious cycle as the added weight put a greater strain on the heart. This was compounded diabolically by the lithium he was compelled to take to forestall the recurrence of mania.

Filming was begun with "The Golden Pince-Nez," about an old Russian invalid, a professor, whom we learn had in his youth betrayed the revolution. His young assistant is mysteriously murdered, and Holmes takes the case. Hardwicke was not available for this one, so the script was adapted to include Sherlock's brother Mycroft, played as always to great effect by Charles Gray. He and Brett epitomized the distinguished Holmes brothers as they might have become, corpulent and aging gentlemen, like the actors. In this instance, it is Mycroft who has the superior insights, dropping two cogent hints, along with a strategic dusting of snuff, that allow Sherlock to unravel the mystery.

Next to be filmed was "The Red Circle," concerning a secret Italian brotherhood of that name, which in history was an offshoot of the Carbonari, a political society in southern Italy in the early nineteenth century. It was another story adapted by Jeremy Paul, whose script waxes a tad sentimental. He creates the character Enrico Firmani, a friend of Holmes and benefactor to his fellow Italians in England. In the course of the plot, Enrico is murdered at the opera house where he works by the villain Black Giorgiano. As the film ends, Holmes is seen there at an opera performance with tears in his eyes for his lost friend. The two Jeremy's were both getting older, which could account for the uncharacteristic bathos.

The first episode of *The Memoirs* to be broadcast was the third one filmed, and that was "The Three Gables." As summer drew to a close, production began; and by mid-September, with autumn coming on, the team went on location to Lyme Park near Manchester, where Lyme Hall would serve as the castle of the dowager Duchess of Lomond.

It was during this shoot that David Stuart Davies visited Brett in his caravan. They had a long discussion of the series, which Davies details in his book. He also writes that Brett was still very heavy, wheezing, and short of breath. In fact the next day Jeremy collapsed on the set and was taken to the hospital. He managed to complete "The Three Gables" only with the aid of oxygen and a wheelchair. When it was done, he was hospitalized for his heart condition, staying over a month. This had the effect of delaying production of the next episode, ominously titled "The Dying Detective."

Those dark days of November were approaching, the time surrounding his birthday, which would never fail to bring back the awful day he was told of his mother's death; and here he was again portraying Sherlock Holmes as desperately ill. In the story, the detective is not really dying, only pretending to have contracted the deadly Sumatran river fever. Culverton Smith, the villain in the piece, is an amateur scientist who studies tropical diseases, and who covets his cousin's property. He kills the cousin by infecting him with the fever; and when Holmes reveals his suspicion, Smith tries the same tactic on him. By persuading Smith that he has succeeded, Sherlock coaxes a confession from him; and with Scotland Yard listening at the door, the trap is sprung.

Thus channeling Holmes in this peerless performance, Brett thrashes around on the settee in the Baker Street flat, a shawl over his night clothes, slipping in and out of delirium, and clutching his body in sudden spasms of pain. Considering the terrible struggle he was having with his own health, both physical and mental, and irrespective of his own commitment to the series, the only word for this script is pernicious. Was it ignorance of mental illness, indifference to the well-being of the starring actor, recklessness as to consequences? Again the writer was Trevor Bowen, who had also adapted *The Eligible Bachelor*.

The shooting of this film ended in time for Jeremy's birthday. He would be sixty, a milestone, and a party was planned. According to Davies, he became ill at this event, suffering another psychotic break, a "white out" as Jeremy described it, like the one in 1986. The next day, 4 November, he was back in Charter Nightingale.

The galling thing about a mental hospital or a psychiatric ward is the common practice of subduing patients with medications that can themselves cause psychosis; thus the more a person is drugged, the greater the justification for keeping him hospitalized. The doctors at Charter Nightingale understood that Jeremy needed care for his heart problem, so they called in a cardiology consult. But Jeremy needed more than a consult, and he knew it. He also deduced that the drugs were making him worse; so while furtively disposing of the pills he was supposed to swallow, he gave a convincing portrayal of a placid patient, thereby foiling the psychiatrists.

Escaping the psychiatric hospital, he went straight to the Harley Street Clinic where he was treated for what by now had been diagnosed as cardiomyopathy. A bizarre observation, macabre even, is that these two institutions are equidistant on either side of Baker Street in London: Charter Nightingale to the west and Harley Street to the east.

While Brett was in hospital, the next episode, "The Mazarin Stone," had to be filmed without him. Charles Gray stepped in at the last minute to take the case as Mycroft Holmes. Together with Hardwicke playing Dr. Watson as always, the two did a creditable job under the circumstances, solving the mystery of a 110-carat diamond stolen from the Whitehall Museum. The script even incorporates elements of another Conan Doyle story, "The Three Garidebs," in quite a complex plot that stretches the original beyond recognition. The thief, Count Sylvius, played by Jon Finch, is apprehended as he is boarding a ship to Amsterdam. Mycroft discovers the jewel concealed in the head of the Count's cane, and with a wide grin at the miscreant, tosses it high into the air. Of course, he catches it and all is well with the Empire.

Brett was able to return to Manchester in time to add scenes to the beginning and the end of this extraordinary episode, explaining Holmes's absence and alluding to his mystical "third eye" with which he would watch over his brother's shoulder. The film that followed, "The Cardboard Box," would be his last as Sherlock.

* * *

Linda Pritchard was a godsend to Jeremy. She was devoted to him: going for cigarettes in the middle of the night if he ran out; pacing the floor with him when his manic state would not let him rest; working crossword puzzles with him to focus his racing mind; and listening as he rambled about philosophy and religion, his favorite topics. On occasion she did feel the sting of his angry moods, when he could be hostile and offensive. She was the rare person, though, who not only understood that illness was the cause of these behaviors, but had the patience and compassion to tolerate them. When manic depression is not managed or has become worse over time, even a person's closest friends and relatives may plead self-defense in severing ties. Not only are there the angry outbursts but also the blustering, haughty, overweening conceit. Such distortions were entirely antithetical to Jeremy's natural personality. The starkness of this contrast must account for the fact that in his case so many people seem to have continued to love him.

Now it was 1994, and Brett was determined, come what may, to complete the final series, *The Memoirs*, with "The Cardboard Box." Granada would then have done forty-two of the fifty-four Sherlock Holmes mysteries of Conan Doyle. Linda could not have been the only one who thought it foolhardy to continue in his condition, but there was no stopping him. He would be reunited in this film with Joanna David, who starred with him in the miniseries *Rebecca* in 1979. Here she plays Susan Cushing, the eldest of three sisters, who comes to Holmes when the youngest, Mary, goes missing. The only sister to have wed, Mary has evoked the insane jealousy of the third sister, Sarah, who develops a fixation on Jim Browner, Mary's sailor husband. Sherlock's interest is piqued when Susan opens a parcel on Christmas Eve to find a cardboard box containing two human ears preserved in raw salt.

This dark tale about a crime of passion draws upon Sir Arthur's maritime experience, when as a young man, immediately following his medical training, he was employed briefly as a ship's surgeon by the African Steamship Company. In the tale, the truth slowly emerges that the sailor, Jim Browner, has murdered his wife Mary and her lover, and has sent their ears, one from each victim, intended for Sarah as a grisly token that he knows how she undermined the marriage and promoted her sister's infidelity.

Redeeming himself, Trevor Bowen was faithful to the original in this adaptation, and the ending is a close paraphrase of Doyle's text. Watching as police pull the bodies from an icy river, Holmes says, "What is the meaning of it, Watson? What is the object of this circle of misery and violence and fear? It must have a purpose, or else our universe has no purpose and that is unthinkable. But what? That is humanity's great problem to which reason so far has no answer."

No more fitting closure to Brett's long tenure as the quintessential Holmes could be conceivable. This speech is the very iteration of the profound and disturbing questions which had dogged the actor himself his lifelong: the lives of exemplary people, such as his mother and his second wife, cut short; the terrible suffering he both experienced and witnessed, inflicted by disease whether of body or mind. Why? Apparently, like Holmes, he found no answer, and in this respect his affinity with Sir Arthur is underscored. From the years 1918 to 1919, Conan Doyle lost his son Kingsley, in his late twenties, and his younger brother Innes, then in his forties, both to the flu pandemic which followed immediately upon the Great War.

It was then, in the last decade of his life, that Doyle became actively involved in spiritualism, firmly believing that psychic phenomena should make people "realize that there was something beyond all this."[158]

Jeremy offered to Linda the notion that through suffering we learn to appreciate life and to have compassion for others; but that is a rationale, not a justification. It is difficult to infer his actual thoughts on such things, because he did not write about them. We know, however, that he was intelligent and highly intuitive, and that he had an interest in the Eastern religions, which embrace a far deeper understanding of reality. Surely it is at least possible that he had touched upon Buddhist ideas of oneness, of the true self, of an ultimate nature of transcendence that renders paradoxical our dualistic perceptions of pain and pleasure, life and death. He would have known of karma, that suffering is just the effect of a cause, however outrageous it may seem to us. It is suggestive, as Linda makes a point of emphasizing, that Jeremy in spite of his struggles never expressed self-pity. That in itself should tell us that he had some knowledge and understanding of Buddhist precepts—and Quaker humility. We should recall that the founder of Quakerism, George Fox, through all the trials of his wanderings never cursed fate, but to the contrary felt the love of God all the more strongly.

Thankfully, "The Cardboard Box" did not deal with madness, yet it took a toll on Brett. For example, because of his heart he could only work every other day; and by the time he returned to London, he was once again slipping into a black mania. His doctor wanted him to return to Charter Nightingale, and even threatened to commit him involuntarily, which he could do legally for a period of six months. Thus coerced, Jeremy of course acquiesced, so there followed another few weeks in the psychiatric hospital.[159] The lithium had been stopped, replaced with another medication, perhaps an anti-seizure drug. These have now been found effective in manic depression for some patients, and in fact Jeremy's mood swings stabilized over the next many months. His heart condition, however, grew steadily worse.

He had company in his ill health, just what misery is said to love. His old friend Robert Stephens at age 63 was the perfect case of karma maturing; after a life of debauchery, his liver and kidneys were succumbing to the effects of alcoholism. In September that year he had transplant surgery. The previous year he was a huge success as King Lear with the Royal Shakespeare Company, which had been hailed as his "comeback" after his career had been in the doldrums for some time. This was also the period of the AIDS epidemic that was devastating urban gay communities. Gary Bond tragically fell victim, his health failing in 1994. Jeremy visited his erstwhile domestic partner in hospital, and they sang together. We venture a guess that it was something by Noel Coward, at whose seventieth birthday tribute they had met in 1969. Perhaps it was "Time and Again," which Jeremy had performed with Anne Rogers that night, or the so romantic "Someday I'll Find You." Tears would have flowed. But if either could recall the lyrics to Coward's "Mad Dogs and Englishmen," they would roar with laughter, to their mutual benefit.

A visit to Robert's bedside, we daresay, would not have been the least maudlin, given the irreverent, hardened personality that comes across in his memoir, written around this time.[160] He and Jeremy likely remained friends, each with his own personal trials.

We also like to think that Jeremy had occasion to see his cousin Daphne every so often. Free at last from the onerous work of the Holmes series, home from hospital, and feeling better than he had in a while, he was so pleased to hear her voice on the phone.

"Jeremy, darling, after surviving ten years in Manchester, you need to celebrate," she proclaimed.

"Aren't you sweet, Daphne, thank you. What do you suggest?" he responded.

"High tea at the Savoy, tomorrow afternoon, you and I. What do you say?"

"I'll be there, dear!" Daphne could always lift his spirits.

The elegance of the Savoy Hotel had graced many family celebrations over the years, beginning with his taking leave of Eton, a true cause to celebrate. Then there was the Coronation Ball in 1953, a romantic wedding night with Anna, his fortieth birthday with

Gary, and his fiftieth when his brothers took him and Joan. The place held considerable nostalgia for Jeremy. He was already seated in the Thames Foyer, where tea is served, when Daphne arrived. She had grown a bit stocky at age 65, but her greying hair was complimented by a sky blue spring suit, and a double strand of pearls was matched by a round pearl brooch.

"Oh, Daphne, you are a sight for sore eyes!" They embraced warmly. "You always look stunning, darling!"

"Thank you, Jeremy love." She studied his face, once so beautiful, sculpted now by a long habit of suffering. "How are you faring now that you're home?"

"Linda looks after me, sees that I take all my pills. She's my guardian angel." Daphne recalled how her Aunt Betty, Jeremy's mother, liked to say he had the face of an angel. She smiled at the poignant thought of that long ago day at Berkswell Grange when she was allowed to hold her infant cousin.

"I'm glad to hear it," was all she said, "and how is David?"

"I think he's angry with me. I couldn't keep my promise to stay out of hospital."

"He's just frustrated, Jeremy. We all are: wanting to help, not knowing how, worried sick about you." Daphne was clearly distressed. Her dear cousin was still overweight, his breathing labored, particularly when he talked. "But now you can relax, get more rest, retire from acting!"

"No, no, no! I'd be bored to death, Daphne, you know that," he protested, even knowing he might well have no choice. "Tell me about Martin, please," he went on, changing the subject, "the wonderful success he is having in television."

The while they conversed, they were sampling the finger sandwiches, the fresh scones with clotted creams, and of course the best tea, in a bottomless pot. Daphne was all too happy to rave about her son, who was costarring in a popular situation comedy called "Men Behaving Badly," involving three flat mates, one of whom is a young woman, and the awkwardness arising when both young men develop romantic feelings for her.

"I am so proud of him, Jeremy, and you can be too. He has always considered you a role model. Have you seen the show?"

"I caught one or two episodes. It is hilarious; Martin is a natural at comedy, as I always knew he would be." Jeremy paused, refilling their cups while considering his next words. "I hope he wasn't type cast." The character, Gary, is an oafish, sex-crazed lout, whom Martin played to the hilt.

Daphne laughed, then confessed, "Well I will admit that you were right about boarding school. It was not the best influence, but the bullies taught him to laugh at himself. Isn't that what comes across in this role?"

"Oh yes, it is cleverly written, but so vulgar, honestly."

"Right again, darling, however we can't be prudish. It's the way the world is moving." The plaintive look of futility and despair on her cousin's face gave Daphne a start. Familiar as she was with his uncanny expressiveness, she had never seen him so sad. "Buck up, old man!" she admonished, and he managed to flash that quick smile of his.

* * *

Perhaps it was the echo of Daphne's words, or maybe the title intrigued him, but when he was offered a part in a film called *Mad Dogs and Englishmen*, Brett accepted. He played Tony Vernon-Smith, a drug lord and brothel owner. Joss Ackland, who had appeared with Jeremy in "The Copper Beeches," one of the early episodes in the Holmes series, was Sam Stringer, a corrupt narcotics officer. Plot-wise the film is a Shakespearean tragedy. Stringer has incestuous feelings for his daughter Sandy, who he discovers is not only addicted to heroin, but also is the drug lord's girlfriend. Sandy's friend Antonia, meanwhile, is an upper class young woman who has fallen into her same plight of addiction and prostitution. The two bear a close resemblance. Antonia is wooed by an American named Mike, working as a delivery boy, who tries to rehabilitate her. It ends with Stringer, the vengeful father, busting into the brothel and fatally shooting its owner. In the dark, bullets flying, he also shoots a woman who appears to be Antonia. To his horror, he has killed his daughter Sandy.

The subject matter is salacious, lewd. There is nudity, female only, but far more graphic than the sex is the violence in the lower echelons of the drug trade. Brett plays the role as perfectly as he had done every part in his long career, and he had played his share of villains. But fans of his Sherlock Holmes were aghast that he would lend his talents to this picture, as though it sullied Holmes himself. Simply because Brett was such an excellent actor, this inversion of his magnum opus is jarring, though it is amazing that he was able to work at all. When the film was released in June of 1995, he told the press he was the mad one to appear in *Mad Dogs and Englishmen*.[161]

We feel obliged, nonetheless, to note certain aspects of the script that would have had resonance for Jeremy. For one thing, the angry eruptions that became a kind of signature in these later years were used to good effect. Then there is the speech he gives Mike regarding class, about which Americans, he says, know nothing. Mike calls Antonia an aristocrat, for which he is upbraided by Tony, who points out that as a prostitute she has to remain accessible to the public; and to conduct one's affairs in public is the opposite of aristocratic. Later he pronounces that "this world is disintegrating."

Heaped upon his personal adversities was the added fact that Brett's world *had* disintegrated. A courtly time of refinement, manners, morality, led in all spheres by truly talented people, was replaced by a world overtaken by the tawdry, sordid, and brutish, given to the craven glorification of mediocrity, and serving only expediency. Might his appearance in this movie have been a subtle jab at the prurient tastes indulged by an industry intent upon profits at the expense of decency? He may have seen it as his crown of thorns; the view is not without merit.

In spite of his steadily worsening heart disease, Brett took a small part in an MGM production of *Moll Flanders*, based on the eighteenth century novel by Daniel Defoe, of which the subtitle is a synopsis: "Twelve years a whore, five times a wife, twelve years thief, eight years felon, grew rich, lived honest, died a penitent." Defoe was thought to have taken the story from a London criminal he met in Newgate Prison.

In this film adaptation, Jeremy played the father of Jonathan, an artist. His scene was filmed on location in Ireland, and just to get there and back was a strain physically, leaving him to face the necessity of retirement. It was then 1995.

He and Linda, being natural optimists, fully expected that his heart problem would be successfully treated with medication indefinitely, especially as he would no longer have the stress of working. Summer came and the hot weather was not pleasant for him; breathing was harder, and he tired very easily. But the two enjoyed several relatively quiet months of domestic tranquility: cooking together; watching their favorite television shows, opera, horse racing, and old movies.

On 11 September he had medical appointments, his psychiatrist and his cardiologist. Linda would now accompany him in order to hear the doctors' instructions firsthand. At the psychiatrist's they discussed Jeremy's retirement from acting following a career of over forty years. He expressed his regret and frustration, stemming from the sense that he had so much more to offer his audience, but was mollified by the reminder that his work in large part was on film and would thus be available well into the future.

At the next appointment, his regular doctor was away, so he was seen by a younger cardiologist, who upon examining Jeremy recommended an increase in medication. This information, related in Linda's book, would suggest that Jeremy's heart condition was not optimally managed, though it seemed to Linda he already was taking enough pills. Without trying to second guess the physicians, we would simply observe that many doctors tend to be overly conservative in prescribing heart medications, fearing side effects, when a higher dose might well provide better relief of symptoms. It can be a trade-off between a better life and a longer one.

The day was exhausting and discouraging, particularly for Jeremy. He was too tired to help with dinner when they returned home and unable to eat much anyway. He stretched out on the sofa after supper, relieved to rest at last and to breathe easier. Linda was very concerned and wanted to sit with him. He expressed his deep gratitude for the loving care she continued to give him, but insisted that she go to bed. As she had work the next day, she went reluctantly.

Jeremy fell asleep on the sofa. Sometime in the middle of the night, the wee morning hours of 12 September, he seemed to hear a whispering voice, "Wake, wake up," and he did.[162] But he did not awaken in his apartment on Clapham Common, nor in some celestial heaven. He awoke in his bedroom at the Grange in Berkswell. A soft spring breeze billowed the white curtains at the open window, bringing the scent of wisteria in bloom. He felt complete peace, no pain or struggle, no fear. A state of bliss.

* * *

When Linda came down early, Jeremy was still on the sofa. Cold. Dead. She was devastated, shaken to the core. But as the reality set in, she was able to go through the motions required by such a situation in the mechanical, detached manner the mind will adopt in self-defense. Paramedics came minutes after she called the emergency number, then two policemen, who made her a cup of tea and stayed until her parents arrived. Jeremy's general physician also came, presumably to sign a death certificate. In the midst of it, Linda was able to call some of Jeremy's family and friends. The news was shocking, but in a way that was immediately qualified. "Of course, we should have expected it," came the reaction, "clearly his health had been deteriorating." His body was cremated, and a private funeral was held. Then on 29 November, a Wednesday, there was a memorial service at the Church of St. Martin in the Fields, arranged by June Wyndham Davies.[163] A testament to the respect and renown he held in the theatre world, the attendance was four hundred people, many of whom were luminaries of the British stage and screen. David Burke and Edward Hardwicke were both there, and Michael Cox. His son David came with his mother, and cousin Daphne brought her son Martin, who wept openly during the service. Several friends gave speeches of remembrance, including Denis Quilley, and his bridge partners, Penelope Keith and Charles Kay. Patience Collier, the fourth at bridge, had died at age 77, eight years previously.

Robert Stephens, who had also been in failing health, had died just two months after Jeremy and a month prior to the memorial service. To the end, he was a man who never lacked for personal drama. That very year Patricia Quinn had finally agreed to marry him, having stuck with him for more than a decade. Then he was knighted. Thus representing him at the service for his old friend Jeremy was his widow Lady Patricia. Robert's ex-wife Tarn Bassett, still a close friend of Jeremy's, was also there and read the poem "Death is nothing at all."

If as the Tibetans believe one's spirit lingers in the old haunts for a time following death, Jeremy would have been there enjoying this service, filled as it was with stories of the great good fun he had brought to the people he loved, not to mention the beautiful music. There was the Mendelssohn solo "O for the Wings of a Dove," which he had sung with the Eton Chapel Choir as a boy soprano, and a violin solo played by Katherine Gowers based on the theme her father Patrick had written for the Sherlock Holmes series.[164] This was the same haunting variation played in "The Final Problem" as Holmes goes over the falls. The service ended with the "Amen Chorus" from Handel's Messiah, which followed a blessing from Reverend Huggins, Jeremy's eldest brother John, who also shared fond memories.

Then life went on, as it somehow always does. In the next six years, David Huggins wrote and published three novels. The last of the three was titled *Me Me Me*, written in the first person and concerning a young Brit from a family of actors, who goes to Hollywood to help his grandfather compose a memoir. A novelist not uncommonly draws upon his own life. David's mother even states in her own memoir that his characters are not far removed from some of the vain, egocentric actors among those she has described. But the worrisome remark by David's protagonist in this short book is that he learned early in life to say whatever the adults wanted to hear. David inherited the penthouse on Clapham Common; when he married in 2001 the wedding was held there. That same year his last novel came out. Were his demons laid to rest?

Anna Massey's life became more stable after her second marriage, and she lived until 2011, passing on at the age of seventy-four. The same year, Edward Hardwicke died; he was seventy-nine. Daphne Clunes was also seventy-nine when she died in 2007. Martin continued his great success in television, growing into a very different role as the phobic and repressed Doc Martin in the eponymous series. Jeremy's first grandchild, Daniel Huggins, was born in 2002, and a second, Iris, three years later.

About a week before he died, Brett broadcast an appeal on the radio for the Manic Depressive Fellowship. He described the disorder and his own personal struggle, emphasizing that he had been successful in life in spite of it. In coming forward with his story, he hoped to give courage to others so afflicted. At the memorial service that followed his death, Myra Fulford, representing the Fellowship, gave an address in which she praised his willingness to champion their cause. Let us not neglect to mention that there was a reception that day after the service at the Player's Theatre, and let us in closing invite readers to entertain the possibility that Myra approached Reverend Huggins to express her deep sympathy.

"Thank you, Myra, you are so kind," the reverend responded. The room was crowded with theatre people, and the two were standing at the bar that had been set up for this occasion. He was nursing a Scotch, and she had a glass of red wine. "Your address was most informative and appreciated." He motioned to the bartender for a refill, then continued, "You know, many people seem to believe that it was the role of Sherlock Holmes that pushed my brother over the edge; and among ourselves—the family that is—we wonder if it was the death of his wife Joan ten years ago, after which he declined steadily. What do you think, given your expertise?"

"Well, Reverend," Myra began, slowly pondering a serious question, "the circumstances of a person's life will naturally have some psychological effect, but we now understand that serious mental illness is a disease of the brain, as organic as any other disease." She paused, sipping her wine. "We also have learned that manic depression is genetic in many cases, and, key to your question, it can often become more serious with age."

"So he may not have needed a push."

"Exactly my point, though hardship is certainly not helpful," Myra was warming to the subject, or it may have been the wine, "which leads me to a question related to your field, Reverend, if I may be so bold."

"By all means, Myra."

"As I have learned more about your brother's life, I am struck by how ill-starred he was: his mother's death, his wife's, the rheumatic heart damage in his early years that haunted him when he needed lithium to control his manic depression. Do you think God was testing him?"

Now it was John's turn to ponder slowly. "The question of the ages," he said. "Jeremy was enamored of the Eastern religions, and their doctrine of karma lets God off the hook. Whatever happens is simply the effect of some cause, and my brother seemed to accept what life brought in that spirit. But I agree that if ever a man was less deserving of being ensnared in the web of fate, it was Jeremy. Maybe karma is in fact the mysterious work of God. Suppose for example that Jeremy's mental disorder, as you say, was predetermined and destined to grow serious with age. Had he not had heart damage he might then have survived only to end his days in an institution."

"So not a test but a mercy. And your mother?" Myra persisted.

"Just a hail storm."

"You are a wise man, Reverend, and it has been a pleasure meeting you, as it was an honor to have known your dear brother," and they shook hands as she excused herself. John took his drink and, tired of standing, went to sit with Michael Cox, whom he knew to be a fellow Sherlockian.

"A terrible loss, old chap," Michael observed, then putting a hand on John's shoulder, "How are you holding up?"

"Passably well, Michael, thank you. Jeremy was suffering so much; we knew the end was near."

"Your brother was a great man, Reverend, loved by all who knew him. Look at the hundreds of people who filled the church today, the wonderful, funny stories told by his close friends. He brought laughter and joy and will continue to do so." Michael stopped, studying

John's face. He had heard that the elder Huggins was the one who had grown up loving the Holmes mysteries. "He was the consummate Sherlock Holmes, don't you think?"

"Oh yes, indeed, and you of all people must take credit for it," John replied.

"No sir, you can blame my wife!" Cox jested. "She gave the seal of approval on that casting decision."

"When I was a boy, Michael, I read all the Sherlock Holmes stories, loved them, like yourself I understand." Cox nodded, and John continued, "I am gratified that Jeremy will be remembered for his part in this excellent series, and yet"—he paused to finish his Scotch—"he had a long career before taking that role. He was a talented classical actor. He loved Shakespeare; he loved to sing and had the most glorious voice." Cox kept quiet and listened, a little surprised at this companion's earnestness. "But he was more, my friend," John went on, "much more than an actor. He was a uniquely beautiful man, in body and in spirit. He was his mother's son. He had all her best qualities: he was gracious and charitable, generous and fun loving; shared her Quaker values of hard work, humility, chafed at class distinctions. She lived on in him, as our father said after she died. Today I feel as though she has died again."

Deeply touched by this speech, Michael took the reverend's hand, and using his first name, said softly, "I am so sorry, John, so very sorry."

Then Reverend Huggins got up slowly. "I'm going for another Scotch."

Cox called after him, "Make it a double!" and John glanced back with a smile.

The hymn sung that day in the Church of St. Martin in the Fields could not have been more fitting, so much so that we suspect it must have been suggested to the choir director by Reverend Huggins himself. It was "Lord of the Dance," composed by songwriter Sydney Carter in 1954. Christ is sometimes referred to as the Lord of the Dance, in a mystical sense similar to the Hindu goddess Shiva, whose dance creates and destroys the universe as we know it. Carter based the hymn on an old Christmas carol in which Jesus tells his own story verse by verse, and calls the day of his birth his "dancing day." The tune is that of the Shaker hymn, "Simple Gifts."

The very idea of the Son of God dancing is heterodox in much of sectarian theology, but not among the Quakers. In fact the Shakers in America were an offshoot of Quakers in Manchester, England, known there as the Shaking Quakers. Thus did this hymn draw upon the vibrant roots of Jeremy's heritage, reflecting as well his own unorthodox spirituality. He loved to dance!

His brother John, coming out of the Players Theatre that typically chill and foggy November day, may well have had a spring in his step, even after the third Scotch, and no doubt a tear in his eye, humming the refrain:

> Dance then, wherever you may be,
> I am the Lord of the Dance, said he,
> And I'll lead you all, wherever you may be,
> And I'll lead you all in the Dance said he.

Let us, dear readers, remember Peter Jeremy William Huggins the way the old cleric would surely have wished, as that uniquely beautiful man, who was more than an actor.

*****************************FINIS********************************

Conclusion

To write a biography is somewhat like finding figures in the clouds: "That one looks like a horse, now it's a dog!" From a sky full of whirling shapes and faces, the myriad details of a person's life, the author must choose images that may shape a credible picture. Even the known facts will represent but a fraction of all that went into that life, so the author must be careful to draw upon those that will tell the true and essential story. This will depend largely on the author's purpose.

A good deal of biography is purely historical, and such work, which must be carefully researched and referenced, is vital to academia. But an author may also write a biography to convey his idea of the person based on what is known. He may, as I have done, employ a fictional style using the historical facts of the subject's life. Such a work is known as a fictional biography, or a biographical novel. Told as a story, the person's life seems more immediate, and our appreciation is enhanced.

Historians tend to disparage historical fiction, and it is true that readers often slip too easily into mistaking the fiction for fact. Yet even the writer of history is selective with regard to facts, which must then reflect his personal viewpoint, even if inadvertently. I might point out, furthermore, that a scholarly biography requires some degree of intrusion on the heirs or descendants of the subject, which an author might understandably want to avoid.

The current rector of Berkswell Parish, the Rev. Dr. Mark Bratton, wrote on this debate in the Parish Magazine on the occasion of Remembrance Day in November 2015. He told of an interchange he had heard on the radio between historian Niall Ferguson and novelist Jane Smiley, in which Ferguson complained that the novelist "makes things up." Smiley countered that the history writer can never be completely certain of historical reality, and that fiction may often convey the deeper truths of human life. In his article, the rector embraces the latter opinion, citing the Gospels as an example, since they carry the message of Christ even if they are not historically factual.

In my story of Jeremy Huggins, it is this deeper meaning I have tried to capture. But it is fiction based on fact, a portrait I have seen emerge from my exploration of reliable sources, enumerated in a reference list that follows. Especially helpful among the many sources consulted have been the memoirs of people close to him, including Anna Massey, Robert Stephens, Martin Clunes, and Linda Pritchard. I have also used certain websites that were well referenced or that could be cross referenced. Interviews that he gave as well as much of his work in film and television, still accessible on the internet, were of great value. I did not rely on the press to any extent, since show business news suffers a famous lack of credibility, and even serious critics will always have their own slant. The lovely people in Jeremy's hometown of Berkswell were an enormous help to me, answering questions and guiding me to resources I would not otherwise have found. These individuals are listed in the acknowledgements.

It has been a labor of love, and of respect, in which I have taken care to be sensitive to Jeremy's family and friends and to avoid the effrontery of presuming to know his mind. I have made the effort to be open in separating fact and fiction, making clear the basis of any suppositions. Where I have used fictional narrative, I have told you my reasons and sources. If I seem to have overused the conditional clause—too many *might-haves* or *quite-possibly*'s—at least it spares the reader from questioning either my source for that information, or my temerity in asserting it. Where I do make an audacious claim, I have endeavored to use endnotes alerting readers to what is factual and the source for it, or explaining what information led me to make it. The nature of Jeremy's personal relationships was not possible to know with any certainty, particularly with close family members who were private people. I have tried, therefore, to read between the lines in those books that have been written about him, drawing bold inferences at times in the manner of Sherlock Holmes himself. In some cases I suggest only a probability, reflecting Jeremy's own character, or bearing upon some aspect of his story.

Apologies may be in order to theatre buffs and Sherlockians for the many summaries of plots which we could agree should be common knowledge. In my defense, I would suggest that the life story of Peter Jeremy William Huggins may come to have wider appeal.

While this portrait of him is mine as the author, I hope fondly to have persuaded readers of its accuracy, or at least its validity. If some complain that had I only consulted the tabloids I would have seen a very different image in the clouds of history, they can go themselves to my sources, or simply have a careful look at the photo of Elizabeth Huggins, *nee* Butler, daughter of Edith Cadbury Butler. He was the beloved son of this superlative woman, a half Irish descendent of a prominent Quaker clan; and in that picture we see beyond any doubt the woman and mother she was: gracious, refined, caring, and accomplished. That portrait and the second frame from the Marcus Tylor backstage photo shoot of Jeremy Brett, the picture on the cover of this book, were the matches that lit my determination to tell the compelling story of his life.

He was ensnared early on in the inexorable fate that closed slowly around him. The diving event in polluted water at Eton, the ear infection, rheumatic fever, heart damage, his mother's death—he survived all that. Much later, another death, another beloved woman. A mood disorder, which until then had been handled tolerably well, now required the very drug that would destroy his already damaged heart.

His courage in the face of adversity is a worthy example for us all, though not so uncommon. He never felt himself singled out, but remained sensitive, regardless of his personal pain, to the suffering of others. What really cries out forcefully for our attention, however, is that this entanglement, a veritable Grimpen Mire of misfortune, was visited upon such a very gifted and remarkable person. First there was his extraordinary physical beauty, then his skill as an actor, how adroitly he moved into the mind of a character, after discerning with perfect intuition the writer's intent. That the method of *becoming* a character contributed to his undoing seems clear to me; others may debate it. After all, his persona already projected an unusual duality that was at once charming and disturbing. His bisexuality blended masculine and feminine seamlessly; his bipolarity held up the two faces of Janus, the tragic and the comic, appropriate for an actor, terrible for the man.

My interest here was not in Jeremy Brett the famous actor. Celebrity itself surrounds a person in unreality. The life of a celebrity can be distorted in as many ways as mirrors in a funhouse. My focus is in giving the full picture of Jeremy Huggins the man, telling his whole story, not only that of his amazing career. The device in Chapter One of hiding the stage name may seem transparent, but my intent is simply to steer the reader away from this celebrity aspect, if only temporarily. Those early childhood years in Berkswell, with his pony, his beloved Nanny Clifford, his vivacious mother, were the happiest of his life. The story of that time, blessed for a child even with the war raging, should be read without the distracting thought of who Peter H. would become.

A compelling story is one that stays with you, never leaving your mind, demanding to be shared. I will not be so specious as to suggest a moral to this one. I only hope you will have laughed and cried in reading it as I have in writing it. Perhaps in some small way it will also increase the understanding of bipolar disorder, and even of the rainbow spectrum of human sexuality, or inspire some young writer in a future generation to author the strictly factual version. In the end, knowing his story, how shall we remember this man? Several people have written, and many fans believe, that Jeremy Brett has been underrated as an actor. Among others, Edward Hardwicke, David Stuart Davies, Kevin Jackson in The Independent, October 1993, have held in the strongest terms that it is a disgrace that he did not receive recognition from the British Academy of Film and Television Arts, the BAFTA award. To my mind, this fact says more about the tawdriness of this process than about Brett's unquestionable talent.

MORE THAN AN ACTOR

He will be remembered for his acting for generations. Granada's Sherlock Holmes is still shown on television, where it is discovered by new fans. These films and much of his earlier work are also available on the internet, from his Freddy Eynsford-Hill in *My Fair Lady* to Tony Vernon-Smith in *Mad Dogs and Englishmen*, and in between: *The Good Soldier, Rebecca, The Picture of Dorian Gray, The Ideal Husband, The Merry Widow, Macbeth*, and more. Jeremy's classic and stunning good looks surely can never be forgotten, particularly as they graced a man as noble inwardly as outwardly. That angelic face he was born with became, when he grew to manhood, that of a very strong *archangel*. In writing this biography, I have sought to convey the nature of a very special person, so that readers may always remember Jeremy as I shall: the son of Elizabeth Cadbury Butler. His memory is inseparable from hers. When she brought flowers to the bombed out Coventry Cathedral in 1940, she did not leave a calling card. Jeremy Brett did not seek awards. While he loved his fans, he needed no recognition. He was his mother's son.

Acknowledgements

FIRST AND FOREMOST MY SINCERE gratitude must go to certain kind individuals associated with St. John the Baptist Church of England, Berkswell Parish: Julie Bramley of the primary school, who gave me the address of Mr. John Webb; Janet Roberts, parish administrator, who fielded my inquiries most patiently; and Wendy Burns, curator of the Berkswell Museum, who sent me pictures of the memorials honoring Colonel and Mrs. Huggins, including the screen in the Lady Chapel and the lych-gate in the churchyard.

Likewise my many thanks to John Webb, a resident of Berkswell for the entirety of a long life, who was enormously helpful, sending photocopies of the articles and pictures relating to the Huggins family from *Berkswell Miscellany, Volume V*, which was nowhere else to be found. His own autobiography, *From the Other Side of the Fence*, was invaluable in setting the backdrop of village life during World War II and afterward, as have been his regular contributions to the Parish Magazine, which he shares with me.

In writing about the years at Eton College, Eleanor Hoare, the archivist there, set me straight on various points. I am indebted for her obliging and sympathetic responses.

My thanks to Glyn Price, chairman of the Berkswell & District History Group, who located for me a surviving member of the Offshoot Group, responsible for writing and publishing the annual *Berkswell Miscellany*. She was one of three who visited Jeremy Brett backstage at Wyndham's Theatre in 1988. Respecting her wish not to be mentioned, I refrained from naming any of the three.

Certainly I cannot fail to acknowledge Marcus Tylor, whose incomparable photographs were a source of inspiration, with thanks for his permission to use two of them on the covers of this book; and likewise Linda Pritchard, not only for her own informative memoir, but also for her help with photographs–and words of encouragement. With the kind assistance of these good people, I have endeavored to honor the memory of a great man.

In some way perhaps, this effort may serve to inspire a future biographer.

Sources

Books

A. Barrister of the Inner Temple. *Eton Portrait Gallery*. Williams & Son, London, 1876.

Conan Doyle, Sir Arthur. *The Complete Sherlock Holmes Vols. 1 and 2*. Barnes & Noble Classics, New York, 2003.

Dandelion, Pink. *An Introduction to Quakerism*, Cambridge University Press, Cambridge, 2007.

Davies, David Stuart. *Bending the Willow*. Calabash Press, British Columbia, 2010.

Deane, Hamilton. *Dracula. The Vampire Play in Three Acts*. Samuel French, New York, 1933.

DuMaurier, Daphne. *Rebecca*. Harper Collins, London, 1938.

Gibbs, D. E. *Berkswell Through a Looking Glass*. Published privately by the author, Warwickshire, 1989.

Green, Philip. *A Haircut and a Shave*. Vantage Press, New York, 1974.

Haining, Peter. *The Television Sherlock Holmes Third Revised Edition*. Virgin Books, London, 1994.

Hildred, Stafford, & Tim Ewbank. *Martin Clunes, The Biography*. John Blake Publishing, London, 2010.

Huggins, David. *Me Me Me*. Faber and Faber, London, 2001.

Hutton, Mike. *Life in London, 1950s*. Amberley Publishing, Gloucestershire, 2014.

Jamison, Dr. Kay. *An Unquiet Mind*. Vintage Books, New York, 1995.

Lycett, Andrew. *The Man Who Created Sherlock Holmes: The Life and Times of Sir Arthur Conan Doyle*. Weidenfeld & Nicolson, UK, 2007.

Massey, Anna. *Telling Some Tales*. Random House, London, 2006.

Milburn, Clara. *Mrs. Milburn's Diaries*. Peter Donnelly, ed. George G. Harrap & Co., London, 1979.

Morgan, Kenneth O. *Twentieth Century Britain*. Oxford University Press, Oxford, UK, 2000.

Paul, Jeremy. *The Secret of Sherlock Holmes*. Players Press, California, 1989.

Pritchard, Linda and Mary A. Warner. *The Jeremy Brett—Linda Pritchard Story*. Rupert Books, Cambridge, 1998.

Stanislavsky, Constantin. *Building a Character*. Routledge, New York, 1949.

Stephens, Robert. *Knight Errant: Memoirs of a Vagabond Actor*. Hodden & Stoughton, London, 1996.

Stoker, Bram. *Dracula*. Barnes & Noble Classics, New York, 2003.

Tylor, Marcus. *A Roll with Jeremy Brett*. Blurb, California, 2010.

Webb, John. *From the Other Side of the Fence*. Troubador Publishing, Market Harborough, UK, 2003.

Ziegler, Philip. *Olivier*, MacLehose Press, London, 2013.

Periodicals

Berkswell & District History Group. *Berkswell & Balsall Visited & Revisited*. Publication no. 4, November 2006.

Herbert, Rosemary. "Interview with Jeremy Brett: the Armchair Detective." Volume 18 no. 4, pages 340-350, New York, 1985.

Offshoot Group, Berkswell Historical Society, *Berkswell Miscellany, Volume III, 1987, & Volume V, 1989*.

Websites (Listed in approximate order of chronological relevance)

Birmingham Central Library (calmview.birmingham.gov.uk)
Balsall Common Primary School (balsallcommonprimary.co.uk)
Property history—Berkswell Grange (zoopla.co.uk)
Berkswell Parish Church (berkswellchurch.org)

Berkswell School (berkswellschool.org.uk)
Berkswell History (berkswell-history.org)
Henry William Huggins (wikitree.com)
Childhood photos—(jeremybrett.livejournal.com)
Eton College (etoncollege.com)
British Newspaper Archive (britishnewspaperarchive.co.uk)
British History Online (british-history.ac.uk)
AbeBooks—UK (abebooks.co.uk)
Warwickshire Heritage and Culture (heritage.warwickshire.gov.uk)
Balsall Heath Local History Society (balsallheathhistory.co.uk)
Berkswell Genealogy Resources (forebears.io/england/warwickshire/berkswell)
The Genealogist (thegenealogist.co.uk)
The Grove, Highgate Village (rightmove.co.uk)
British Universities Film and Video Council (bufvc.ac.uk/screenplays)
Internet Movie Database (imdb.com)
Noel Coward Gala—tracks (noelcoward.net)
Gary Bond (thewonderfulworldofgarybond.com)
BBC Archive (bbc.co.uk/archive)
Day of the Week (dayoftheweek.org)
British Musical Theatre Archive (mustclosesaturday.co.uk)
IBDb: Broadway Information (ibdb.com)
The Brettish Empire—Lisa Oldham (brettish.com)
Google News Archive (news.google.com)
Societe Sherlock Holmes de France (sshf.com)
Martin Clunes (buffalopictures.co.uk)
Woodmen of Arden (longbowarchers.com)
Sherlock Holmes (bakerstreetwikia.com)
Royal Shakespeare Company (rsc.org.uk)

(Many websites were consulted in researching details of this biography, including standards like Wikipedia and Google Maps. Given above are the less obvious sources. Abe Books, for example, was the best for out-of-print material.)

Videos

On disc:
MPI Home Video:
    The Adventures of Sherlock Holmes
    The Return of Sherlock Holmes
    The Casebook of Sherlock Holmes
    The Memoirs of Sherlock Holmes

Oscar Wilde Collection (BBC Video)
Macbeth (Kultur Films)
The Good Soldier (Acorn Media)
Rebecca (Cinema Caverna)

On YouTube: (Channels given)
Gypsycyn:
    An Act of Reprisal - 1965
    The Merry Widow - 1968
    The Rivals - 1970
    Haunted, "The Ferryman" - 1974
    Number 10, "Bloodline" - 1982
    Macbeth - 1982
    Berkswell Grange - 2012
Cehache:
    The Prodigal Daughter - 1975
    The Merchant of Venice - 1974
    Rebecca - 1979
PoisonApple37:
    Jeremy Brett Interview - 1988
    Interview with Jeremy Brett and Edward Hardwicke
British Pathe:
    The Coronation of Her Majesty Queen Elizabeth - 1953
    Noel Coward's 70th Birthday – 1969
Affairs of the Heart - 1974 (Marlene Cole)
Joseph and his Technicolor Dream Coat - 1972 (Damien Slatterly)
Jeremy Brett and Twiggy - 1975 (SillyGirlBlue)

The Gentleman Factory - Eton College BBC - 1980 (Nick Higgins)
Eton College Documentary - 1993 (tituscesaer)
Sir Laurence Olivier: Great Acting -
    1966 interview with Kenneth Tynan (Gassalacsa4)
Jeremy Brett/Edward Hardwicke Interview (PLbrettfan)
Jeremy Brett NPR Interview - 1991 (macolleague)
Jeremy Brett - The Wogan Interview (JBrettsgirl)

Endnotes

Chapter One

1. Mrs. Elizabeth Huggins, *nee* Butler, a member of the Cadbury family.
2. Ellen Clifford was nanny for the four Huggins boys, serving the family for fifty years.
3. The Huggins family lived in Berkswell in the West Midlands of England near Coventry.
4. Henry William Huggins was promoted to lieutenant colonel at the outbreak of World War II in 1939, prior to which he was Major Huggins. I have elected to refer to him as Colonel throughout the story, however.
5. The Cadbury family enterprise began not with chocolate but tea.
6. Peter Jeremy William Huggins, known by his stage and screen name, Jeremy Brett.
7. Jeremy's maternal grandmother was Edith Cadbury Butler, wife of Arnold Butler, and second child of Richard and Emma Cadbury.
8. This place was Holly Lodge in Berkswell. Much of the information concerning Jeremy's childhood, and the family photos, comes from the periodical *Berkswell Miscellany Volume 5*, which I frequently reference.
9. Lily Knight, whom I have assumed was one of the live-in staff.
10. Jennie Vines was a housemaid.
11. Joyce Jakeman, the housekeeper, may also have lived in.

12   Miss Katherine Lant owned Nailcote Hall until her death in 1938.
13   I surmise that Jeremy's cousin Daphne was the daughter of an aunt on his father's side. The Colonel had a brother, Leslie, and two sisters, Gladys and Margaret, the latter being of an appropriate age.
14   Daphne Acott was Jeremy's first cousin, five years older. She married actor Alec Clunes, and their son, Martin, also became an actor.
15   The oldest parts of the Church of Saint John the Baptist, Berkswell Parish, date to the twelfth century.
16   This was Rev. Arthur L. Whitaker, rector of Berkswell Parish from 1924 to 1950.
17   Jeremy had two aunts on his father's side, Gladys and Margaret (see note 13), and three great-aunts on his mother's side, one of whom was also Margaret. His grandmothers, to add to the confusion, were both named Edith.
18   Lou Wilcox frequently drove family members.
19   Church organist Arthur Goode.
20   A historic and exclusive archery club in Meriden, dating from the eighteenth century, is called the Woodmen of Arden. This area in the midlands of England was known in medieval times as the Forest of Arden. Colonel Huggins and all four of this sons were members.
21   John Webb has been a most helpful correspondent, and his autobiography, *From the Other Side of the Fence*, very informative.
22   Tom Houghton was the family gardener.
23   We know there was an Airedale, and Jasper was a popular name for a dog at that time, so an educated guess.
24   Maud Watson (1864–1946) was the daughter of Berkswell rector Rev. Henry Watson. Her Wimbledon victory was in 1884.
25   This man was Frank "Skinner" Horn, colorful and beloved of children.
26   The village of Berkswell is located at the crossroads of Meriden and Coventry Roads.

27 Colonel Charles Joshua Hurst Wheatley owned the Berkswell Estate and lived in Berkswell Hall.
28 Sir Charles Hyde owned newspapers in Birmingham and was a supporter of the community, especially the local Boy Scouts. The Moat, where he lived, is another historic property in Berkswell.
29 There was by the side of the road a gate known locally as the "black gate," which was used infrequently for occasions such as this, when it often had to be rescued from the vines. This information was per Mr. John Webb, who made his living in the nursery business.
30 The Royal British Legion is a charitable organization founded in 1921 to support veterans and members of the armed services.
31 The incidents of Jeremy riding both the pony and the donkey into the Grange are reported in *Berkswell Miscellany, Volume 5*. The narrative details are fictional.
32 Mrs. Clara Milburn kept a wartime diary, which was discovered after her death by the husband of a granddaughter and published in 1979. Out of print but available used, it has been an invaluable resource of information, even about the local weather!
33 Mr. Western. This information appears in *Berkswell Miscellany, Volume 5*.
34 This was Miss Kenderdine. There is still, at this writing, a Kenderdine Montessori School in Coventry.
35 Not until after Elizabeth Huggins's death was it learned that she had placed the flowers anonymously on the altar of the bombed-out Coventry Cathedral.
36 Ann Gay was a neighbor child, who lived with her family at Nailcote Hall, which changed hands after the death of Miss Katherine Lant in 1938.
37 The photograph appears in *Berkswell Miscellany, Volume 5*. The tale of bullying and of Jeremy's revenge is fictional, intended to convey the difficulties a child with a speech impediment may be expected to encounter, as well as the exceptional kindness of Jeremy's mother.

38 The Cameo Theatre, originally called Balsall Palace, was in nearby Balsall Common.
39 Daphne Acott grew up to become the secretary of Orson Welles.
40 Information on this production came from the online archive of the Royal Shakespeare Company. I have attempted to be factual in all such theatrical references.
41 Saints Crispin and Crispian, martyred in the third century AD, are thought to have been twins.
42 The Stowe School, mentioned earlier.
43 Miss Record, at the end of Baulk's Lane, was known to scold Peter for this trespass.
44 Mrs. Christobel Wheatley was ten years younger than her husband and just forty-five when he died. She lived on at Berkswell Hall for another forty years, continuing to play an active role in the Parish.
45 Claude Elliott, called the Emperor by the students, was the first Head Master of Eton who was not clergy. He was replaced by Robert Birley in 1949.

Chapter Two

46 I found no information on Mrs. Huggins's attitude regarding Eton, but surmised in light of how she was described by her son and others that it might have been negative.
47 Hawtrey House is one of two student residences built in 1845, the first to be built specifically for that purpose. Details of this kind regarding Jeremy's Eton years were provided by the Eton Archivist.
48 The Lent Half is from mid-January to late March. Though there are now three terms, they are still called Halves.
49 The interview with Danny Danziger appeared in the Independent on 12 October, 1992.
50 Francis Cruso was noted for his translation of Aristophanes's *The Frogs*.
51 The word used at Eton for caning or flogging.

52 The Eton slang boys use for teachers and administrators.
53 Fellow actor Robert Stephens, whom Jeremy met at the Manchester Library Theatre in 1954. Stephens reports on their friendship in his memoir *Knight Errant*.
54 Durnford House is near Hawtrey and is the other residence built in 1845.
55 In fictional parts of the story, I have sought nonetheless to use probable or possible locations and contemporaneous events.
56 He tells this story to Rosemary Herbert in the interview for the Armchair Detective, Fall 1985.
57 The New Theatre is now the Noel Coward Theatre.
58 Jeremy related this interchange with Guthrie but did not give particulars. There was a production of *Tamburlaine* in London in September of 1951. But Jeremy turned eighteen on 3 November, and he was known to have had oral surgery to correct his speech at the age of seventeen. Perhaps it was a very eventful year, but I nevertheless decided to place the meeting earlier.
59 I chose this name because a Dr. Ralph Oliver, president of the Warwickshire Lawn Tennis Association in 1984, was pictured in a publication of the Berkswell & District History Group. Might he have been the son of the local doctor?
60 1982: *Confessions of an Actor* by Olivier.
61 Rev. Henry Bursell replaced Reverend Whitaker as rector in 1950. D. E. Gibbs of Berkswell Parish, in his book *Berkswell Through a Looking Glass*, provided exhaustive parish records, including the chronology of rectors going back to 1249.
62 Jeremy did attend Central School with actresses Wendy Craig and Mary Ure, but this incident is fictional. It demonstrates the kind of support for which fellow actors expressed appreciation.
63 It is difficult to surmise whether the Huggins family would have gone to London on this grand occasion, or perhaps would have preferred to avoid the hubbub. Details of the coronation of Elizabeth II are from newsreels, still readily available on the internet, *British Pathe* being a good channel.

64 Jeremy related this episode about his father and the boots, but without any particulars, though he did say in an interview that it occurred in Manchester.
65 This theatre was formerly the St. James Cinema, once owned by Anna's grandfather. It is a few blocks from Ebury Street and, at this writing, is again known as St. James Theatre.
66 An old chain of tea shops, which I speculate may have been there at the time.
67 Daphne Acott actually married Alec Clunes in 1956, but I chose to move it up a year for the narrative. The information about Alec's activities during the war is from the biography of his son Martin.
68 Anna Massey wrote of the wedding in her memoir but did not give the date. The Terrence Rattigan play at the Globe opened 8 May, 1958, a Thursday, so I am proposing either 10 May or the week after.
69 I could not be certain this was true, but Stephens's memoir makes no mention of the wedding, although he was in London at the time.
70 In her memoir, Anna credited voice coach Iris Warren with helping her acting career and her self-confidence.
71 Anna's memoir does not mention a christening, but I considered that the families must have met at some occasion.
72 We know that Elizabeth Huggins was visiting a bishop in Wales when she died in this car accident. The topography of Wales suggested to me that it may have been the bishop of Swansea, who was then Rev. John Thomas. It is not known how the family was notified, so this version and the Bishop's relationship with the rector are my invention.
73 Sources indicate only that Michael was an artist, with no other details about his life.
74 I presume that there would have been a memorial service. The choice of Woodbrooke, where Colonel and Mrs. Huggins had met, is sentimental.

75 To quote D. E. Gibbs of Berkswell in his book *Berkswell Through a Looking Glass*, "A brilliant conversationalist, she could always be counted on to say the right thing at the right time."

76 I could find no attribution for the name of Jeremy's beloved dog, so I used the coincidental similarity with impresario Binkie Beaumont. An internet source cites a radio interview with Brett in 1991 in which he stated that Mr. Binks had been dead for about sixteen years and that he died at the age of seventeen; therefore, he would have lived from 1958 to 1975.

Chapter Three

77 Here Robert is referring to the playwright John Osborne, who had a way of antagonizing people.

78 It is possible but improbable that such a production took place. We know that Jeremy Brett was in Montreux, but not how he acquired his love of opera. I wanted to use this famous Puccini aria from *Turandot* for its unique evocative quality.

79 My tale of the romance in Montreux is fictional, based on Anna Massey's memoir recounting that he was in Montreux and that he told her he had met a man there. The trip to Tenerife is also based on her account.

80 Without knowing exactly where in Notting Hill he lived, I chose Ladbroke Square because of the gardens.

81 This story is quoted on the website JeremyBrett.info.com, though without specific attribution.

82 The chronology is uncertain here since Stephens did not make it to Chichester in the summer of 1963, and it is unclear whether Brett returned in subsequent years. But Stephens's memoir does claim that Brett was at the Manor House with him and Tarn, and the arrangement serves the narrative. With the Isle of Wight being a short hop across the Solent from Chichester, it has seemed to me an ideal place to take children.

83 They were nonplussed to learn that their songs had later been dubbed in by Marni Nixon and Bill Shirley.

84   One source for this quote is an interview with Rosemary Herbert, conducted in New York in April 1985 and appearing in the fall edition of the Armchair Detective.
85   2 February.
86   This being Linda Pritchard, who will be introduced in the next chapter.
87   Easter, which always falls on the first Sunday after the first full moon of spring, had just passed.
88   A Tibetan term for a stage after death for souls who, having not achieved enlightenment in this life, must return for another try.
89   The first Earl of Aylesford sponsored the Woodmen of Arden at its founding in 1785, near his family seat, Packington Hall.
90   The Wheatley family was well loved in Berkswell, as was Jeremy's family, and they would have known one another. The exact nature of his relationship with Mrs. Wheatley is not something I could discern, but I do hope my surmise is close.
91   The number 625 in this title referred to a type of high-definition transmission.
92   That Brett broke his nose in *As You Like It* is a fact. It is my guess that it might have taken place in this combat with the wrestler, and Waterloo Hospital is nearest to the Old Vic. It is also on record that Olivier paid to have it set properly.
93   On the internet there is always more information to be mined. I have stopped short, however, of matters not relevant to the scope of this book.
94   It was not until the 1980s that caning was phased out at Eton. The last "beating" is believed to have been in 1984.
95   As of this writing, a track of this song and others from the review may be heard on www.noelcoward.net. Newsreels of the birthday at the Savoy are presently available compliments of *British Pathe*.
96   A Gary Bond website states of this meeting that "the attraction was immediate and intense."
97   The performer Danny LaRue was known for his singing and for cross-dressing.
98   Released internationally as *Outback*.

99 A television version was made in 1972.
100 The geography is unclear here. Stephens's memoir puts the Meridiana Hotel near their home in Queen's Elm Square, while at this writing there is a hotel with that name on Argyle Street in a different part of London.
101 Anna Massey writes in her memoir that following their divorce, Jeremy took their son on "trips," and Martin Clunes's biography tells of Jeremy's generous personality and his support after the death of Martin's father. The particulars of this outing, however, are fictional.
102 When Martin Clunes decided to go into acting, Jeremy offered to pay for cosmetic surgery that would lessen the prominence of those ears. Martin declined and was successful in spite of them.
103 Martin Clunes biography mentions this film as figuring into his decision to become an actor.
104 This information is from Stephens's memoir.
105 Coward was knighted in 1969.
106 After *Design for Living* in 1973, until 1988, all but one of Brett's appearances on stage were in Canada and the US. The one stage role, at the Yvonne Arnaud Theatre in Guildford, England, was in 1977 in the musical *Robert and Elizabeth*, about the Brownings, which also ran in Ottawa. A complete chronology of his performances on stage and screen, taken from his own records, is appended to the memoir of Linda Pritchard.
107 Kingsley Amis (1922–95) was a London-born contemporary author. He was knighted in 1990.
108 There was no indication that either Gary or Jeremy saw this musical, but it was popular in the gay community and developed a cult following.
109 The car, described in a Boston Globe interview, was actually a 1978 model, but I place it here for the sake of the narrative. She may, after all, have had a similar car and tag prior to that.
110 Brett's performances at the Stratford Festival in Canada, his meeting with Joan Wilson to film an introduction to *The Rivals*, and his participation in *Piccadilly Circus*, all took place around

this time. While my chronology may not be precise, it seemed reasonable to place them together.

111 And he did. The man was E. J. Taylor, an American artist, with whom Gary Bond lived from 1979 until his death from AIDS in 1995. Thanks to a growing acceptance of gay relationships by then, Taylor is mentioned in Gary's obituary by British newspapers the Guardian and the Independent.

112 A short-lived series starring Rick Moses, it had just four episodes.

113 This information comes from Anna Massey's memoir, while the dialogue is of course fictional.

114 In his biography, Martin Clunes tells these tales about his adolescence.

115 David Huggins did become an illustrator and graphic designer and wrote three novels.

116 Stephens characterizes these bridge evenings as "old maidish."

117 Penelope Keith described just such a Christmas party, including the scavenger hunt, at the memorial service for Jeremy in 1995.

118 This is the full name of the king of the Transylvanian vampires, who was "the last of his tribe."

119 A Boston Globe article from 1980 quotes Joan as saying, "We see each other in different places—wherever we happen to be."

120 Palmer House is just the other side of State Street from the Shubert Theatre. One source quotes him as mentioning the Ambassador, which is two miles north. I imagine him staying closer.

121 The source for this quote and the one in the next paragraph is a fan website called the Brettish Empire, maintained by Lisa L. Oldham.

122 Geoffrey Dingle was rector of Berkswell parish from 1966 to 1988.

123 Bela Lugosi starred in the original Broadway play in 1924 and then the movie. In London, Dracula was played by Raymond Huntley with playwright Hamilton Deane as Van Helsing.

124 About two years later, Mrs. Wheatley went to live in a nursing home. The Hall was converted to apartments in 1984. There

125 was a memorial service for her at Berkswell Church in February 1988, after a private funeral.
125 According to legend, the superstition dates to the play's origin, when an actor was killed with a real dagger that had been mistaken for the prop. Thereafter, if Macbeth's name is uttered in the theatre, disaster might befall.
126 In his book *Bending the Willow*, David Stuart Davies touches on this dispute over copyrights that delayed the Granada series.

Chapter Four

127 Colonel Moran hunted in India; *shikari* is Hindu for "hunter."
128 This was his day-to-day uniform; it would be a black jumper in cold weather, often with a red rose pinned to it.
129 In this film, Prospero is a New York architect who is in a midlife crisis and retreats to a Greek island.
130 The Reagan visit is a fact, and we know that Brett was in Barbados reading Doyle. His encounter with Colbert is fiction—as far as I know.
131 I make frequent reference to *Bending the Willow*, published by Calabash Press. It is not a biography of Brett, but information on chronology has been very helpful, as well as extensive quotes from interviews with key people, including the star.
132 This scene was taken from *The Sign of Four* before they knew they would eventually be using that story.
133 I have assumed that Jeremy remained in the house in Notting Hill, with his son occupying the loft, because Anna Massey reports that their son moved into her Holland Park house when Jeremy moved to Clapham Common.
134 This quote is attributed to TV Guide, in the Brettish Empire, a website maintained by Lisa Oldham. The site references primarily books and American newspapers.
135 The series *The Adventures of Sherlock Holmes* was released in the States beginning in March 1985.

¹³⁶ I do not have information about where Joan Wilson received treatment, but being in Boston, this is an educated guess.
¹³⁷ This incident was described by Jeremy in *Bending the Willow* and other sources.
¹³⁸ The apartment is described in Linda Pritchard's book, and pictures are accessible on the internet.
¹³⁹ This description was given by Jeremy in an interview with Don Freeman, theatre critic for the San Diego Union, appearing in the paper on 14 May, 1985.
¹⁴⁰ The Brettish Empire (see note 134) reports this story.
¹⁴¹ These details of Joan Wilson's death, while fictional, are based on common experience. The quotation of her last words to her husband comes from Peter Haining's book *The Television Sherlock Holmes*.
¹⁴² This quote is also on the Lisa Oldham website.
¹⁴³ June Wyndham Davies is not related to David Stuart Davies, author of *Bending the Willow*.
¹⁴⁴ Hardwicke describes this meeting to Davies in *Bending the Willow*, including the jazz club and what he viewed in retrospect as Brett's manic state.
¹⁴⁵ From Shakespeare's *Henry V*.
¹⁴⁶ This version of events is fictional. It may well be that he was no longer playing bridge.
¹⁴⁷ The interview with Marilyn Willison appeared on 18 February, 1990. It is quoted on the Oldham website.
¹⁴⁸ This location shoot, over two hundred miles east of Manchester, is mentioned in Peter Haining's book. The use of thirty-five-millimeter film was an unusual quality for television.
¹⁴⁹ Hardwicke tells this story in the Davies book.
¹⁵⁰ Tylor published these photos much later in a book, *A Roll with Jeremy Brett*, describing this backstage shoot in the preface.
¹⁵¹ Linda Pritchard's memoir concerning their relationship, published in 1998 in collaboration with Mary Ann Warner, is an unsophisticated but moving account.
¹⁵² Throughout the book, where there has been no information about venues, I have chosen existing ones that likely may

153 Martin Clunes's biography tells how he was inspired by his cousin's fame. Waiting at an airport on one occasion, he took comfort upon seeing Jeremy's face on television in a Sherlock Holmes episode, even though it was dubbed in a foreign language.
154 Information about this occasion was reported in "The Colonel's Regiment," the article that appeared in *Berkswell Miscellany, Volume V.*
155 Davies writes in his book that Brett went abroad at this time and had to be brought back by his son. We know that he kept in touch with Joan's children, but aside from the details about the shows then on Broadway, this trip is fictional.
156 Martin's wedding is described in his biography. The account of David's attendance is fictional, included to suggest the likelihood of the family's growing concern regarding Jeremy.
157 This meeting is fictional, included to show the possible family dynamics in this situation.
158 Quoted from a typical speech on the subject by Conan Doyle in the biography by Andrew Lycett, chapter 20.
159 Pritchard's book has a tragicomic account of this incident.
160 I assume that Robert and Jeremy remained friends, though Stephens makes scant reference to a relationship in the latter half of his book.
161 The film was released in the States with the title *Shameless*.
162 Buddha is sometimes referred to as "the man who woke up." When pressed to describe nirvana, he offered the one word: *bliss*.
163 The Order of Service may be seen on the Brettish Empire, Lisa Oldham's website.
164 Musically inclined fans may have observed that Gowers wrote two themes for the series, this main theme, which he varied for every episode, and a softer one reminiscent of an Irish folk song.

About the Author

THE AUTHOR CHOOSES TO BE known only by the pen name W. Grey Champion. He has always been a writer, although he did not pursue writing professionally. His career did allow him to cultivate that passion and, in retirement, to indulge it. This biography, a true labor of love that was three years in the making, is his second in publication. His first, which appeared in 2015, was a work of creative nonfiction on the subject of Buddhism, entitled *Conjuring Archangel*. He has also written a weekly blog, "From the Moleskine," for many years.

CPSIA information can be obtained
at www.ICGtesting.com
Printed in the USA
LVOW12s1449010418
571875LV00001B/275/P